GW01607991

FRANCIS FRITH'S

# WYRE FOREST

PHOTOGRAPHIC MEMORIES

**CATHERINE ROTHWELL** was a deputy Borough Librarianbefore retirement, and later had charge of all local history and reference work in the District of Wyre, Lancashire Library. A qualified librarian and a Fellow of the Library Association, she is also familiar with the District of Wyre Forest in Worcestershire; members of her family have lived there for nearly 40 years. She has researched regional cookery, and amongst 60 books has published *Wyre Forest Recipes*. Catherine is now widowed with three children and four grandchildren, but still involved heart and soul in local history.

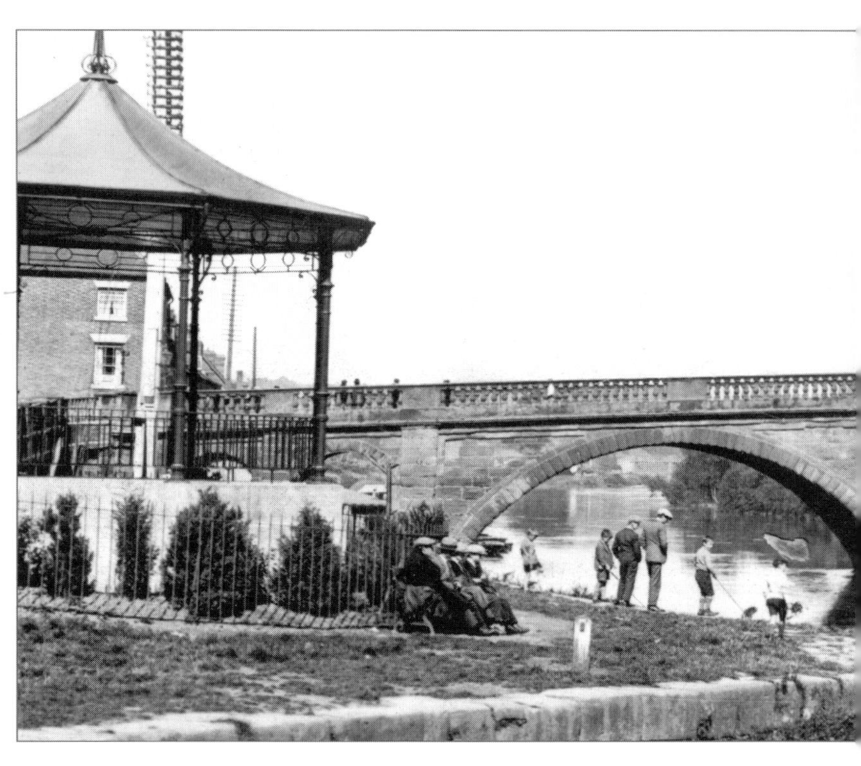

FRANCIS FRITH'S
PHOTOGRAPHIC MEMORIES

# WYRE FOREST

## PHOTOGRAPHIC MEMORIES

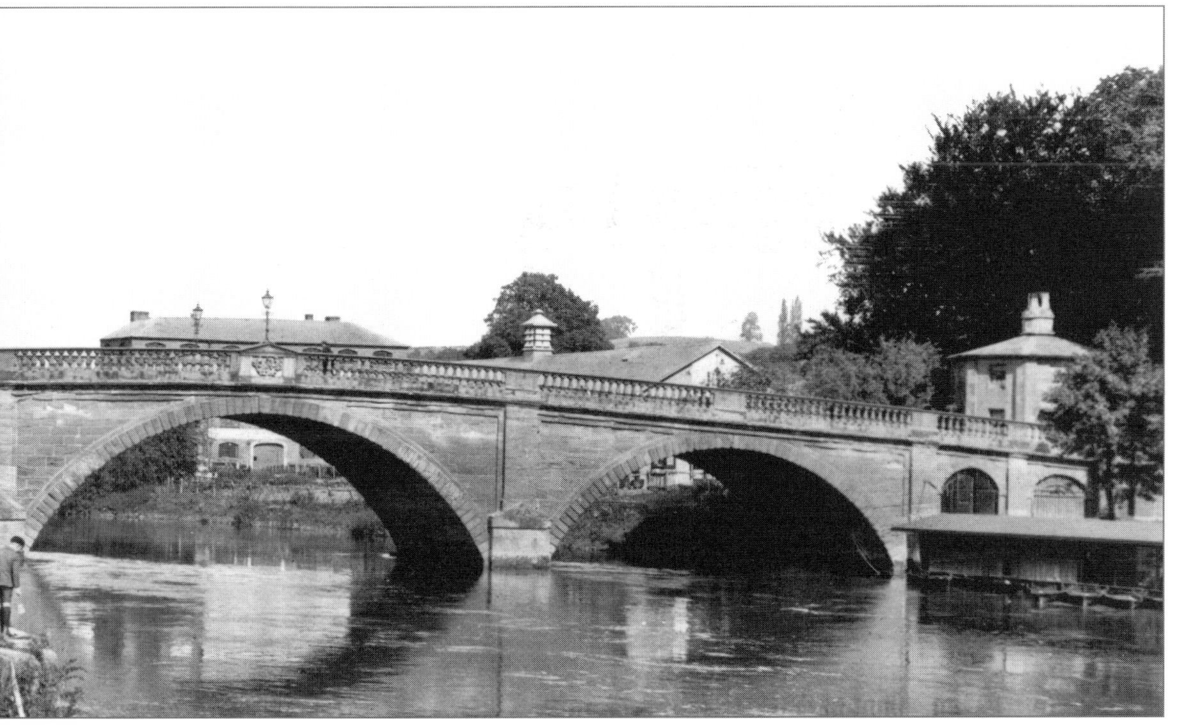

CATHERINE ROTHWELL

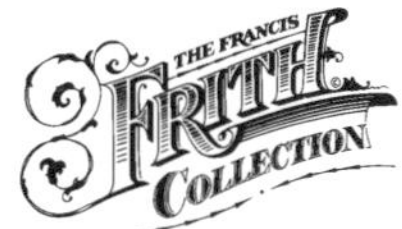

First published in the United Kingdom in 2004 by
Frith Book Company Ltd

Paperback Edition 2004
ISBN 1-85937-804-8



British Library Cataloguing in Publication Data

Francis Frith's Wyre Forest - Photographic Memories
Catherine Rothwell
ISBN 1-85937-804-8

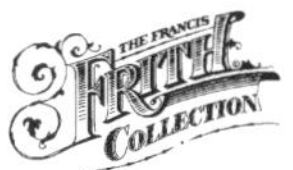


Frith Book Company Ltd
Frith's Barn, Teffont,
Salisbury, Wiltshire SP3 5QP
Tel: +44 (0) 1722 716 376
Email: info@francisfrith.co.uk
www.francisfrith.co.uk

Printed and bound in Great Britain

Front Cover: **BEWDLEY,** *Load Street 1931* 84620
Frontispiece: **BEWDLEY,** *The Bridge c1940* B82008

*The colour-tinting is for illustrative purposes only, and is not intended to be historically accurate*

The recipes and the following images were supplied by
Catherine Rothwell: W643005 (p.17), (W643002 (p.21), S214701 (p.32)
W643004 (p.37), W643001 (p.50), W643003 (p.79)

Image no. K16701 (page 47) supplied by kind permission of the Manager, Harvington Hall.

AS WITH ANY HISTORICAL DATABASE THE FRITH ARCHIVE IS CONSTANTLY BEING CORRECTED AND IMPROVED AND THE PUBLISHERS WOULD WELCOME INFORMATION ON OMISSIONS OR INACCURACIES

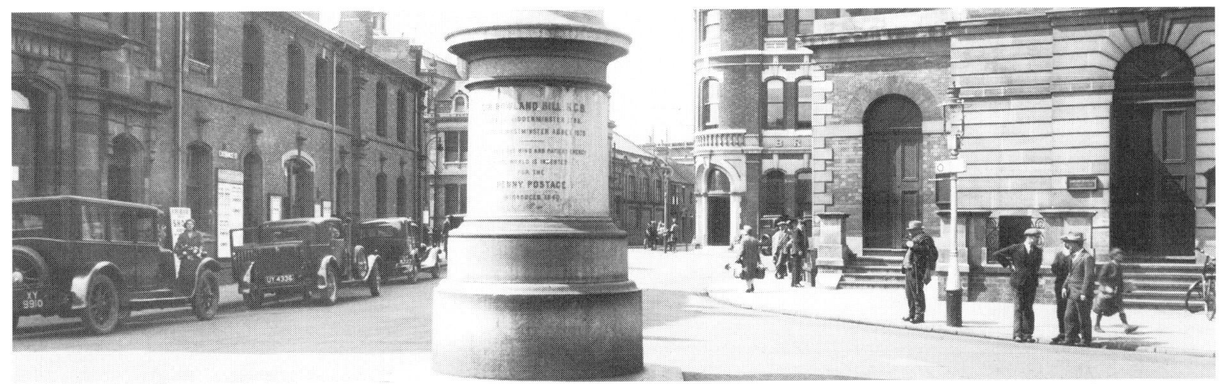

# CONTENTS

# FRANCIS FRITH
## VICTORIAN PIONEER

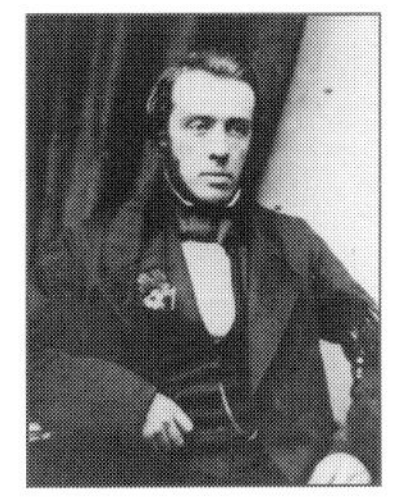

FRANCIS FRITH, founder of the world-famous photographic archive, was a complex and multi-talented man. A devout Quaker and a highly successful Victorian businessman, he was philosophical by nature and pioneering in outlook.

By 1855 he had already established a wholesale grocery business in Liverpool, and sold it for the astonishing sum of £200,000, which is the equivalent today of over £15,000,000. Now a very rich man, he was able to indulge his passion for travel. As a child he had pored over travel books written by early explorers, and his fancy and imagination had been stirred by family holidays to the sublime mountain regions of Wales and Scotland. 'What lands of spirit-stirring and enriching scenes and places!' he had written. He was to return to these scenes of grandeur in later years to 'recapture the thousands of vivid and tender memories', but with a different purpose. Now in his thirties, and captivated by the new science of photography, Frith set out on a series of pioneering journeys up the Nile and to the Near East that occupied him from 1856 until 1860.

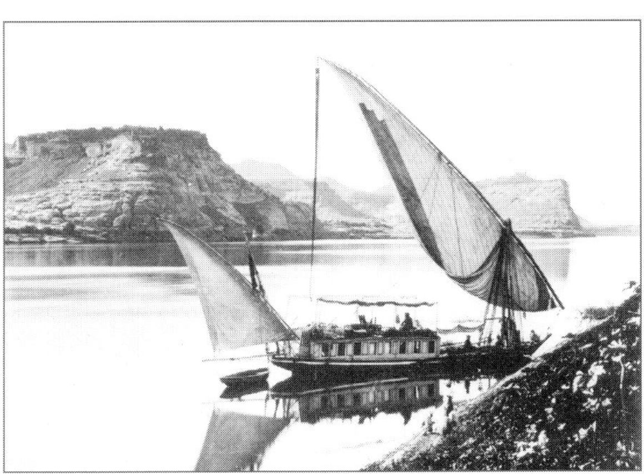

### INTRIGUE AND EXPLORATION

These far-flung journeys were packed with intrigue and adventure. In his life story, written when he was sixty-three, Frith tells of being held captive by bandits, and of fighting 'an awful midnight battle to the very point of surrender with a deadly pack of hungry, wild dogs'. Wearing flowing Arab costume, Frith arrived at Akaba by camel sixty years before Lawrence of Arabia, where he encountered 'desert princes and rival sheikhs, blazing with jewel-hilted swords'.

He was the first photographer to venture beyond the sixth cataract of the Nile. Africa was still the mysterious 'Dark Continent', and Stanley and Livingstone's historic meeting was a decade into the future. The conditions for picture taking confound belief. He laboured for hours in his wicker dark-room in the sweltering heat of the desert, while the volatile chemicals fizzed dangerously in their trays. Back in London he exhibited his photographs and was 'rapturously cheered' by members of the Royal Society. His reputation as a photographer was made overnight.

### VENTURE OF A LIFE-TIME

Characteristically, Frith quickly spotted the opportunity to create a new business as a specialist publisher of photographs. He lived in an era of immense and sometimes violent change.

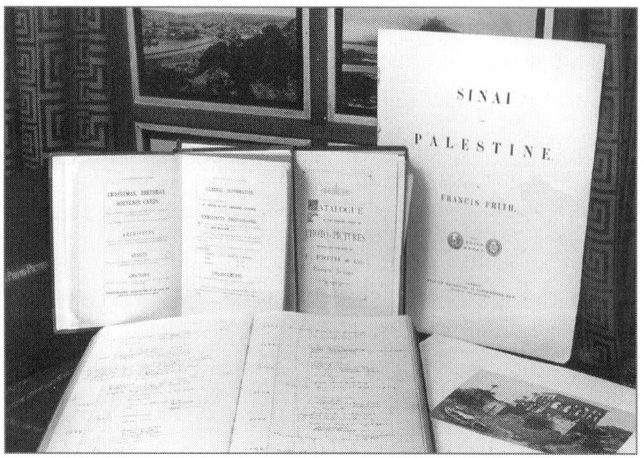


For the poor in the early part of Victoria's reign work was exhausting and the hours long, and people had precious little free time to enjoy themselves. Most had no transport other than a cart or gig at their disposal, and rarely travelled far beyond the boundaries of their own town or village. However, by the 1870s the railways had threaded their way across the country, and Bank Holidays and half-day Saturdays had been made obligatory by Act of Parliament. All of a sudden the working man and his family were able to enjoy days out and see a little more of the world.

With typical business acumen, Francis Frith foresaw that these new tourists would enjoy having souvenirs to commemorate their days out. In 1860 he married Mary Ann Rosling and set out on a new career: his aim was to photograph every city, town and village in Britain. For the next thirty years he travelled the country by train and by pony and trap, producing fine photographs of seaside resorts and beauty spots that were keenly bought by millions of Victorians. These prints were painstakingly pasted into family albums and pored over during the dark nights of winter, rekindling precious memories of summer excursions.

## THE RISE OF FRITH & CO

Frith's studio was soon supplying retail shops all over the country. To meet the demand he gathered about him a small team of photographers, and published the work of independent artist-photographers of the calibre of Roger Fenton and Francis Bedford. In order to gain some understanding of the scale of Frith's business one only has to look at the catalogue issued by Frith & Co in 1886: it runs to some 670 pages, listing not only many thousands of views of the British Isles but also many photographs of most European countries, and China, Japan, the USA and Canada - note the sample page shown on page 9 from the hand-written Frith & Co ledgers recording the pictures. By 1890 Frith had created the greatest specialist photographic publishing company in the world, with over 2,000 sales outlets - more than the combined number that Boots and WH Smith have today! The picture on the next page shows the Frith & Co display board at Ingleton in the Yorkshire Dales (left of window). Beautifully constructed with a mahogany frame and gilt inserts, it could display up to a dozen local scenes.

## POSTCARD BONANZA

The ever-popular holiday postcard we know today took many years to develop. In 1870 the Post Office issued the first plain cards, with a pre-printed stamp on one face. In 1894 they allowed other publishers' cards to be sent through the mail with an attached adhesive halfpenny stamp. Demand grew rapidly, and in 1895 a new size of postcard was permitted called the court card, but there was little room for illustration. In 1899, a year after Frith's death, a new card measuring 5.5 x 3.5 inches became the standard format, but it was not until 1902 that the divided back came into being, so that the address and message could be on one face and a full-size illustration on the other. Frith & Co were in the vanguard of postcard development: Frith's sons Eustace and Cyril continued their father's monumental task, expanding the number of views offered to the public and recording more and more places in Britain, as the

6 St Catherine's College
7 Senate House & Library
8
9 Gerrard Hostel Bridge
30 Geological Museum
1 Addenbrooke's Hospital
2 St Mary's Church
3 Fitzwilliam Museum, Pitt Press &c
4
5 Buxton, The Crescent
6 The Colonnade
7 Public Gardens
8
9 Haddon Hall, View from the Terrace
40 Miller's Dale

coasts and countryside were opened up to mass travel.

Francis Frith had died in 1898 at his villa in Cannes, his great project still growing. The archive he created continued in business for another seventy years. By 1970 it contained over a third of a million pictures showing 7,000 British towns and villages.

## FRANCIS FRITH'S LEGACY

Frith's legacy to us today is of immense significance and value, for the magnificent archive of evocative photographs he created provides a unique record of change in the cities, towns and villages throughout Britain over a century and more. Frith and his fellow studio photographers revisited locations many times down the years to update their views, compiling for us an enthralling and colourful pageant of British life and character.

We are fortunate that Frith was dedicated to recording the minutiae of everyday life. For it is this sheer wealth of visual data, the painstaking chronicle of changes in dress, transport, street layouts, buildings, housing, engineering and landscape that captivates us so much today. His remarkable images offer us a powerful link with the past and with the lives of our ancestors.

## THE VALUE OF THE ARCHIVE TODAY

Computers have now made it possible for Frith's many thousands of images to be accessed almost instantly. Frith's images are increasingly used as visual resources, by social historians, by researchers into genealogy and ancestry, by architects and town planners, and by teachers involved in local history projects.

In addition, the archive offers every one of us an opportunity to examine the places where we and our families have lived and worked down the years. Highly successful in Frith's own era, the archive is now, a century and more on, entering a new phase of popularity. Historians consider the Francis Frith Collection to be of prime national importance. It is the only archive of its kind remaining in private ownership. Francis Frith's archive is now housed in an historic timber barn in the beautiful village of Teffont in Wiltshire. Its founder would not recognize the archive office as it is today. In place of the many thousands of dusty boxes containing glass plate negatives and an all-pervading odour of photographic chemicals, there are now ranks of computer screens. He would be amazed to watch his images travelling round the world at unimaginable speeds through internet lines.

The archive's future is both bright and exciting. Francis Frith, with his unshakeable belief in making photographs available to the greatest number of people, would undoubtedly approve of what is being done today with his lifetime's work. His photographs depicting our shared past are now bringing pleasure and enlightenment to millions around the world a century and more after his death.

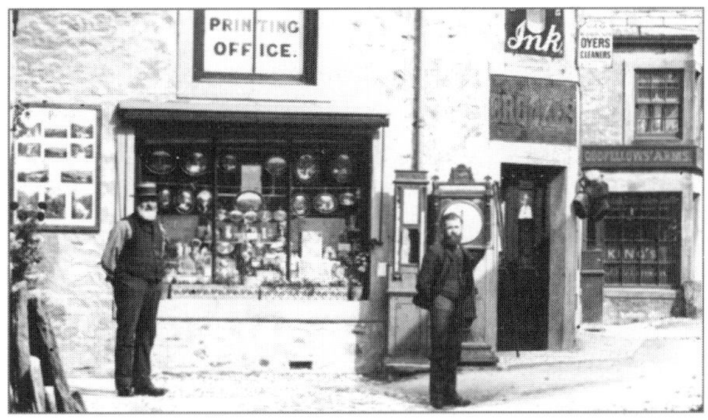

# WYRE FOREST
## AN INTRODUCTION

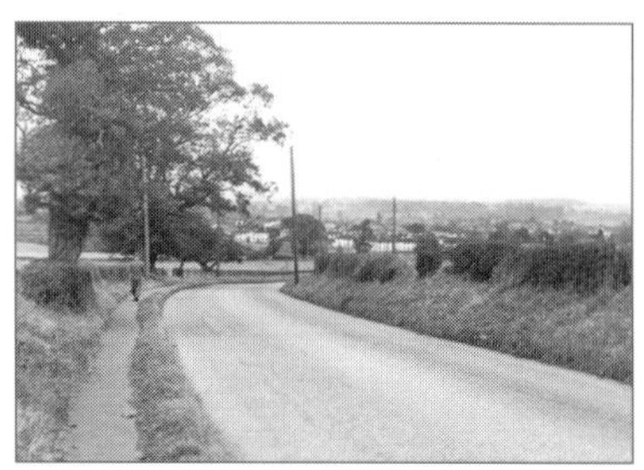

ANYONE fortunate enough to live near Wyre Forest is fortunate indeed, for he or she has 6000 acres of glades and woodland on the boundary of Shropshire and Worcestershire to explore. Bewdley, an historic and intriguing Georgian town, is the main point of access. It is also fortunate that even before conservation became a buzzword, a policy was being assiduously pursued to save 3000 acres of ancient oak in this real old English forest, once a royal chase.

For stressing its beauty and importance with a depth of knowledge unsurpassed on the subject, we must thank Professor Norman E Hickin: as a 9-year-old schoolboy from Birmingham he fell in love with these woody acres, and devoted half a century to recording the forest's flora and fauna in vividly presented words and 200 drawings.

More than thirty years ago, when my late mother and my sister came to live here, I began

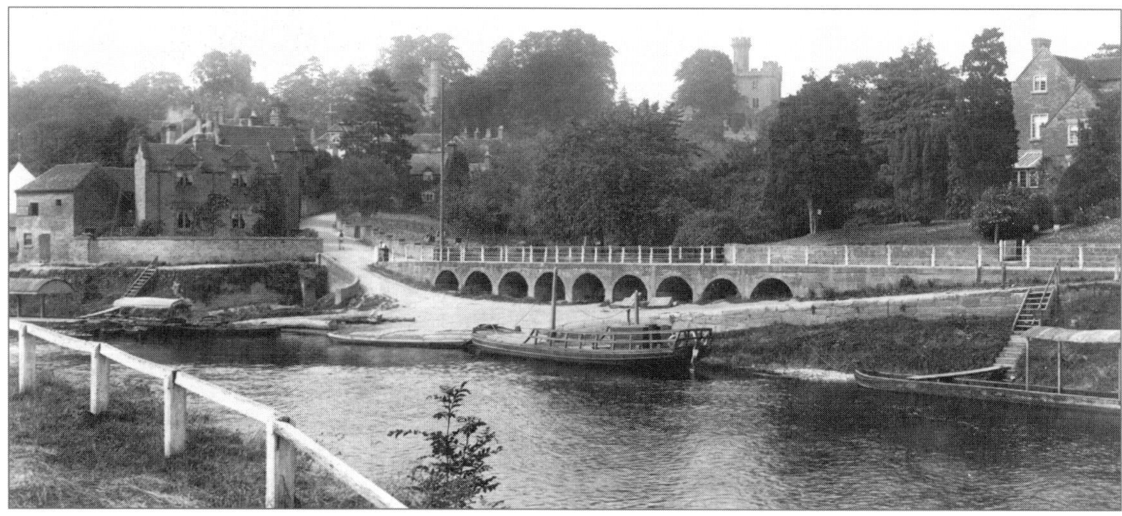

**UPPER ARLEY,** *The Ferry 1904* 51983

to regard it as my second home. This book aims at covering the district pictorially, and it includes towns steeped in history and throbbing with life. For this, thanks are due to another perfectionist, the pioneer photographer Francis Frith.

Now a forest nature reserve, Wyre Forest once supplied oak for the building trade, bark for tanning, and coppiced oak for charcoal burning. Coppicing, practiced for centuries and promoted today by the National Trust, provides a renewable supply of timber, and ensures the continuing life of woodlands.

Once part of a larger forest that covered the West Midlands, Wyre Forest remains one of the biggest areas of woodland left in Britain. In past ages, the forest was a hiding place for outlaws and ruffians who raided the villages which had grown up in woodland clearings. By royal command, Bewdley was recognised as a sanctuary town; the church was a place for fugitives who had shed blood.

With 6000 acres stretching westward from Cleobury Mortimer well into Shropshire, and with forest hamlets like Rock, Pentax, Bliss Gate and Far Forest (the last made famous by Francis Brett Young, a novelist in the thirties), traditional forest crafts flourished. A herd of fallow deer, so much a part of the forest scene, roams at will; the deer are counted and carefully culled to keep the stock healthy. Forest dwellers made combs, spoons, sticks, handles, and bowls from the horn of cast antlers.

A plentiful supply of oak bark and soft water from the river Severn was vital for the leather tanning industry in Bewdley; leather was needed for bellows, clothing, footwear, saddlery, and book binding. At Ribbesford Woods in the 1800s, teams of women did bark peeling. It was a seasonal occupation from late April to June. Newcomers had their 'shins barked' in ebullient peasant style. To avoid this painful rite of passage, treating the team was the best answer. The bark peelers wore flat cloth or straw hats enabling the carrying of big loads on their heads. During the Tudor period, there were 12 tanneries in Bewdley; the last closed in 1928.

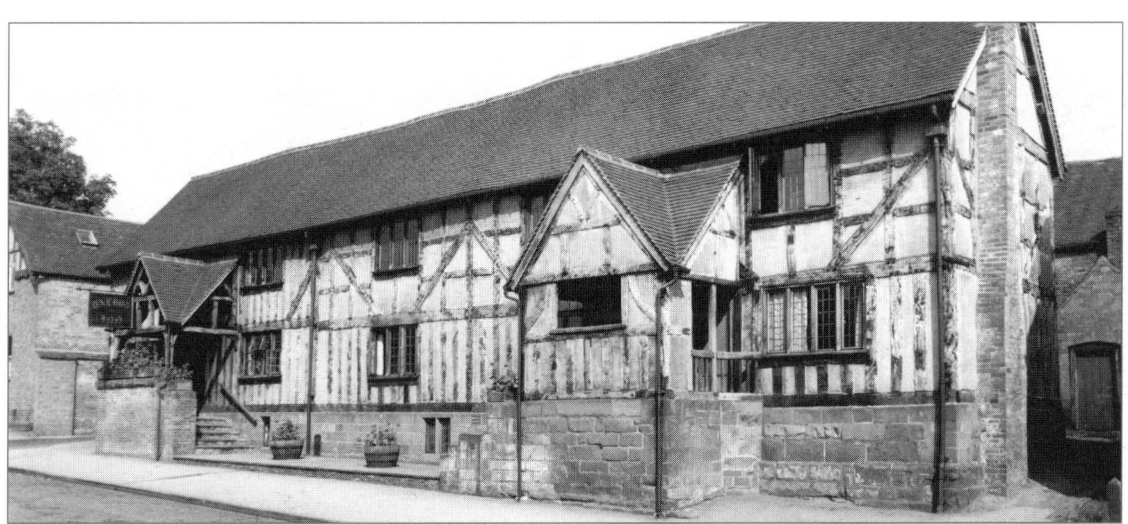

**CHADDESLEY CORBETT,** *The Talbot Inn c1957* C328016

Cookley parish formed the Ancient Order of Foresters in 1862.

On 13 June the great fair for the sale of cattle, horses and cheese was held. Michaelmas goose was a favourite long before turkey. In the early 1900s, large flocks of geese, their webbed feet coated in tar and sand so that they would last out the journey, were driven to the fattening farms.

A Wigan man, Christopher Banks, introduced brass founding and pewter making. Pewterer's Alley in Wribbenhall is named after the pewter and brass foundry, which made what are now collectors' items. Blacksmiths were ever busy at the forges with so many horses necessary for business. Stallions travelled between farms and inns with their stud cards. John Tolley, with his horse and plank-sided Worcestershire cart, was a coal merchant in Dog Lane, along with many other traders operating in Bewdley.

In the hop yards of Bewdley the custom on the last day of picking was to seize the busheler (the foreman) and one of the women and push them into a crib (a basket) to be covered with hops, tossed wildly, and finally 'resurrected' by being tipped out of the crib; this performance was to ensure a good harvest of hops next year.

Norman-French invaders thought the district a beautiful place, 'beau lieu' in French, the origin of Bewdley's name, no doubt; and royalty eyed it favourably. Through the powerful Mortimer family, the manor became part of the private property of English sovereigns. Edward IV granted a charter and coat of arms. Henry VIII granted 3 charters, and for a time his daughters Elizabeth and Mary lived at Tickenhall Palace; Charles I stayed here too during the Civil War. Grateful sovereigns granted privileges. The fact that it was a free borough, allowing freedom from tolls, made Bewdley prosperous. Stourport-on-Severn was also destined to grow from village to lively Georgian town through the 18th-century engineering work of James Brindley. The Staffordshire and Worcester canal and its position at the junction of rivers Severn and Stour meant brisk trade.

At the end of the 18th century, turnpikes greatly improved travel by road. There were

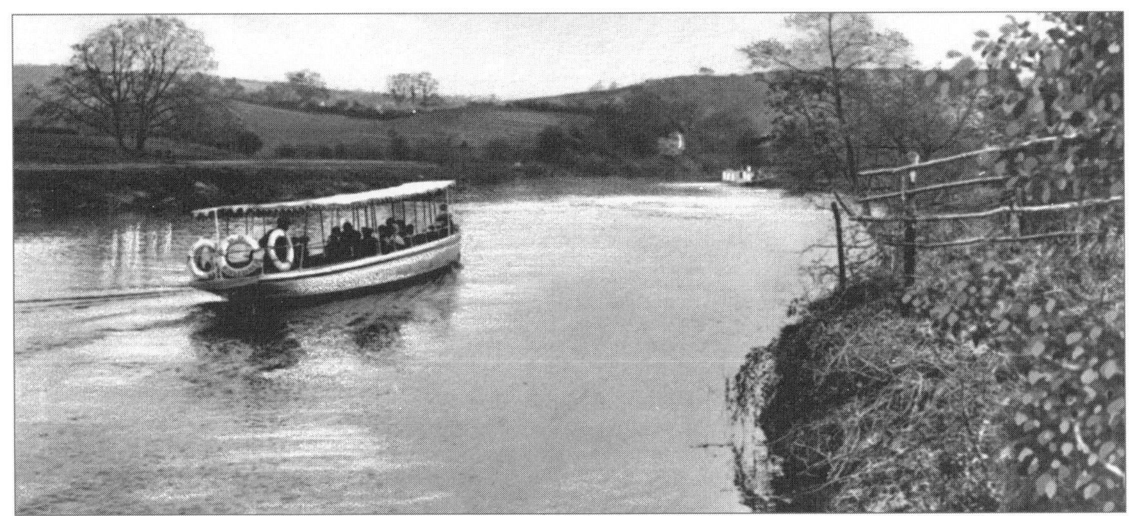

**STOURPORT-ON-SEVERN,** *On the River c1930* S214019

gates at Broadwaters, Sutton, Wolverly, Shatterford and Wribbenhall. Annual takings between 1804 and 1811 rose from £780 to £951. Meanwhile, 'Sabrina Fair' continued to make Bewdley a thriving inland port; the river froze over in severe winters, enabling rollicking winter fairs to be held on the ice.

Amongst great names, Kidderminster's Rowland Hill stands out. He earned worldwide fame and gratitude for his 19th-century carpet-weaving town. Not only did he bring in the revolutionary Penny Post, but his fertile mind made history in the educational world - he and his brother developed the Hazelwood system of education. But there were other benefactors living in and loving Wyre forest district: Richard Baxter, the outstanding preacher and vicar of Kidderminster; and John Brinton, who made possible a pleasant park, a lung for the busy town of carpet workers. Thanks are also due to alderman George Baker, mayor of Bewdley and friend of John Ruskin, the great art critic. Ruskin influenced the Gothic style of Beaucastle, George Baker's home, which was built of locally quarried sandstone and wood from Wyre Forest. When the house was up for sale, a frivolous press claimed that it resembled Dracula's castle. But George had a record of public service to be proud of - he was still in harness at 85.

The Pratt family of Stourport-on-Severn have nobly husbanded land bordering the Severn's bank at Lickhill Manor for over 200 years. Peter Pratt recalls that downstream from the manor house an old stagecoach route crossed the Severn from Arley Kings to Lickhill at Stoney Bottom. Travelling by riverside meadows, the coach swept past Wood Green Farm, where Mr and Mrs Peter Pratt now live. From here the horses had a steady climb over the Bewdley road and the railway at Burlish crossing until Five Ways was reached. The last point of this historic route is now called Kingsway. Could the reason for this name be that it was once used by Royal Mail coaches?

Land management more than ever before is of prime importance. We should be grateful to the Pratt family for preserving their pastures as a bulwark against urban sprawl. Scholars think that the meeting in Wyre Forest of St Augustine 'under the oak' refers either to the Mitre oak or the oak at Rock. Bearing in mind that the Wyre Forest of birch and oak has existed since the ice retreated, does it not deserve the utmost vigilance, care and attention?

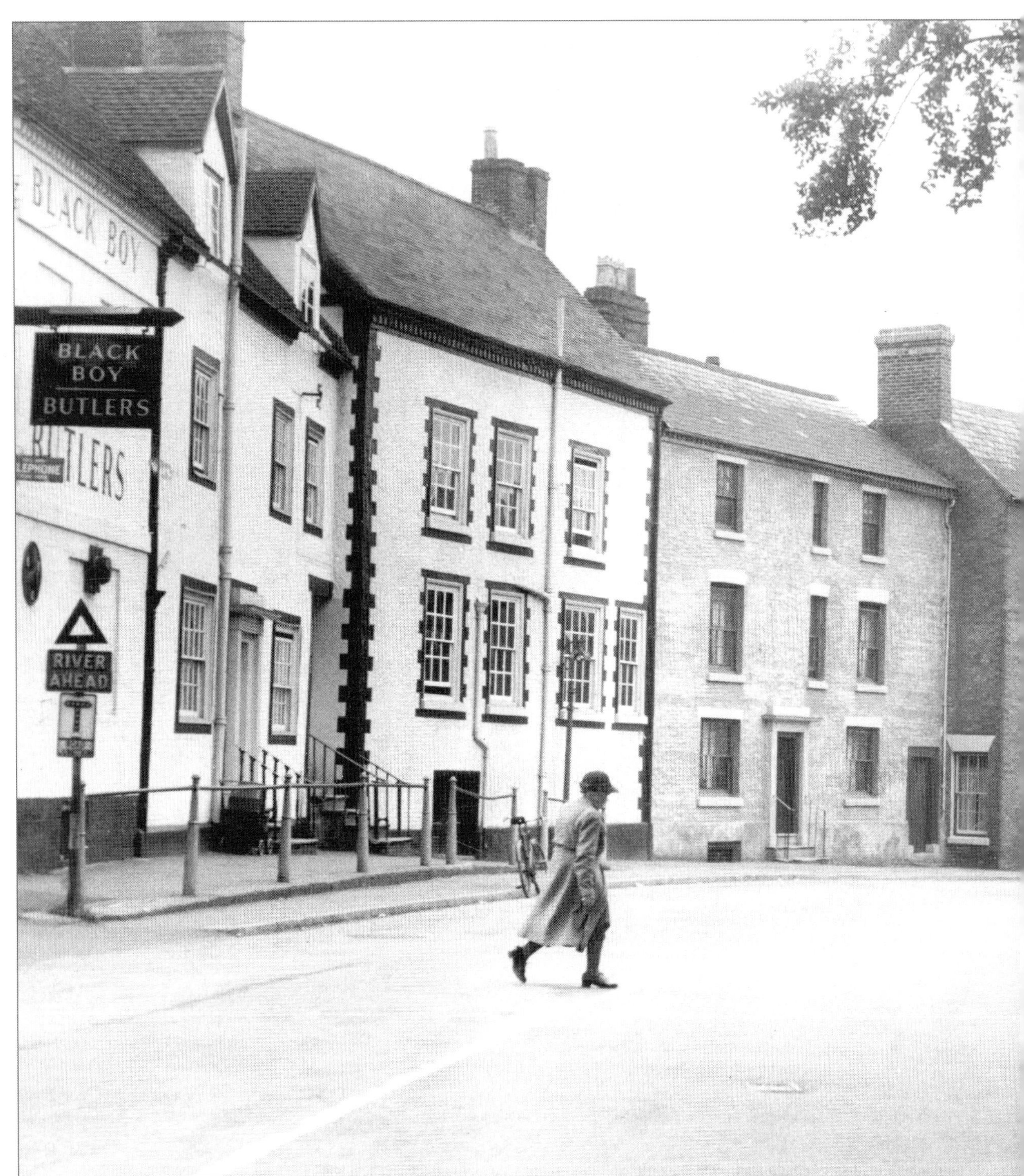
BLACK BOY
BLACK
BOY
BUTLERS
BUTLERS
RIVER
AHEAD

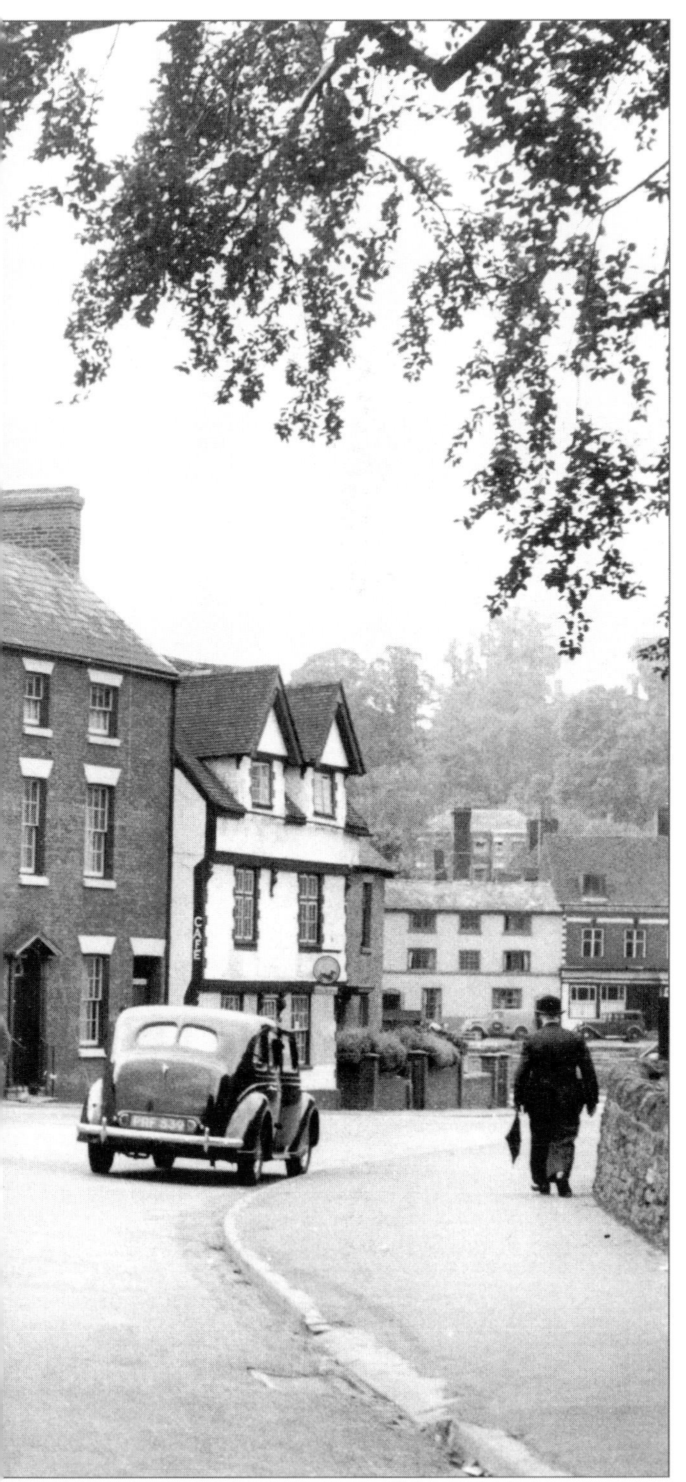

# BEWDLEY, CENTRE OF THE WYRE FOREST DISTRICT

**BEWDLEY**
*Wribbenhall c1950* B82027

The earliest settlement here was established near a well-used track leading to a ford over the River Severn. In the *Domesday Book* this is called Guerbbehall (Wribbenhall). Located on the high ground of Wyre Hill, the settlement had good visibility and safety from floods. The river supplied water, fish and transport. The Old Town Hall, one of the few timber-framed buildings left in Bewdley, is on Wyre Hill, which was then the town centre. This view of Wribbenhall features Butler's Black Boy Inn (left); outside it a warning sign of 'River Ahead' was necessary, as sudden dense fog generated from the river under certain atmospheric conditions can blot out familiar landmarks. Beyond the 18th-century buildings, a café has opened. As yet there is little traffic, and the buildings backed with trees bear out Nicolaus Pevsner's description of Bewdley: 'the most perfect Georgian town in Worcestershire.'

**BEWDLEY**
*Looking North c1940* B82006

This scene reveals a pleasant balance of trees and buildings - these range from Tudor to black and white vernacular architecture. The tower of St Anne's Church on Load Street and the rising hills exemplify what French-speaking settlers regarded as 'a beautiful place' ('beau lieu' in French), the origin of Bewdley's name. In 1724 stocks of iron for Cockley Forge were kept in warehouses at Bewdley.

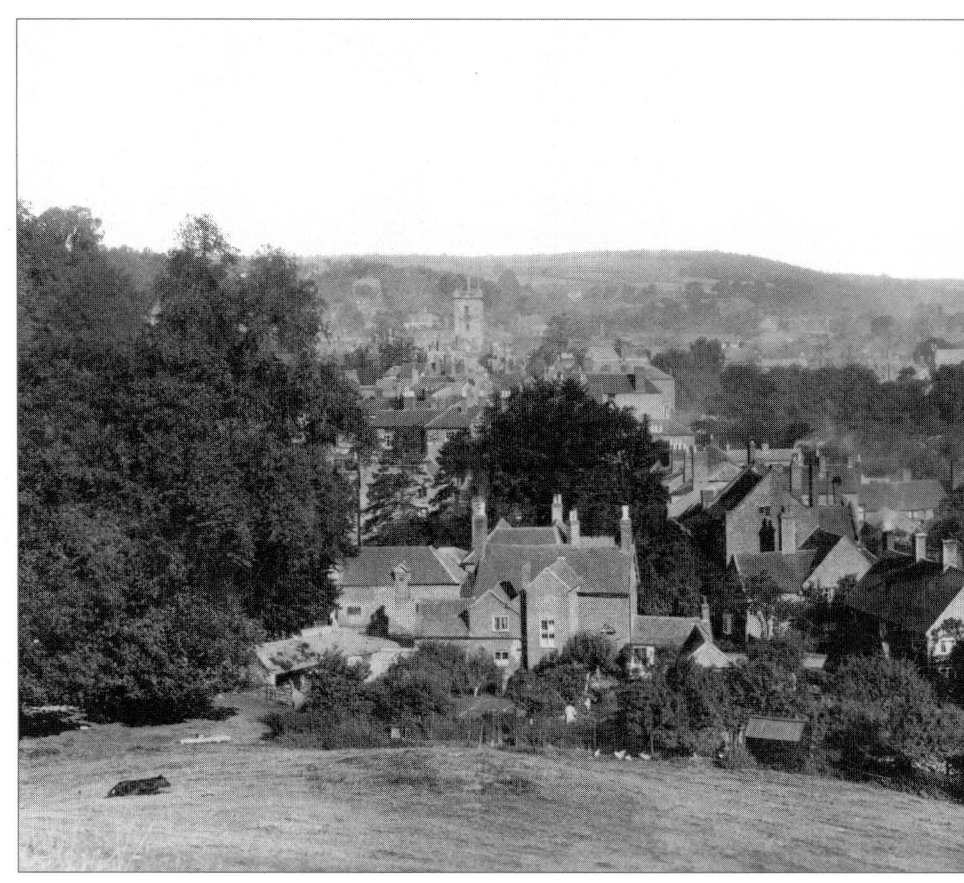

**BEWDLEY**
*Thurston Hotel from the River 1931* 84623

Royal interest in the town and town charters conferred privileges such as freedom from tolls; this was a valuable asset to a town trading by land and river. Both sides of the river were built upon. Success was guaranteed with the natural advantages of the town's position and the great privilege of being a free borough. This general view shows the Thurston Hotel, a free house, next to half-timbered buildings (right). The 6ft-tall Percy Palmer, a well known character from Wribbenhall, was then

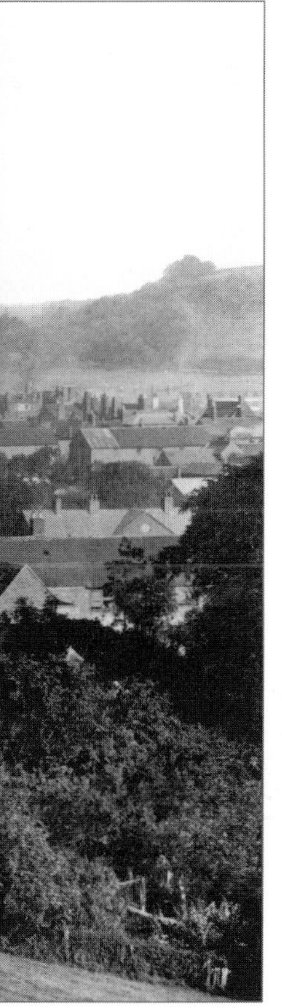

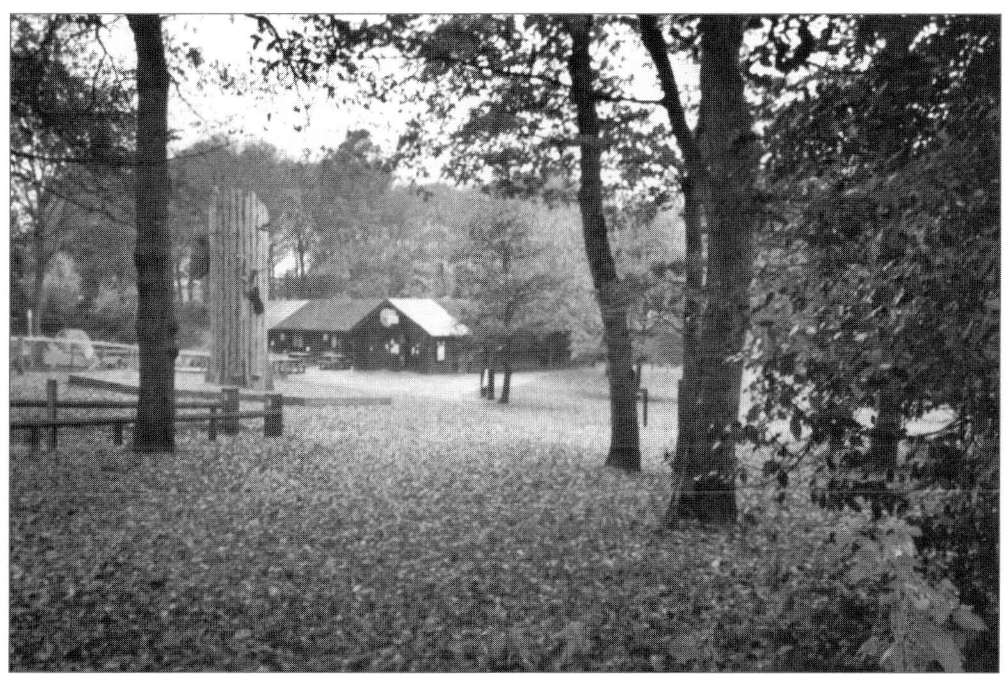

▲ **WYRE FOREST,** *Hawkbatch Visitor Centre, Hawkbatch Woods 2003* W643005

Wyre Forest has a popular visitor centre with a restaurant and shop. It specialises in woodland displays, and organises outings with children in mind. Nature trails throughout the year add interest. Other nature trails in the district are Blackstone Riverside Park, Bewdley; Hartlebury Common at Stourport-on-Severn; Habberley Valley Nature Reserve; and Kingsford Forest Park. All offer acres of beautiful woodland.

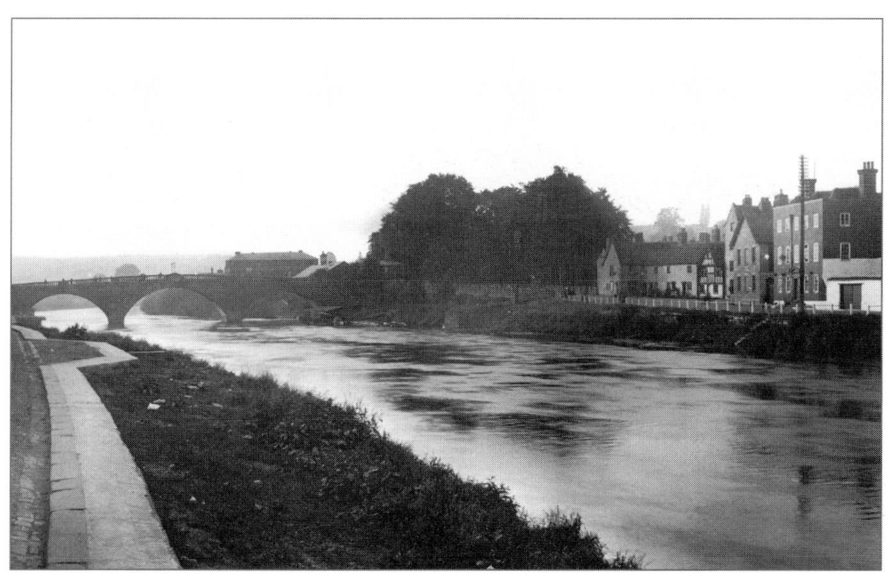

◄ **BEWDLEY**
*The River c1940* B82017

On the far side of the Severn, a boathouse and rowing boats indicate a swing to tourist trade. There were many small iron foundries and tin plate works a century and more ago, but cultivated riverside walks replaced them. In the background is the graceful bridge built by Thomas Telford in 1798. The population in 1930 numbered about 3000. Until 1885, when Bewdley manufactured combs, leather, malt, iron, and brass goods, the town returned one Member of Parliament.

▼ **BEWDLEY,** *The Bridge c1940* B82008

Here we can have a closer look at the famous bridge, with a group of boys fishing by the bandstand (left). Thomas Telford (1757-1834) was the son of a Scottish shepherd; he became famous for his masonry and bridge over the River Severn, and indeed for 1200 bridges, canals, harbours, aqueducts and other feats of engineering. On this spot a local character, Tug Wilson (a great swimmer), organised a race annually from Dowles Ford to the bandstand. He taught many Bewdley children to swim.

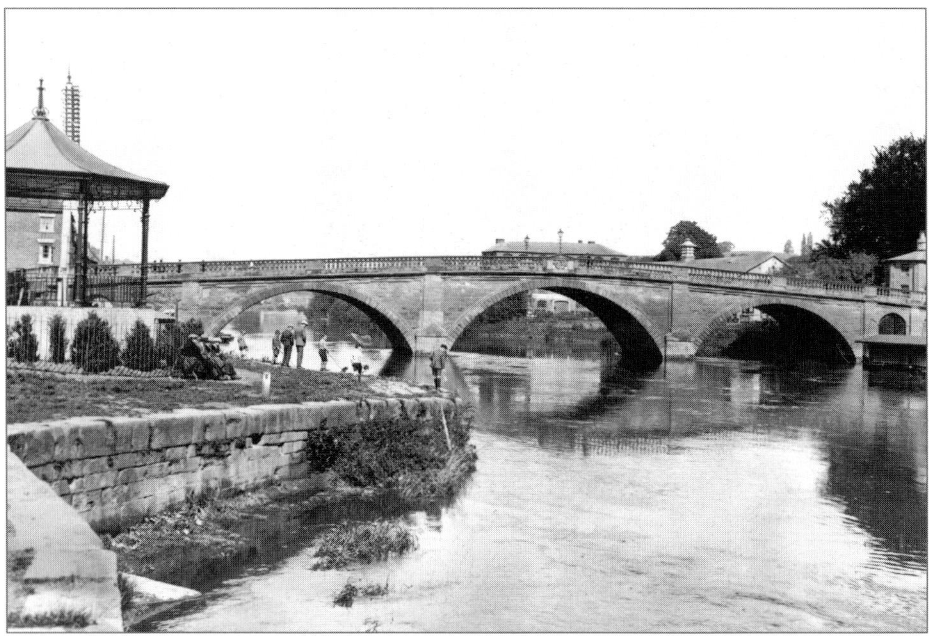

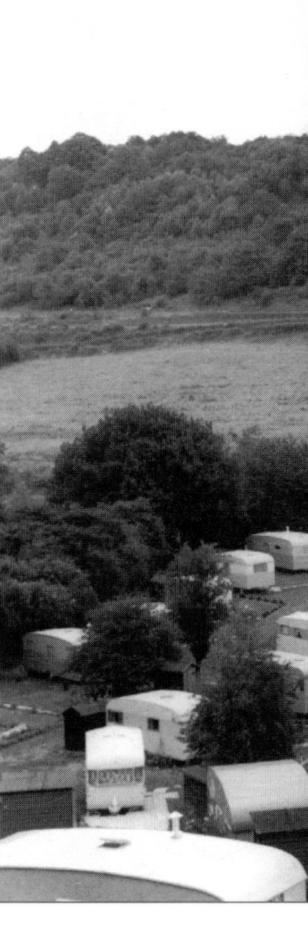

► **BEWDLEY**
*Severnside c1955*
B82069

This picturesque study of the river at Bewdley features a range of architectural styles. Boys leaning on the railings watch swans, but there was always much else to see. In 1880 ships of 60 tons could sail up as far as Bewdley, which could claim to be a seaport, for the Severn, Britain's longest river, is tidal as far as Bewdley bridge.

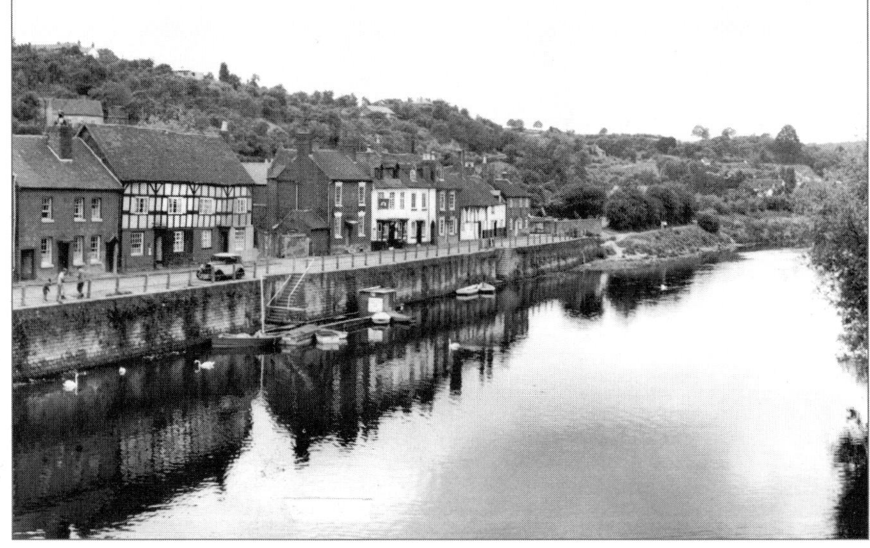

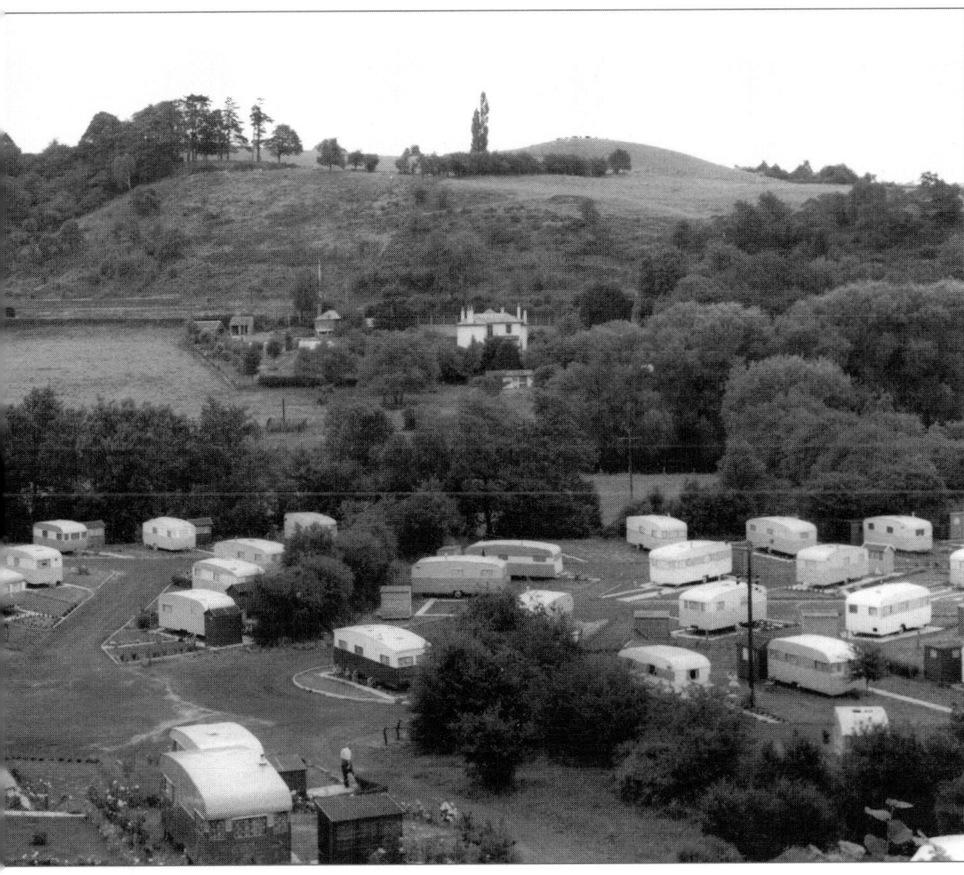

◄ **BEWDLEY**
*The Caravan Park c1965* B82074

Along the banks of the river there used to be many small foundries. On their demise, their sites provided land for recreation and the caravan park. Redstone Caravan Park and Walsh's at Stourport prove popular because of their setting, but flooding from the swollen river could on occasions be dangerous. Various trades were carried on in Bewdley in the past, including coracle making, baskets, wooden wheels, clay pipes, rope making and cap making. Cap making was very big business up to Charles II's reign, because a law of 1571 had made it obligatory for everyone over seven to wear caps on Sundays and holidays. The two main rope works were at Wribbenhall.

► **BEWDLEY**
*Severn Side (North) c1940*
B82209

At intervals on Severn Side, both north and south, steps leading from the sandstone quays were constructed. Warehouses blossomed here from early days, and goods (including wool, wood, coal and other commodities) were conveyed in flat-bottomed trows. Bewdley Rowing Club was on Severnside North. On the left we can see a typical general store, its brick walls covered with tinplate signs offering soup, tea, and custard; confectionery and ice-cream have been added more recently, brought by the motorised delivery wagon.

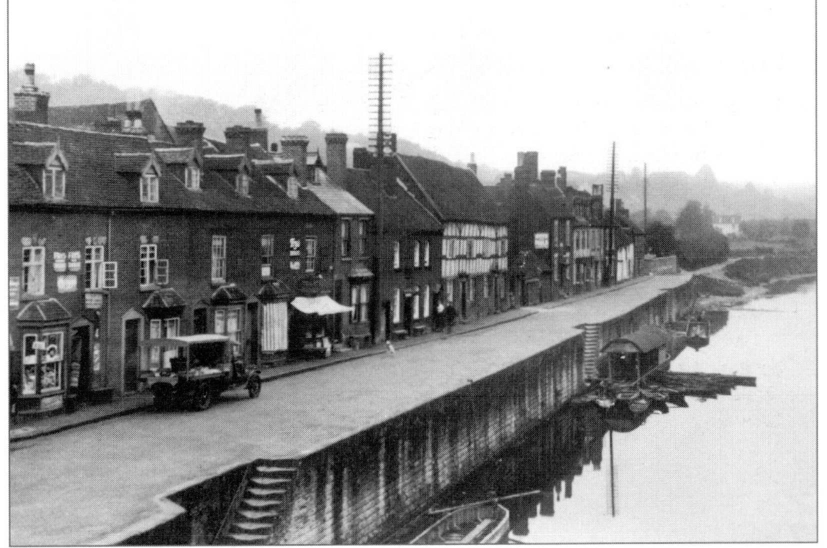

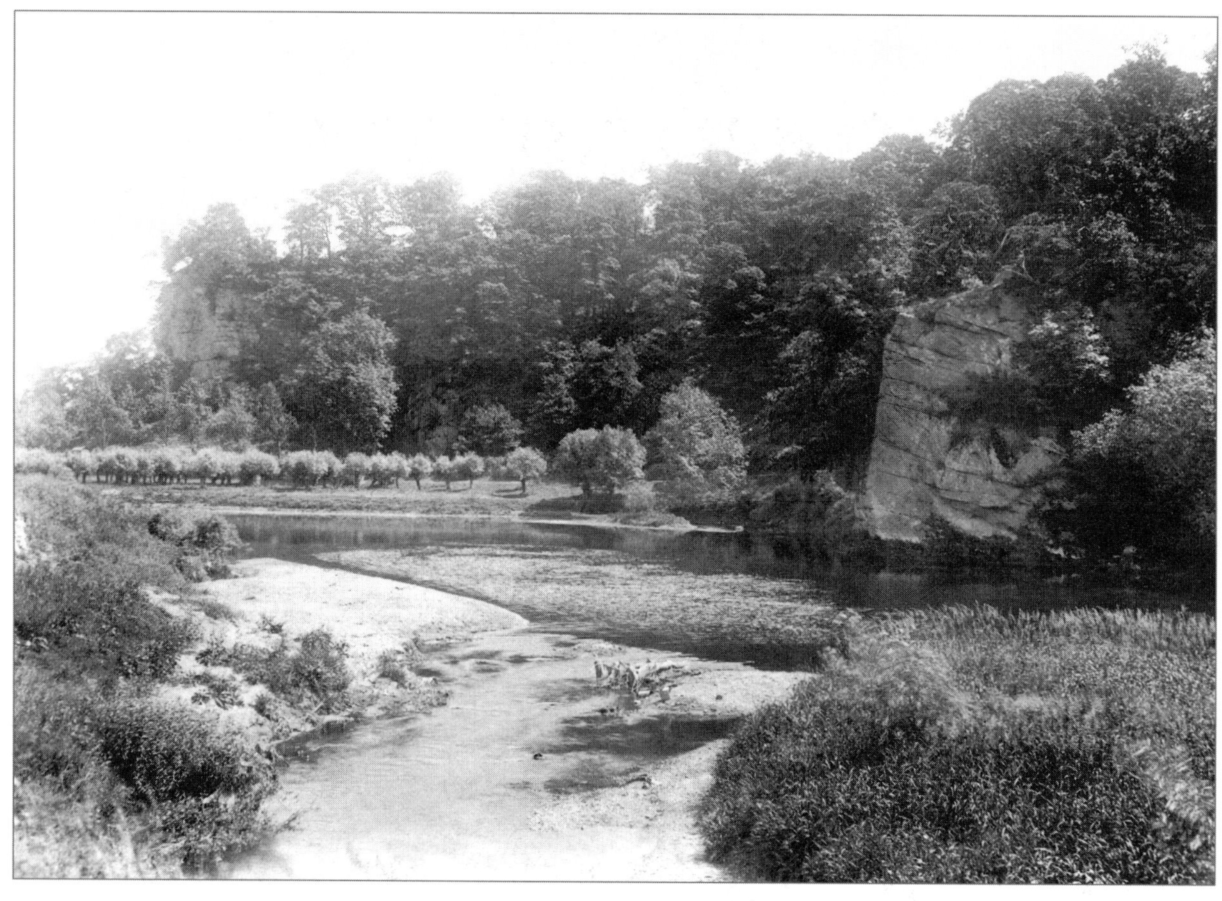

**BEWDLEY,** *Blackstone Rock 1904* 51979

Blackstone Rock, a great outcrop of sandstone rising sheer from the river, is shrouded with trees. Springs bubble up through the underlying sandstone, just as they do at Spring Grove House (now the Safari and Leisure Park). In the 18th century a hermit or holy man lived in a small hollow in the rock. It was a treacherous spot for river currents (the Severn has a tidal bore), and to safeguard their passage the sailors would throw money and gifts from the trows to the hermit, thinking that his prayers would ensure a successful trip. Sometimes as many as 400 trows could be waiting between Bewdley and Blackstone for high tide. The first fair charter was dated 1376, and the fair was held on February 5 each year on the Feast of St Agatha. By the 16th century, when there were three fairs, traffic on the river was further increased.

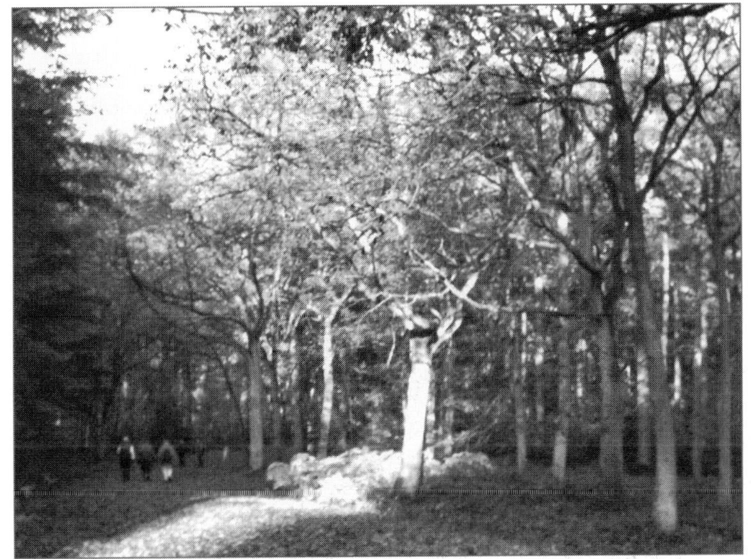

**WYRE FOREST**
*2003* W643002

The track amidst thick leaf mould indicates the path habitually taken by the fallow deer that live in the forest. A herd of 300-400 roams Wyre Forest, and the deer are culled and counted every year to maintain healthy stock. The deer have used these tracks for centuries.

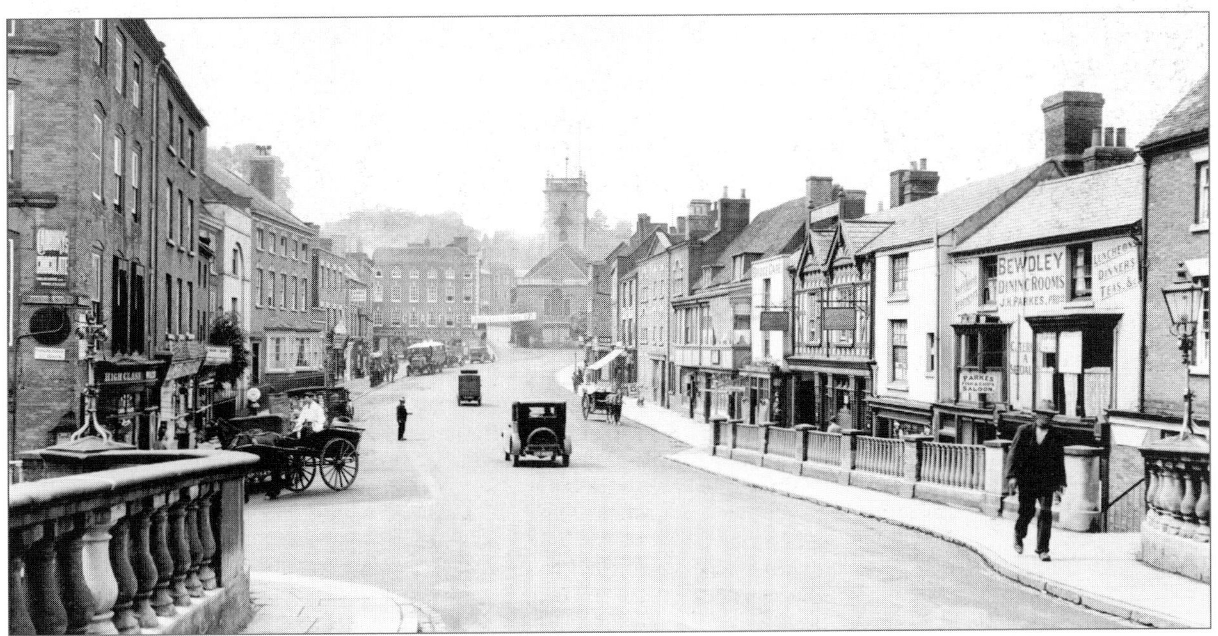


**BEWDLEY,** *Load Street 1931* 84620

A busy day lies ahead. The banner across Load Street indicates a regatta. A white-coated butcher or baker is delivering on the corner of Severnside South (left). Evans' garage and the Chocolate Box higher up face the Bridge Café, a bank, and J H Parkes' Bewdley Dining Rooms across the street. Parkes' Fish and Chips Saloon was a popular part of that establishment. A man is approaching (right) to cross the beautiful three-arch bridge spanning the River Severn built by Thomas Telford with stone taken from the estate of Lord Valentia at Arley and the quarry at Highley. John Simpson, stonemason, of Shrewsbury, oversaw the building, which cost £11,000. Five hundred years ago, this waterway was busier than any in Britain, and Bewdley was one of the busiest inland ports.

▼ **BEWDLEY,** *Load Street c1955* B82032

Here we have a closer view of the classical St Anne's Church, which stands amidst the varied historical architecture which makes Load Street forever interesting. Crawley's the ironmongers (left), the shop window crowded with pots, pans, ladles, corn scoops and deep dishes, is next door to James & Son, grocers, at numbers 45 and 46. The large tin plate signs, 'Old Judge Tea Tips' and 'Silvo' (a metal cleaner) deck the walls. On the other side of the church is Thomas F Timmis, family butcher, established in 1750.

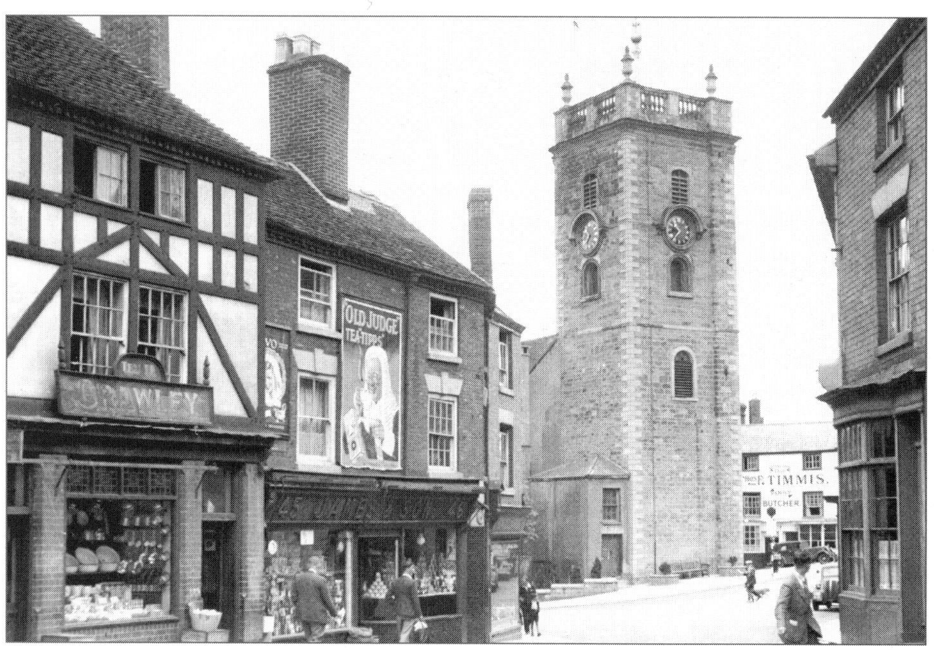


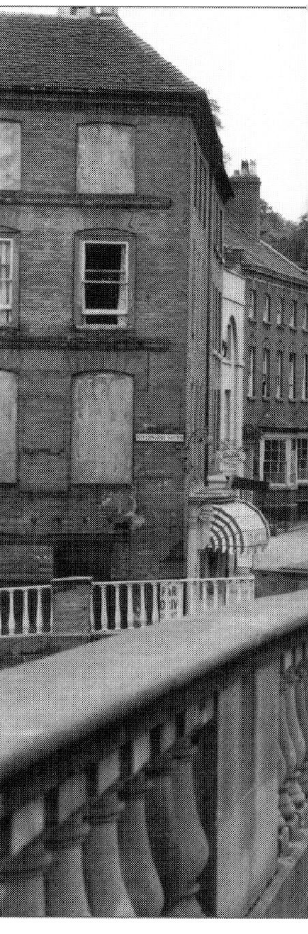

► **BEWDLEY**
*Load Street c1960* B82046

The George Hotel (centre left) was Bewdley's chief coaching inn, and from here coaches left for London and Birmingham in the 17th century. Because there were so many travellers passing through the town, it was said that there was one inn for every six dwellings, including the Pack Horse, the Horn & Trumpet, and the Black Boy. The Black Boy hotel at Wribbenhall was the centre for the barge trade. Weatherhead's shop, a lovely half-timbered building (left), is up for sale. Riding out of the picture is a leather-helmeted and be-goggled motorcyclist with a pillion passenger, a sign of the sixties.

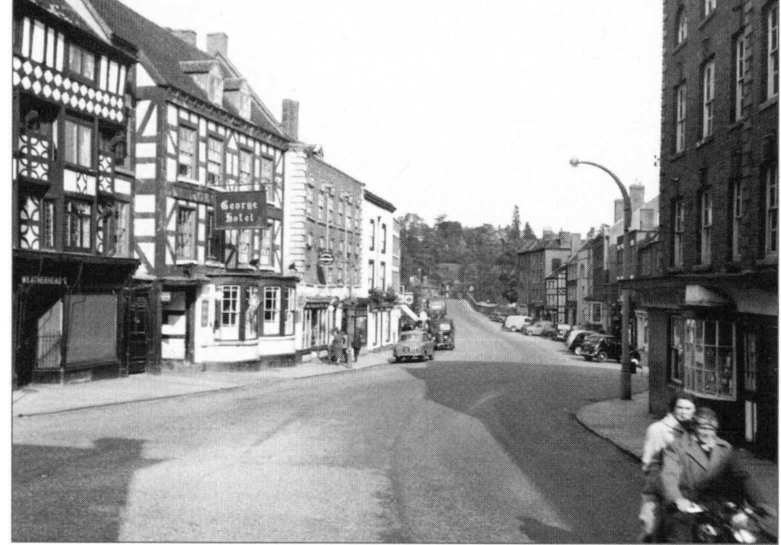

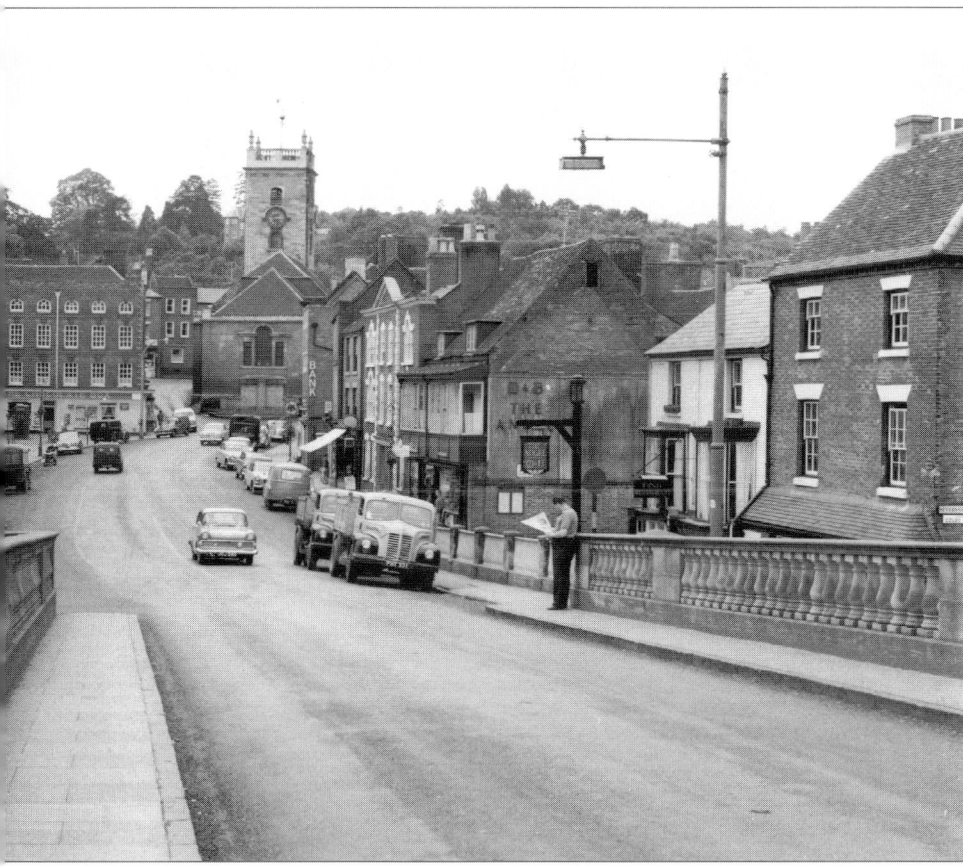

**BEWDLEY**
*Load Street c1965*
B82070

A very interesting building (right) is the Angel, where Charles I stayed for one night in 1645 during the Civil War. The gable end of this inn displays a B&B sign (bed and breakfast). Beyond is a bank, and the Chocolate Box is straight ahead. Severnside North's Coles Quay is to the right.

**BEWDLEY**
*Lower Park, Stanley Baldwin's Birthplace c1965* B82088

Stanley Baldwin earned fame as a Member of Parliament, and became Prime Minister three times. He was born at Lower Park House, Bewdley, in 1867, and succeeded his father as MP for Bewdley in 1908. When he retired, he was created Stanley, 1st Earl Baldwin of Bewdley. He was a first cousin to the poet and novelist Rudyard Kipling, whose mother came from Bewdley. On the left is Lax Lane, where the Pack Horse Inn, an historic hostelry, was the point where pack horse trains assembled. Long strings of mules carried 'Kidderminster stuffs', leather, and ironware. The packmen ate baked rabbit and oatmeal gruel laced with brandy before braving the weather. Lax Lane runs the length of Snuff Mill Brook, which led to an ancient pool.

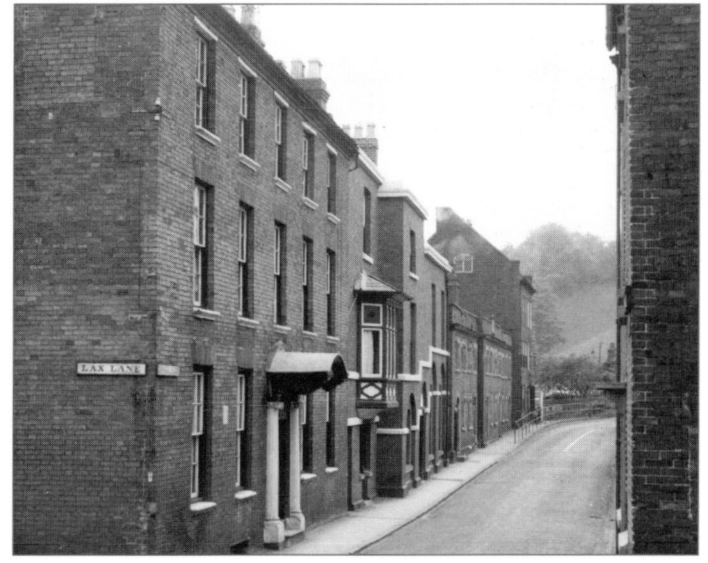

# LENTIL SOUP FROM BEWDLEY

450g/1 lb red lentils, washed and soaked
1½ large onions
2 tablespoons oil
3 crushed cloves of garlic
600ml/1 pint chicken stock
1 teaspoon ground cumin
½ teaspoon ground sea salt
juice of 1 small lemon

Fry onions in oil in a large pan till brown. Stir in garlic. Put in lentils and stock and boil. Stir in cumin. Do not add salt until lentils are softening. Add water if necessary. Stir in lemon juice and serve with a teaspoon of chopped chives or parsley in centre of bowl.

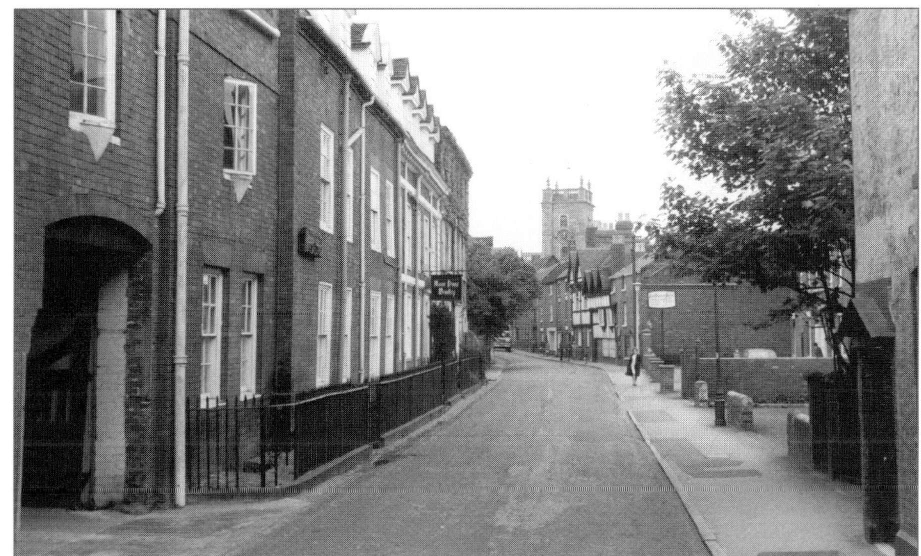

**BEWDLEY**
*High Street c1960*
B82089

On the right is the Redthorne Hotel, and opposite it is the Manor House. A mews area used for coaches and horses in the 18th century lies to the immediate left, with entry by the archway. St Anne's parish church, whose tower rises at the end of the street, is a classical building built c1750. Red brick Georgian houses and black and white vernacular architecture delight the eye in the High Street.

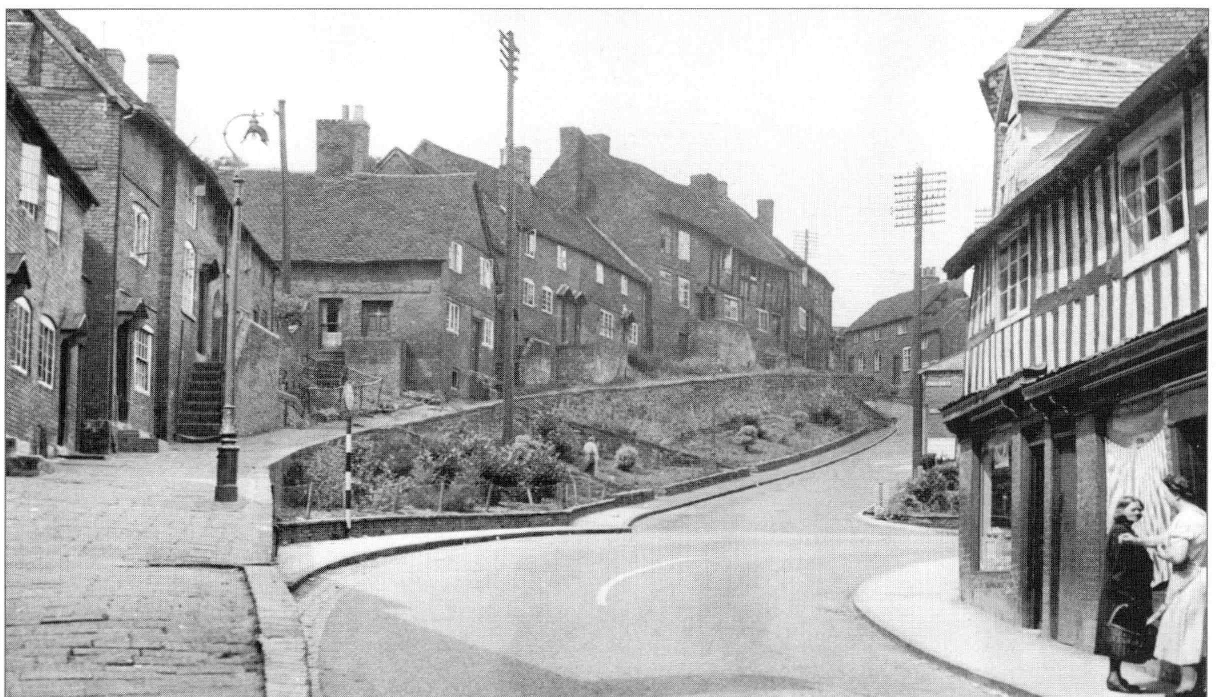

**BEWDLEY,** *Welch Gate c1955* B82033

Welch indicates that we are close to Wales - the spelling is medieval. The building where the two ladies are talking appears to be of Tudor origin. In Tudor times Bewdley was a rich woollen town. Did Henry VIII walk this street? In 1519 a Bewdley girl gave birth to his illegitimate son, later created Henry Fitzroy, Duke of Richmond and Somerset. This boy died of consumption when he was aged only 17. His mother was Betty Blount.

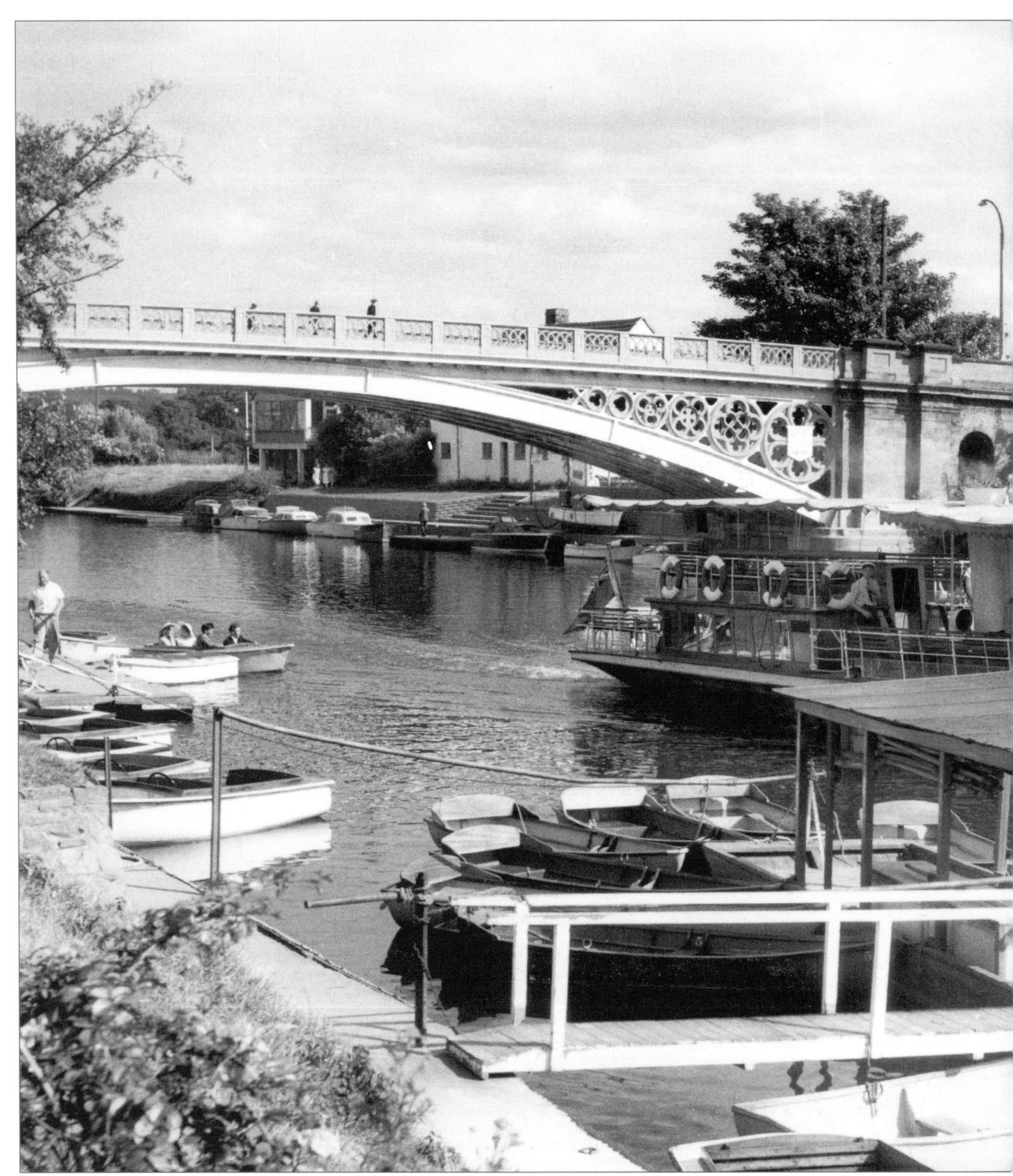

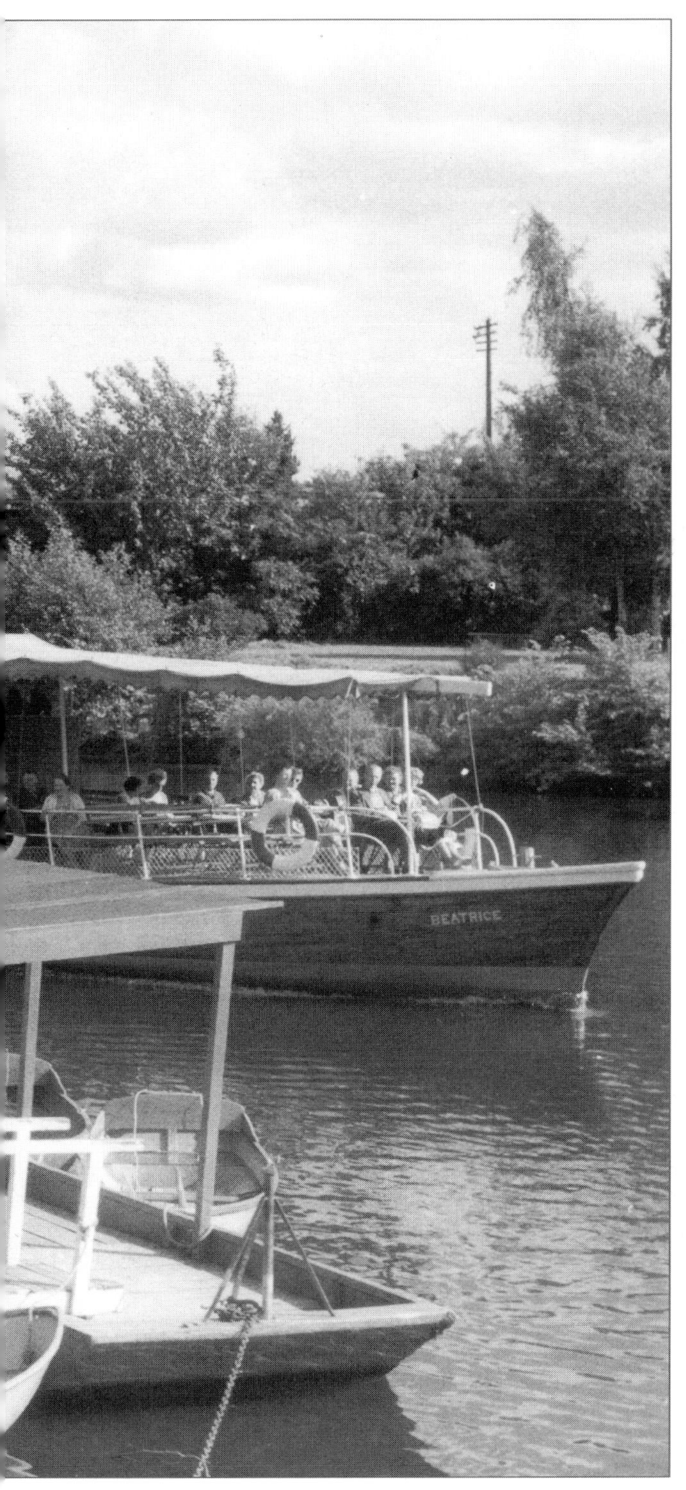


# STOURPORT ON SEVERN

**STOURPORT-ON-SEVERN**
*The Bridge c1960* S214057

In 1880, Stourport had a Local Board of Health to govern its affairs. Twelve members voted on matters relating to health, road maintenance, building, gas and so on. A Young Men's Literary Institute with full membership was running at this time in Kidderminster Road and building up a good library. This Georgian town developed with the building of the Staffordshire and Worcestershire Canal in 1771, but today's scene is mainly a setting for family entertainment: houseboats, riverboat trips, and rowing and power boats at the marina.

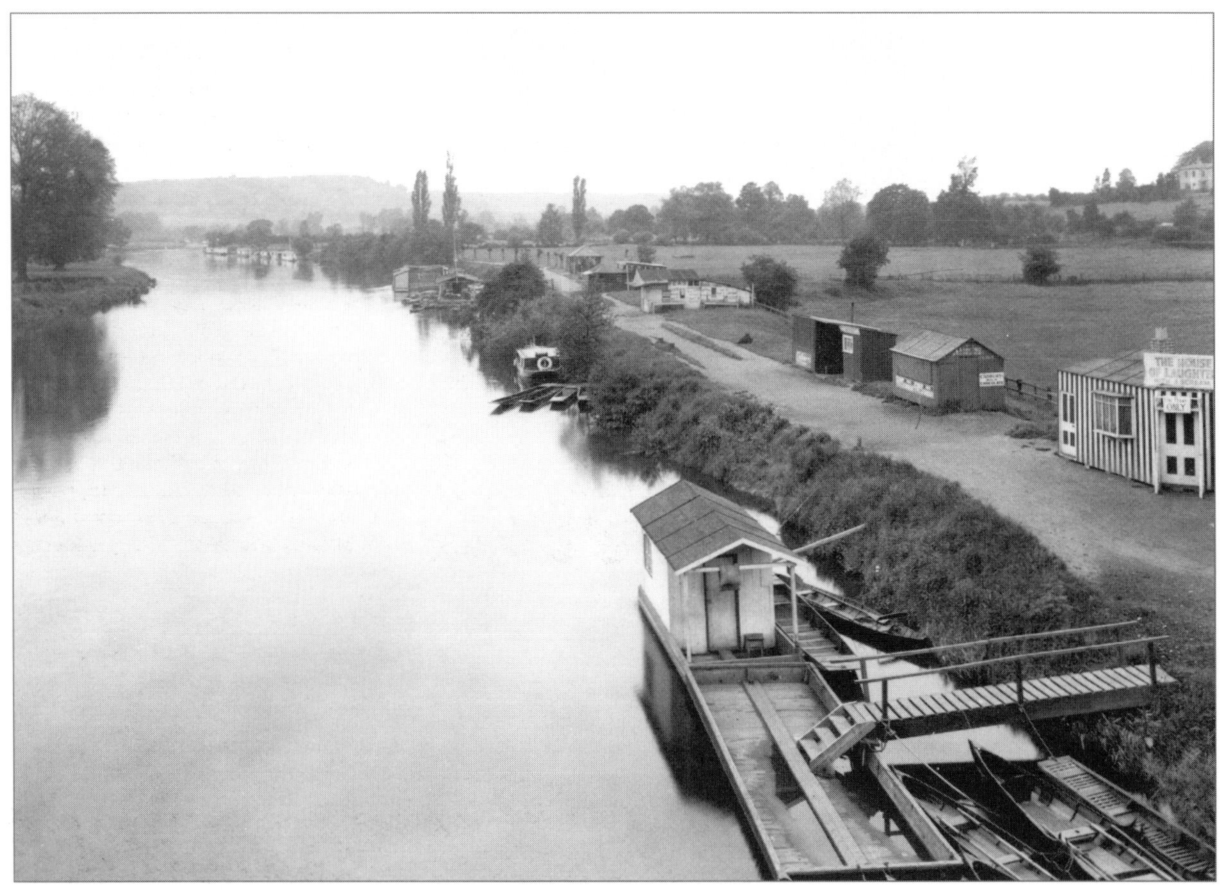

**STOURPORT-ON-SEVERN**
*The View from the Bridge 1931* 84627

This view of a more tranquil river, with small cabins and holiday homes on its banks, indicates the decline of commercial river traffic. The striped cabin far right is captioned 'the house of laughter'. The Baldwin family have been of great influence in Stourport. Alfred, born in 1841 at Stourport near Wilden, was the youngest boy, but he took over the family firm in 1870 as his two half brothers had died. Business revolved round the foundry at Stourport and the forge at Wilden. Baldwin Son & Company produced chains and heavy iron machinery. By 1870 Alfred was living at Wilden House, and took a great interest in the welfare of his workers and their children. A Worcester newspaper reported: 'The youngest child in the village was known to him ... he secured for them well provided and comfortable homes, built schools for the children and a church for them to worship in.' He was MP for Bewdley in the 1890s, and died in 1908. An iron foundry for hollow ware, the Wilden ironworks, carpet weaving, and maltings employed many people hereabouts.

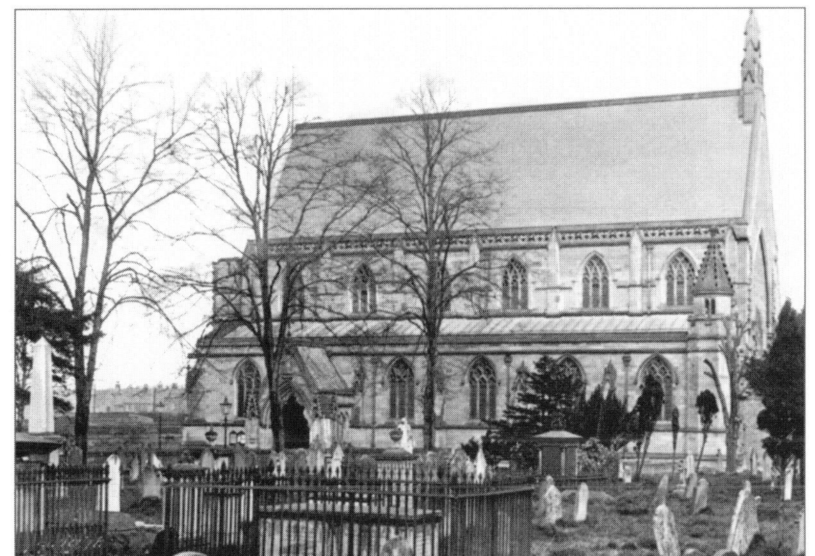

**STOURPORT-ON-SEVERN**
*The Church c1930* S214015

Stourport's church of St Michael stands on a hill, and was built in the Gothic style. It had two bells in 1880, when a splendid brass lectern designed by J O Scott and presented by the vicar coincided with a complete interior restoration of the building. The population at that time was 3500. This church has now gone. There were great plans for a new church by J O Scott, but it proved too expensive, so the old church was demolished and a small, new church, where my mother is buried, was built. It is situated in the Mitton district, the most ancient part of Stourport, not far from Gilgal. The present incumbent of St Michael's is the Rev Barry Gilbert.

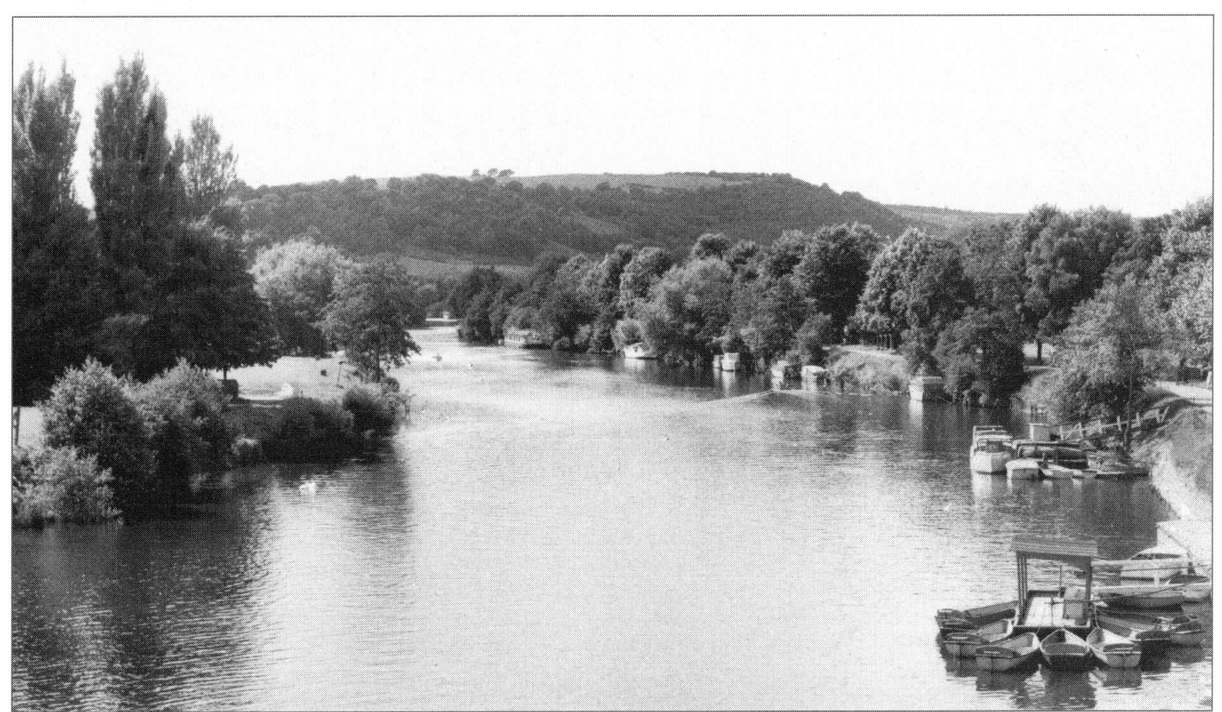

**STOURPORT-ON-SEVERN,** *The River upstream from the Bridge c1960* S214048

The market town of Stourport lies in the borough of Bewdley at the junction of the Staffordshire and Worcester Canal, the river Stour and the river Severn, which led to flourishing trade with other parts of the country. In the 1880s the Severn and Canal Carrying Company advertised daily services to Bristol, Gloucester, Kidderminster and towns further north. On the right are flat-bottomed trows, by 1960 being used for recreation rather than business.

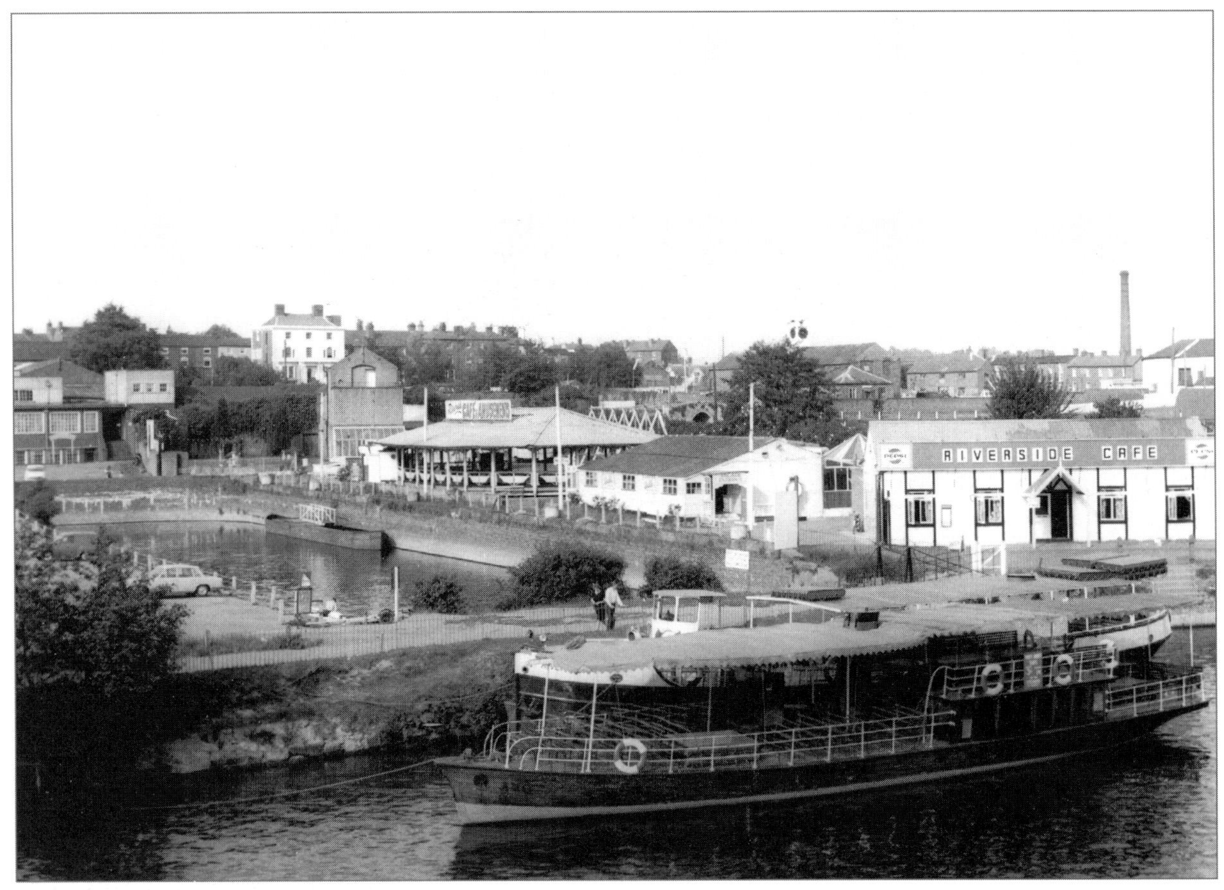


**STOURPORT-ON-SEVERN**
*The River Severn c1965* S214075

Pleasure prevails, with the Riverside Café and an amusement arcade next to the river. The commodious launch *Amo* is waiting to fill up with tourists for a river cruise. The Tontine, overlooking the canal basin, offers traditional draught beers and food, but in 1788 it was owned by the Canal Company; the houses on each side of the original inn were used by hop merchants - there was once a great trade in hops here before the Worcester Hop Market opened. When permission for a canal was refused at Bewdley, James Brindley brought it to Stourport, following the Stour Valley and joining the Severn at this point. Stourport, with its quay and warehouses, replaced Bewdley as an inland port, and although its commercial traffic has gone, it retains its colourful history. The canal bridges are scored and worn by the ropes of the horses that used to pull the narrow boats.

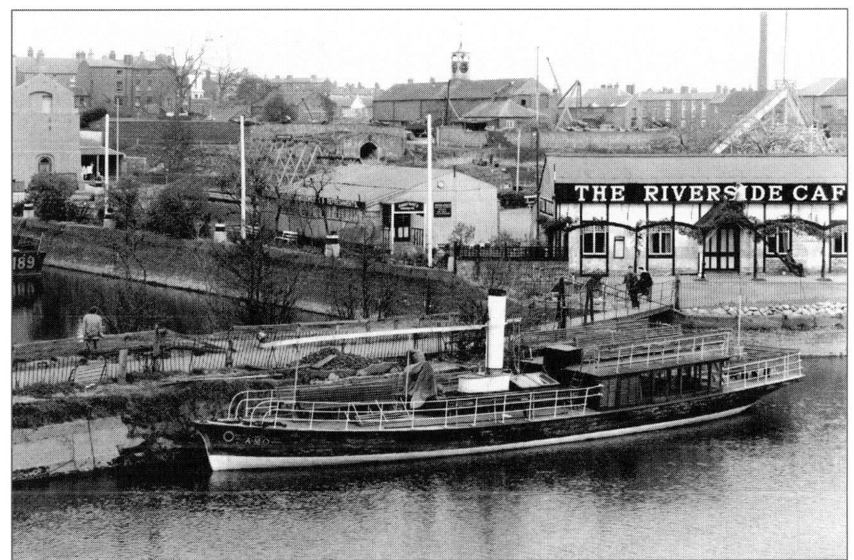


**STOURPORT-ON-SEVERN**
*The View from the Bridge c1955* S214022

Here we have an even better view of the *Amo*, the popular pleasure cruiser, and the Riverside Café, with some demolition work going on in the background. On the second Sunday in May a raft race down the Severn from Arley to Stourport attracts teams from all over the Midlands, and rowing crews from around Britain compete in the mid-August regatta. All year round, a programme of festivals connected with saints' days feature concerts, exhibitions and lectures.

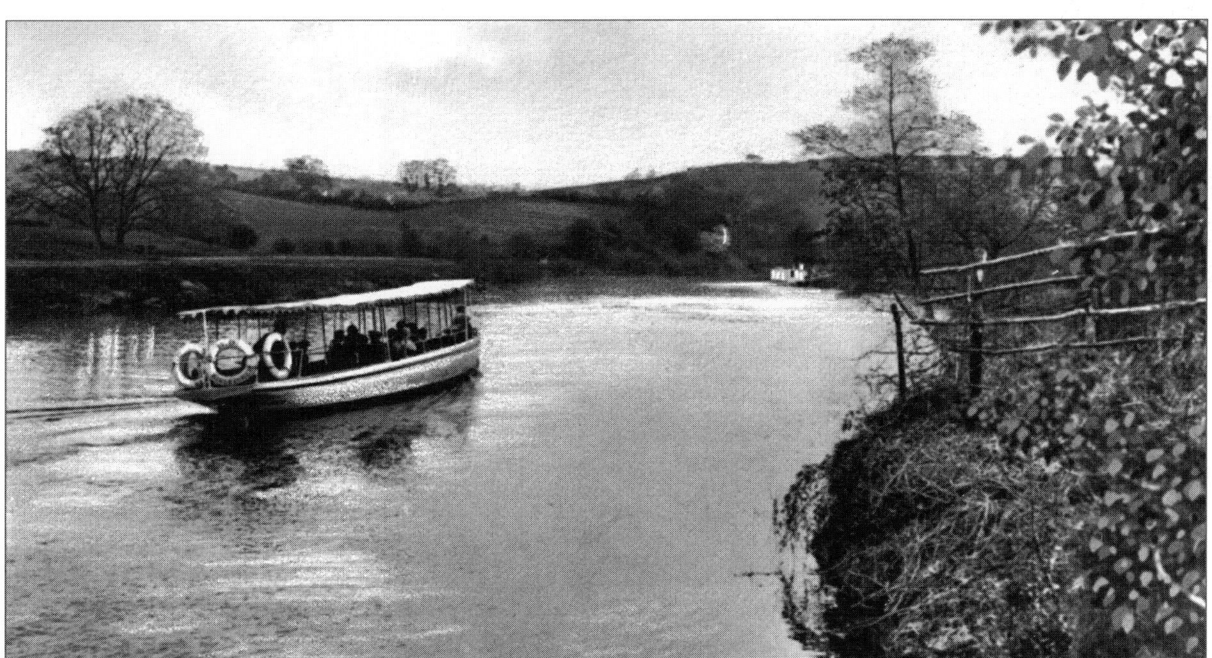

**STOURPORT-ON-SEVERN,** *On the River c1930* S214019

Holiday makers are enjoying a steam launch trip. When the Baldwin family lived at The Mount, near Stourport, young Stanley Baldwin scratched his name on a brick by the chauffeur's cottage. The Mount is now Menzies Stourport Manor Hotel, and the brick on which the lad who became PM Stanley Baldwin carved his name is still there. This country residence was sold by auction at the Lion Hotel, Kidderminster on 15 September 1955. Did they mention a ghost for sale? The story is told in S214701 (page 32). Astley Hall, between Stourport-on-Severn and Great Witley, was another of Stanley Baldwin's residences.

**STOURPORT-ON-SEVERN,** *The Mount, Gothic Doorway 2003* S214701

This Gothic arched doorway was originally the front door of The Mount, which was where Stanley Baldwin lived as a boy. The 19th century house is now a hotel (the Stourport Manor Hotel). On occasions at dead of night, staff are convinced they have seen a lady with long, dark hair and wearing long black period clothes walk down this corridor to what was the arched front door of the Mount, pause on the step and vanish. The night porter was not joking when he claimed her as the ghost of the manor.

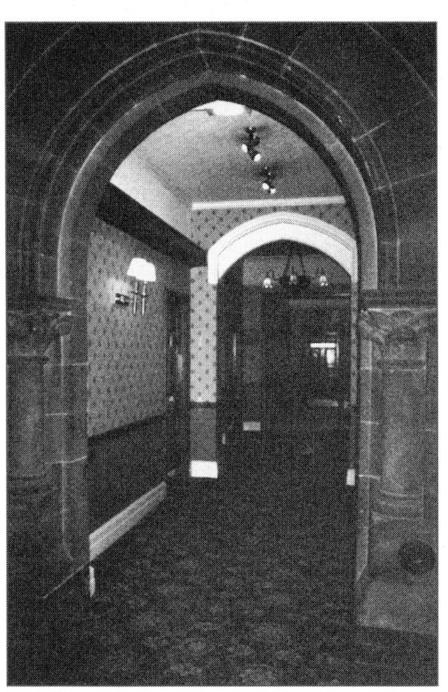

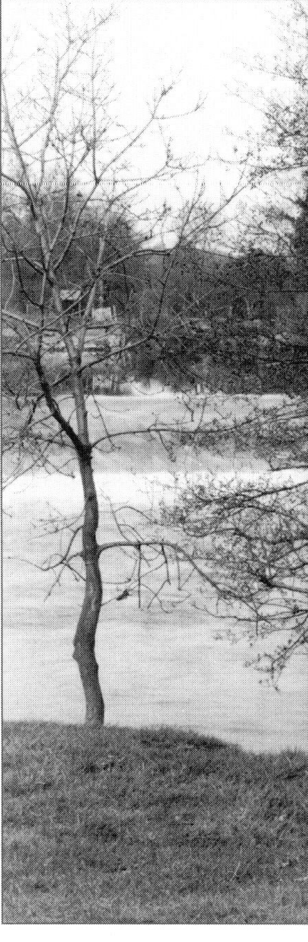

**STOURPORT-ON-SEVERN**
*The Bridge 1904* 51975

Once a busy inland port, the town was known as the 'Venice of the Midlands'. This iron bridge over the Severn river dates from 1870. The canal basin has become the hub of leisure activity. A swimming pool, a sports centre and Stourport Rowing Club are other diversions.

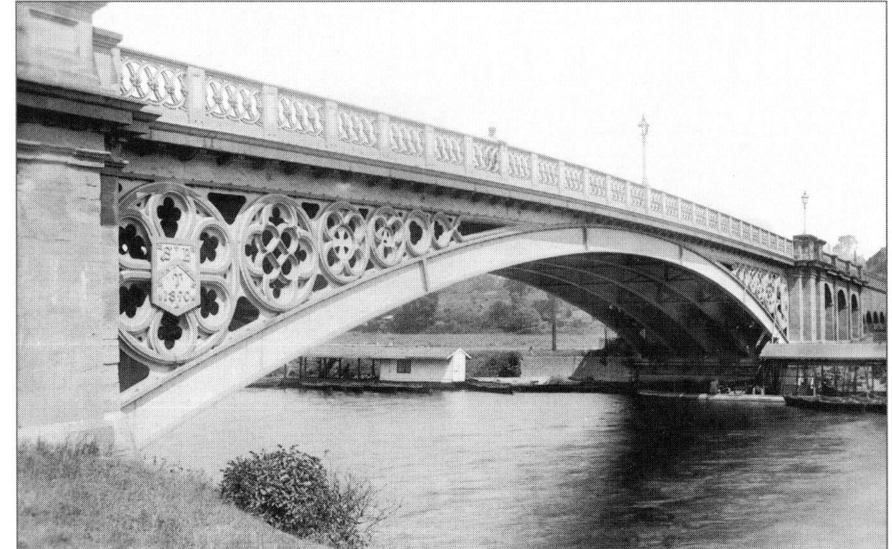

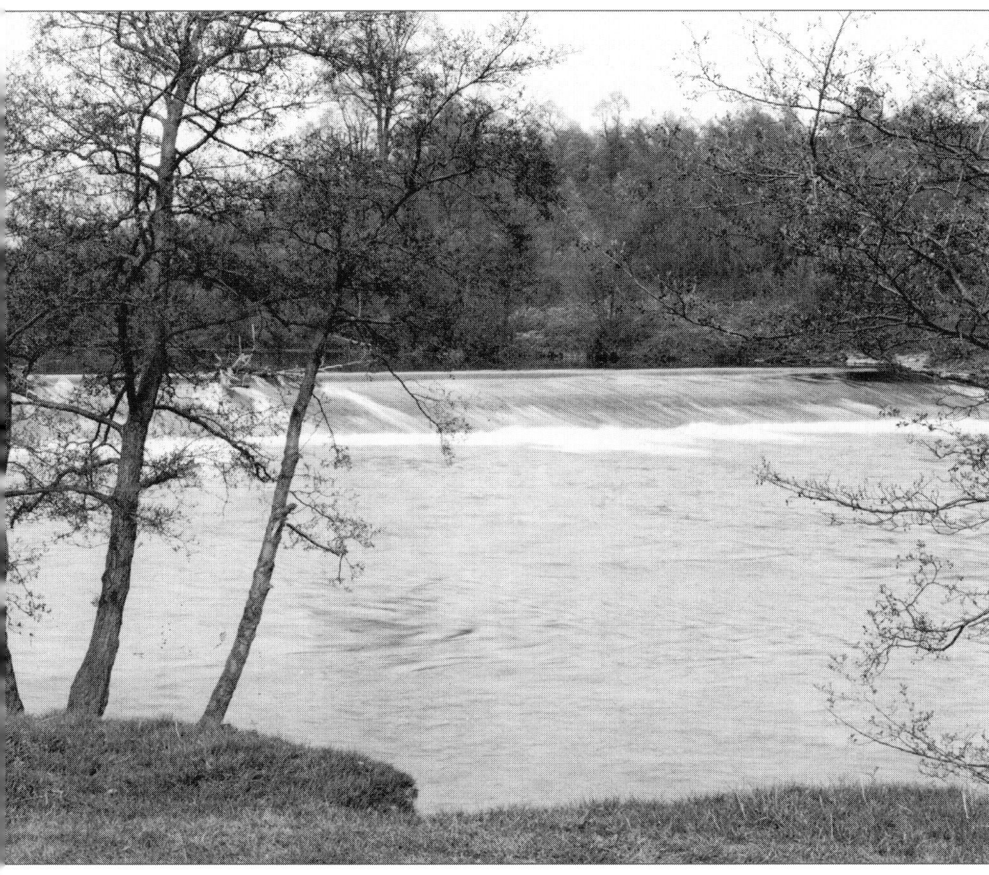

**STOURPORT-ON-SEVERN**
*The Weir c1955*
S214031

The Roman name for River Severn was Sabrina, and the poet Milton in 'Comus' refers to her as 'a gentle nymph ... that with moist curb sways the smooth Severn stream. Sabrina is her name'. This beautiful photograph could echo these words, but fears of the river were not unfounded. Currents have drowned swimmers, and floods have claimed lives and property. Here the power of water is harnessed by the weir to drive mill machinery.

**STOURPORT-ON-SEVERN**
*Bridge Street c1955* S214027

A garage (right) and motor traffic are signs of changing times. The Bridge Inn (left) is not Stourport's only public house; others are the Angel, the Hope and Anchor, the Station Inn, and the Red Lion. The Swan was a posting house. In the 18th century a local man, Samuel Skey, amassed a fortune manufacturing dyestuffs and acid. In 1775 he bought 270 acres of land from Lord Foley and built Spring Grove House, now part of the Safari Leisure Park. A relative of Samuel's, Maria Bicknell, became the wife of the painter John Constable, who made several sketches of the house and the nearby River Severn. Spring Grove remained in private hands until 1970. Its last owner was Major Harcourt Webb, who founded the firm of Webb's Seed Merchants.

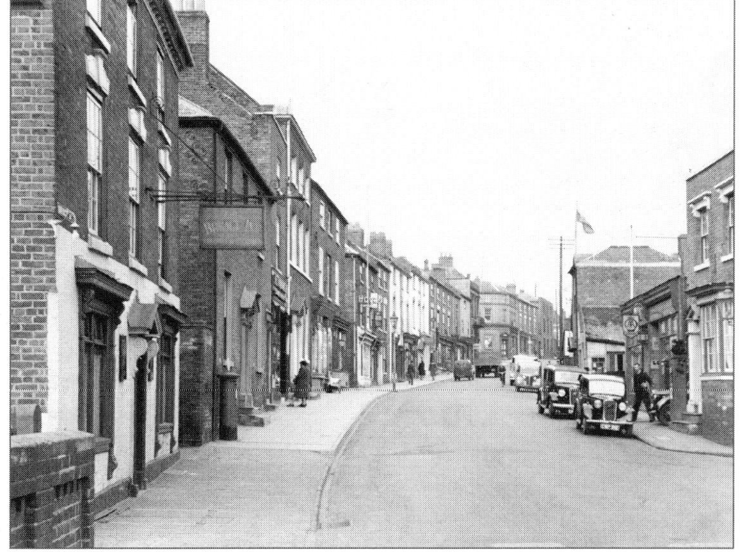

**STOURPORT-ON-SEVERN**
*High Street c1965*
S214077

On the left, behind the three walking girls wearing 60s shorter skirts, is the Wheatsheaf Inn supplied by Banks's ales; next door is S A Wilson, a hairdresser. Immediately to the right, a newsagent advertises Reveille's offer of 'win a year's free groceries'. Weatherhead Brothers Ltd next door, whose shop has lain empty, could rejoice that it had been sold. The barber's pole, beyond the sun blinds, once the familiar sign of the Company of Barber Surgeons incorporated in 1461, had by now disappeared from most towns.

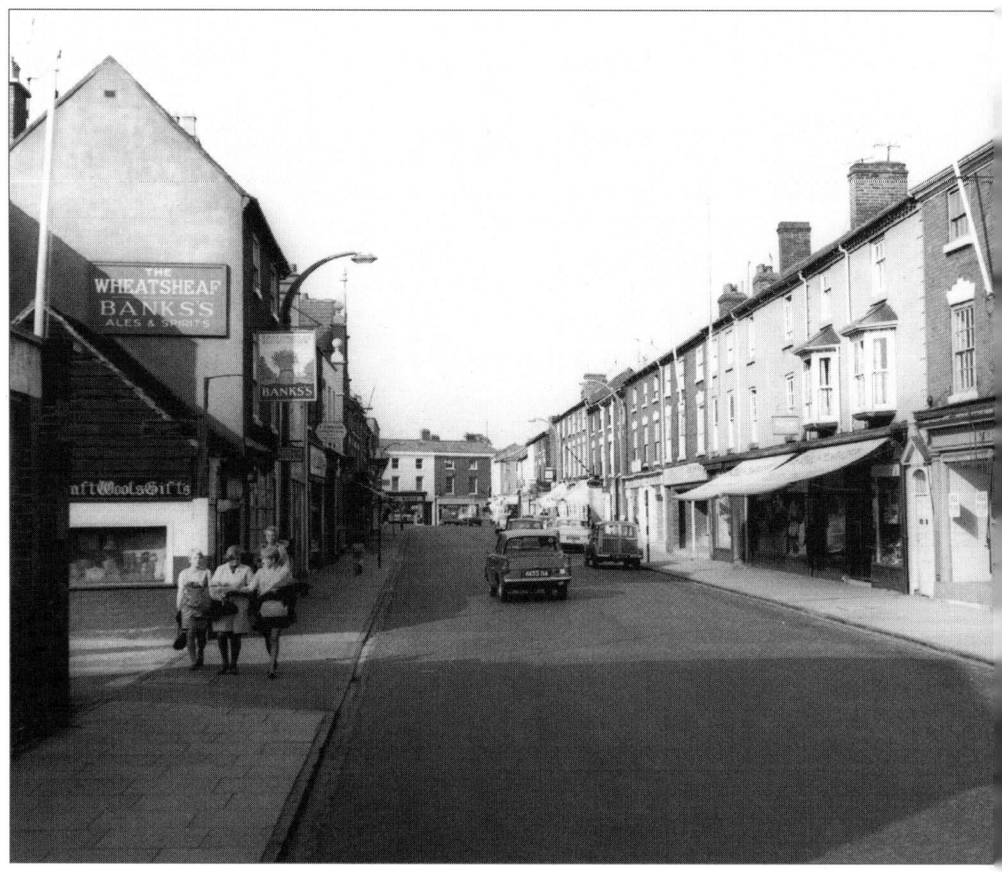


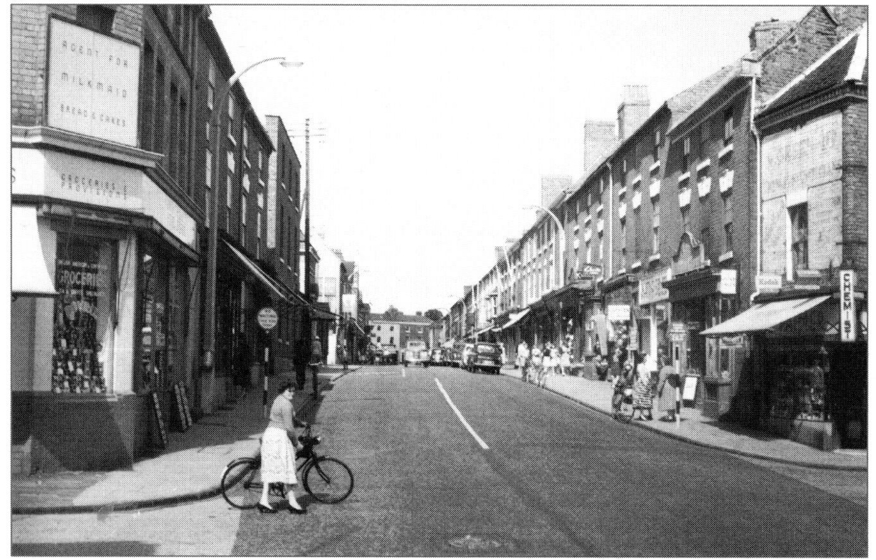

**STOURPORT-ON-SEVERN**
*High Street c1960*
S214046

The grocer's shop on the corner (left) is an agent for Milkmaid bread and cakes. Opposite is a shoe shop and Palmer's the chemist's, who also developed and sold Kodak films. Surprisingly little traffic is evident for such a bustling Georgian town. Canal boats and small inland craft still negotiate the flight of locks joining the canal to the river. The Stourport Steamer Company arrange full day boat trips along the River Severn in season.

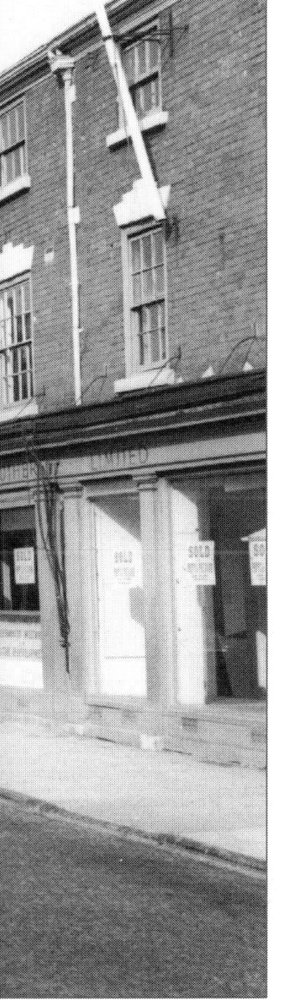

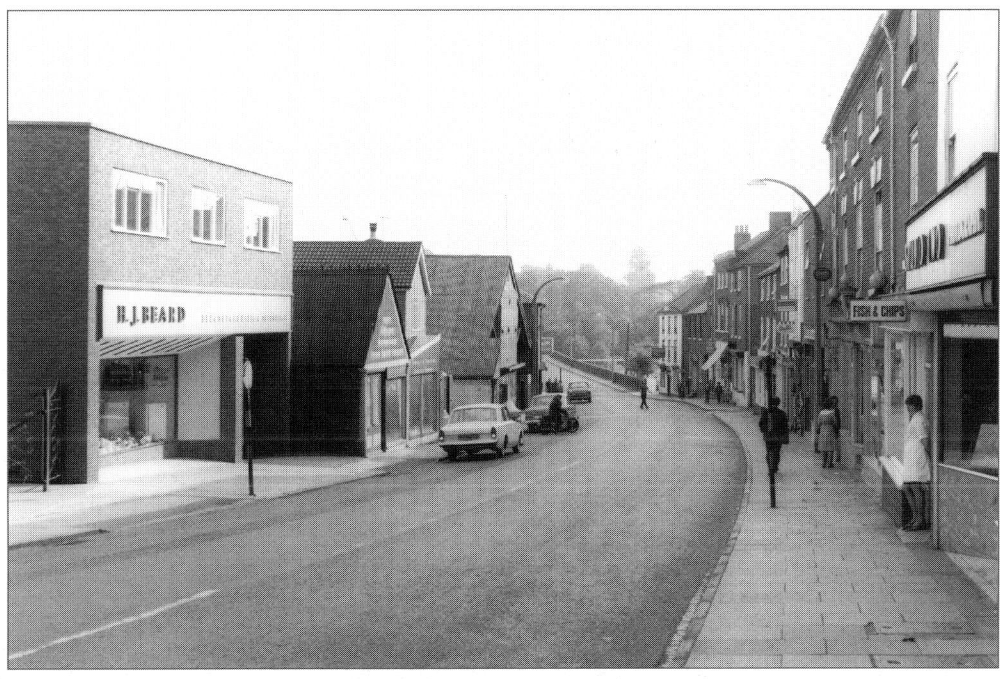


▲ **STOURPORT-ON-SEVERN,** *High Street c1965* S214062

H J Beard's electrical, radio and television shop (left) with its flat roof seems to belong to a new era, ushered in also by the advent of the Civic Centre (see S214065 below). In days gone by, carpets were woven behind the Tontine, and vinegar was brewed next to the carpet works off Severn Street. Parson's Chain Works was at the corner of Hartlebury Road and Worcester Road. Later Midland Industrial Plastics came to the Bewdley road.

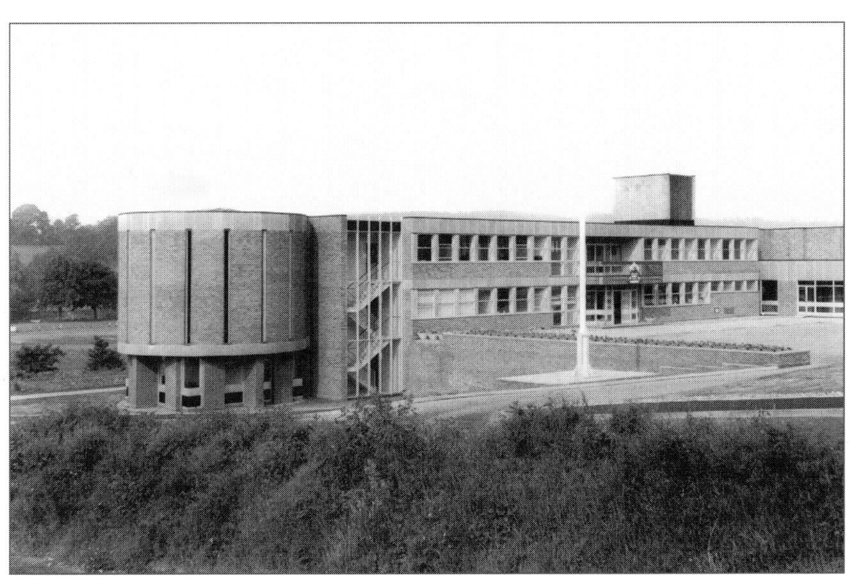

◄ **STOURPORT-ON-SEVERN**
*The Civic Centre c1965*
S214065

The circular tower of the centre is largely glass, a popular choice of architectural style in the 'swinging sixties'. Within is the Council Chamber. In other parts of the building are offices set aside for councillors representing Bewdley, Stourport and Kidderminster, whose rates are set separately according to district. A large hall and stage provides a venue for concerts, lectures, dog shows, pantomimes and events given by the Stourport Choral Society. Behind the Civic Centre land slopes steeply to the river.

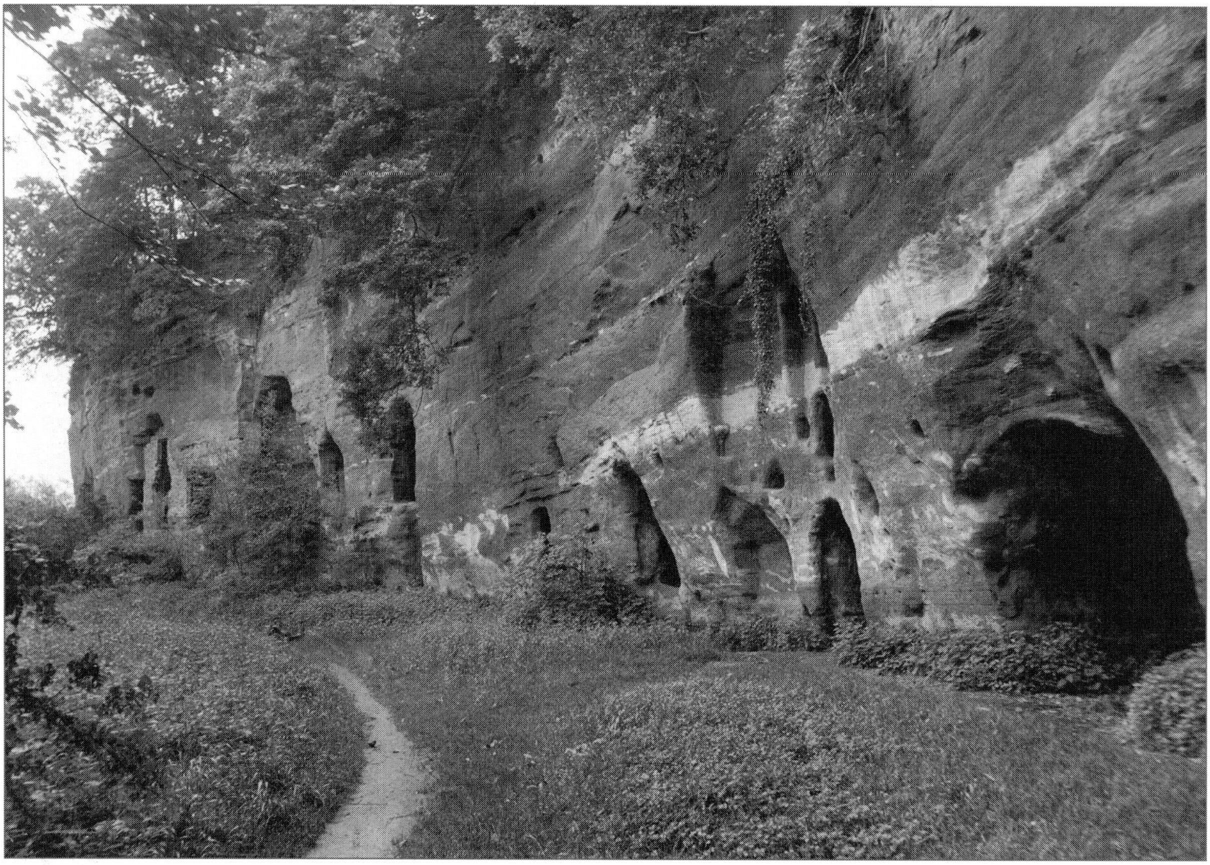

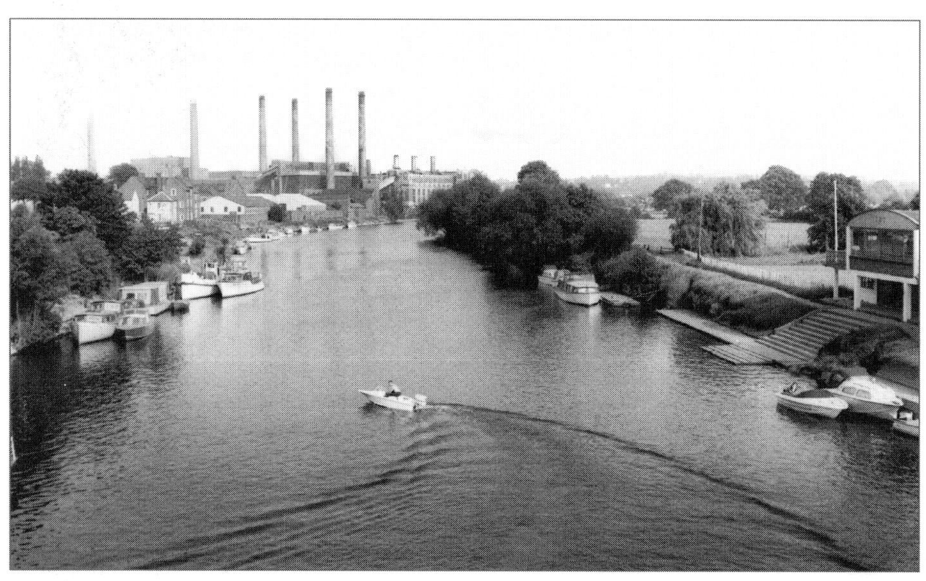

**STOURPORT-ON-SEVERN**
*The River Severn c1965* S214073

We are looking from the Stourport bridge towards Worcester. The tall chimneys against the skyline have now gone - they belonged to the power station. The land has been built upon with an estate of new houses. Also in this area is the Sandy Lane Industrial Estate, near Hartlebury Common.

**STOURPORT-ON-SEVERN** *Redstone Caves 1931* 84629

Three miles from Kidderminster is Habberley Valley. Here a circular way-marked walk can be enjoyed, passing Eastham's Farm and Coppice, Honey Brook and the rock houses carved in a sandstone cliff. They used to be lived in, but not since 1949. The 'redstone' refers to the colour of the sandstone prevalent in the Bewdley and Stourport area. Kinver also has caves like this.

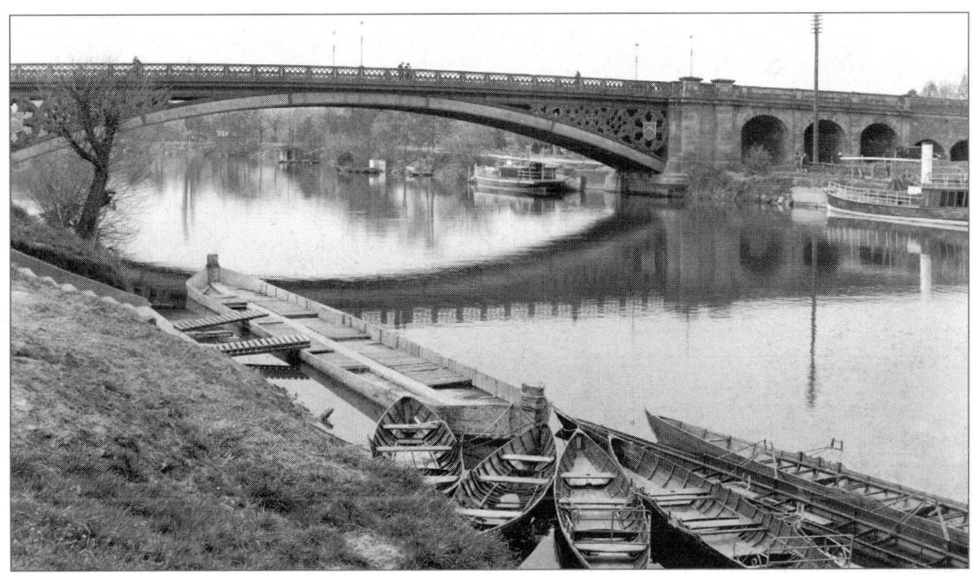

**STOURPORT-ON-SEVERN,** *The River Severn and the Bridge c1955* S214028

From the bridge it was once possible to see a windmill built on a high bluff of rock above the river. A new housing estate has arisen there, and a school called The Windmill School has been built. Wood Green Farm still cultivates acres of pasture on the north bank of the Severn as far as Burlish Top, but changes came about after World War II. The Lucy Baldwin hospital was built in the 1920s, and farmer Peter Pratt recalls that when the river was in flood he had to get the night shift nurses over to the Manor House Annexe - this never flooded, even when the river rose 11 feet above its normal level. If he happened to be on leave in wartime, Peter took the nurses across by rowing boat or by shire horse and cart, together with a churn of fresh milk! An extension to the maternity unit was possible when Mr Rowland Worth vacated the Manor House.

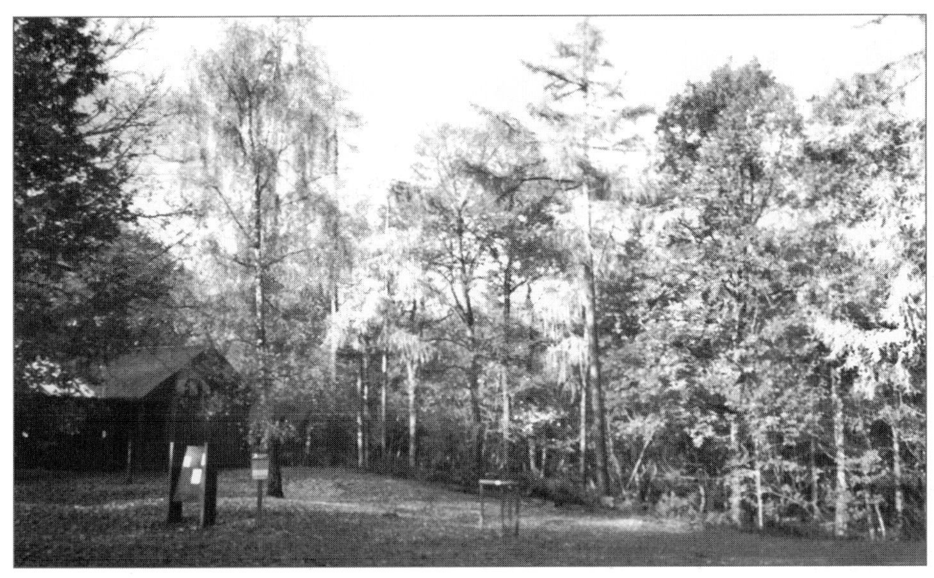

**WYRE FOREST** *Hawkbatch Visitor Centre, Hawkbatch Woods 2003* W643004

Here we see a lovely stand of birch trees mixed with beech, near the Visitor Centre and the car park at Hawkbatch. All the walks through the forest are waymarked and graded according to visitors' age and stamina. Pine cones, bracket fungus, fallen conkers and bluebells in season are a surprise and a delight.

**STOURPORT-ON-SEVERN**
*The Bridge c1965* S214063

On the escutcheon (left), the date of the bridge's construction is given as 1870. The spiral staircase alongside leads to the putting green and fun fair, sited on open meadowland convenient for the annual horticultural show. Walsh's Meadow, bright with cherry blossom in spring, stands near the old Beams Inn, with its outward black and white appearance and old beams within. Gypsies in their brightly decorated caravans were a part of Worcestershire lanes in the last century, and when they came to Stourport to sell their wares they were known to settle in Walsh's meadow.

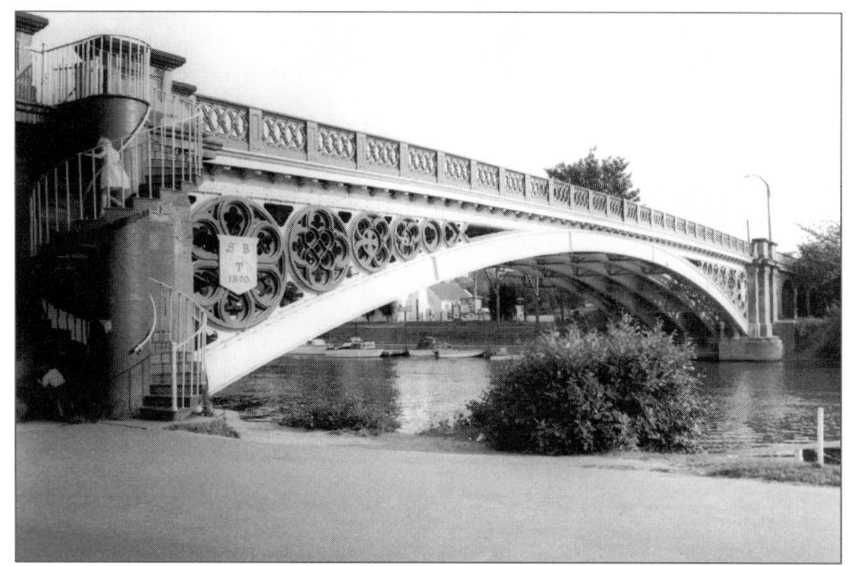


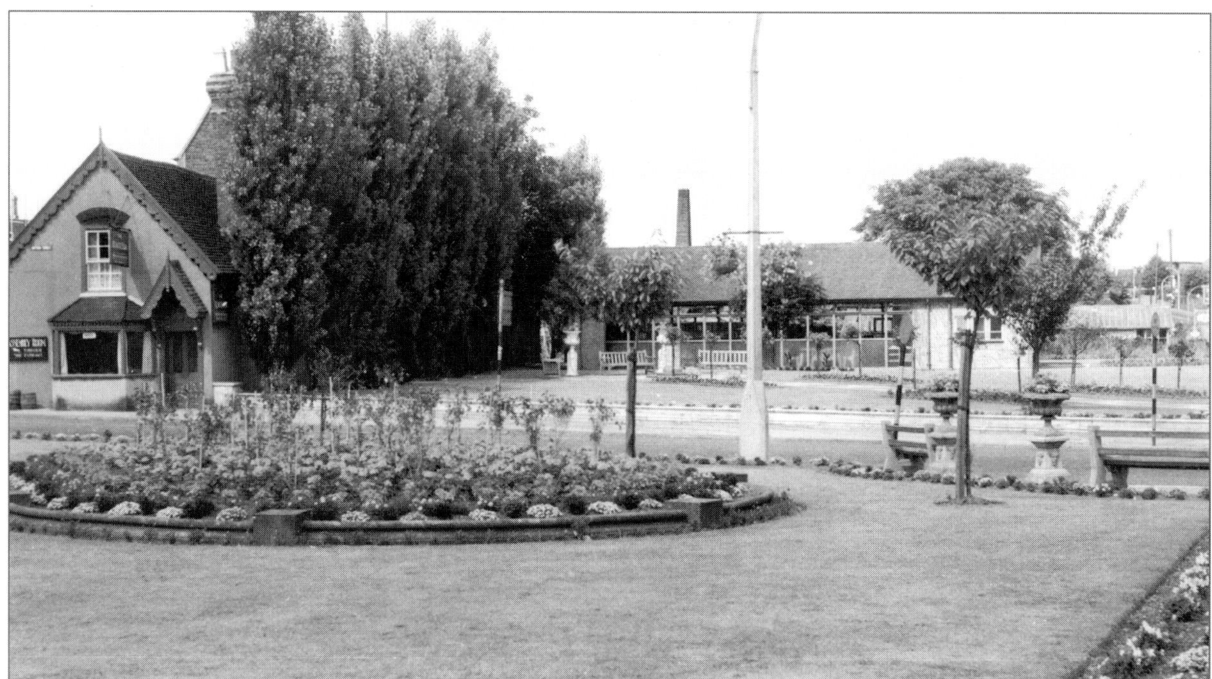

**STOURPORT-ON-SEVERN,** *The Gardens c1960* S214038

The Riverside Fun Fair and the Memorial Park public gardens, with extensive riverside walks, border meadows where fetes are held and floats for the annual carnival assemble. Stourport Rowing Club have their quarters nearby, and the marina provides moorings for sailing craft. As a change from the river, Hartlebury Castle is not far off; the road passes Quarry Bank and the Old Bakery. Bishop Carpenter's gatehouse and drawbridge have gone, but the moat at Hartlebury was described in the 17th century as 'full of water which filleth several ponds stored with fish'.

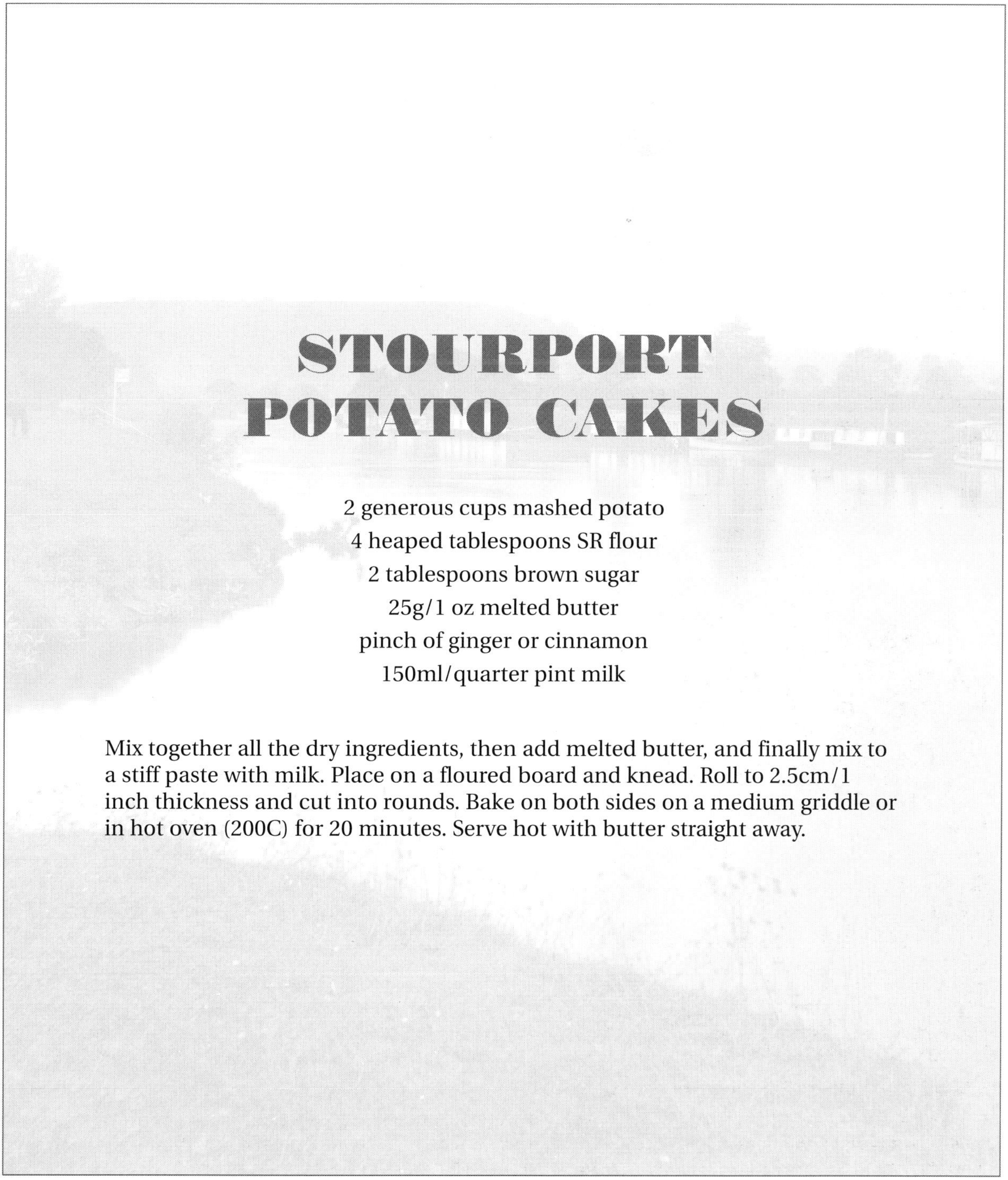

# STOURPORT POTATO CAKES

2 generous cups mashed potato
4 heaped tablespoons SR flour
2 tablespoons brown sugar
25g/1 oz melted butter
pinch of ginger or cinnamon
150ml/quarter pint milk

Mix together all the dry ingredients, then add melted butter, and finally mix to a stiff paste with milk. Place on a floured board and knead. Roll to 2.5cm/1 inch thickness and cut into rounds. Bake on both sides on a medium griddle or in hot oven (200C) for 20 minutes. Serve hot with butter straight away.

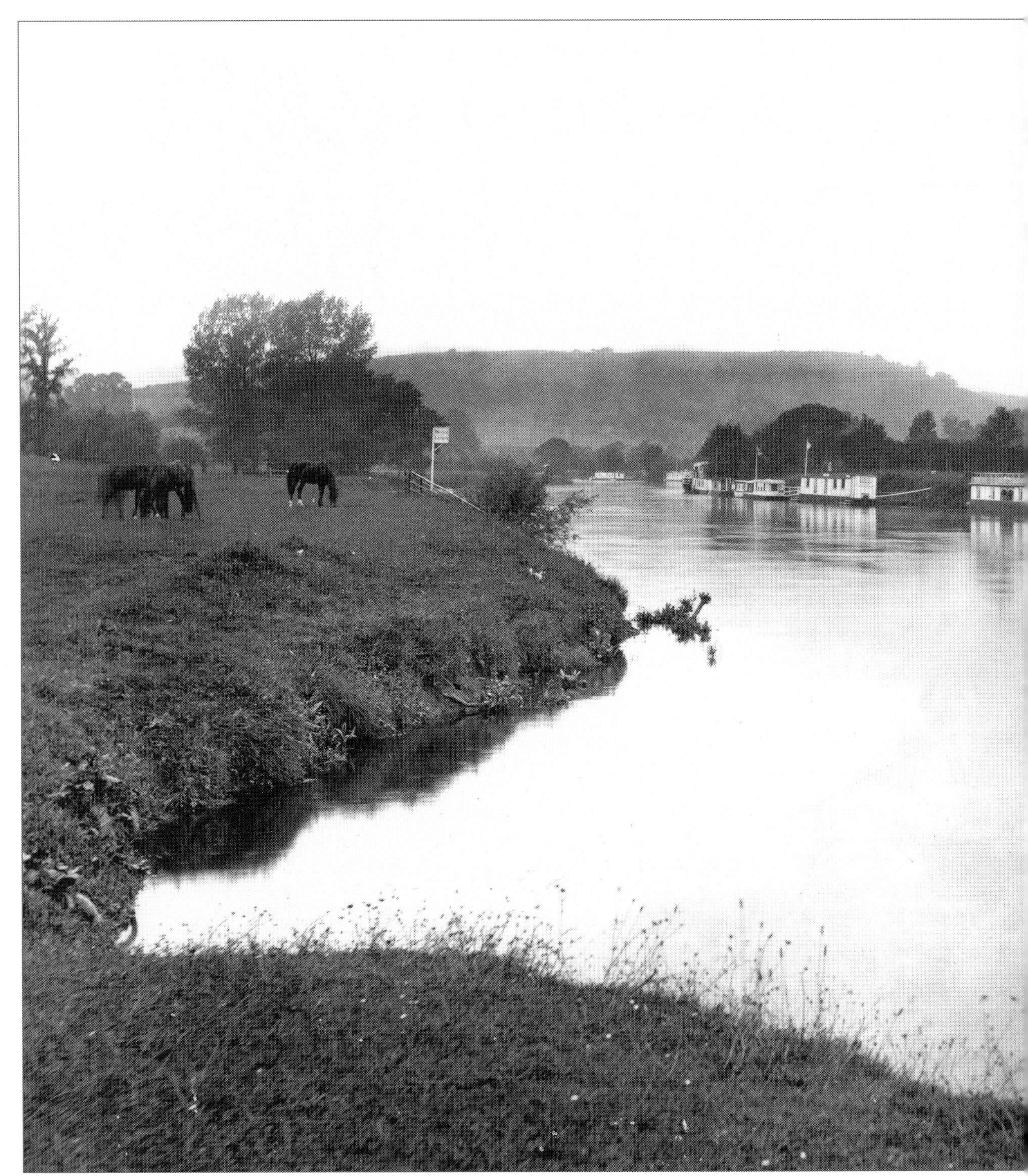

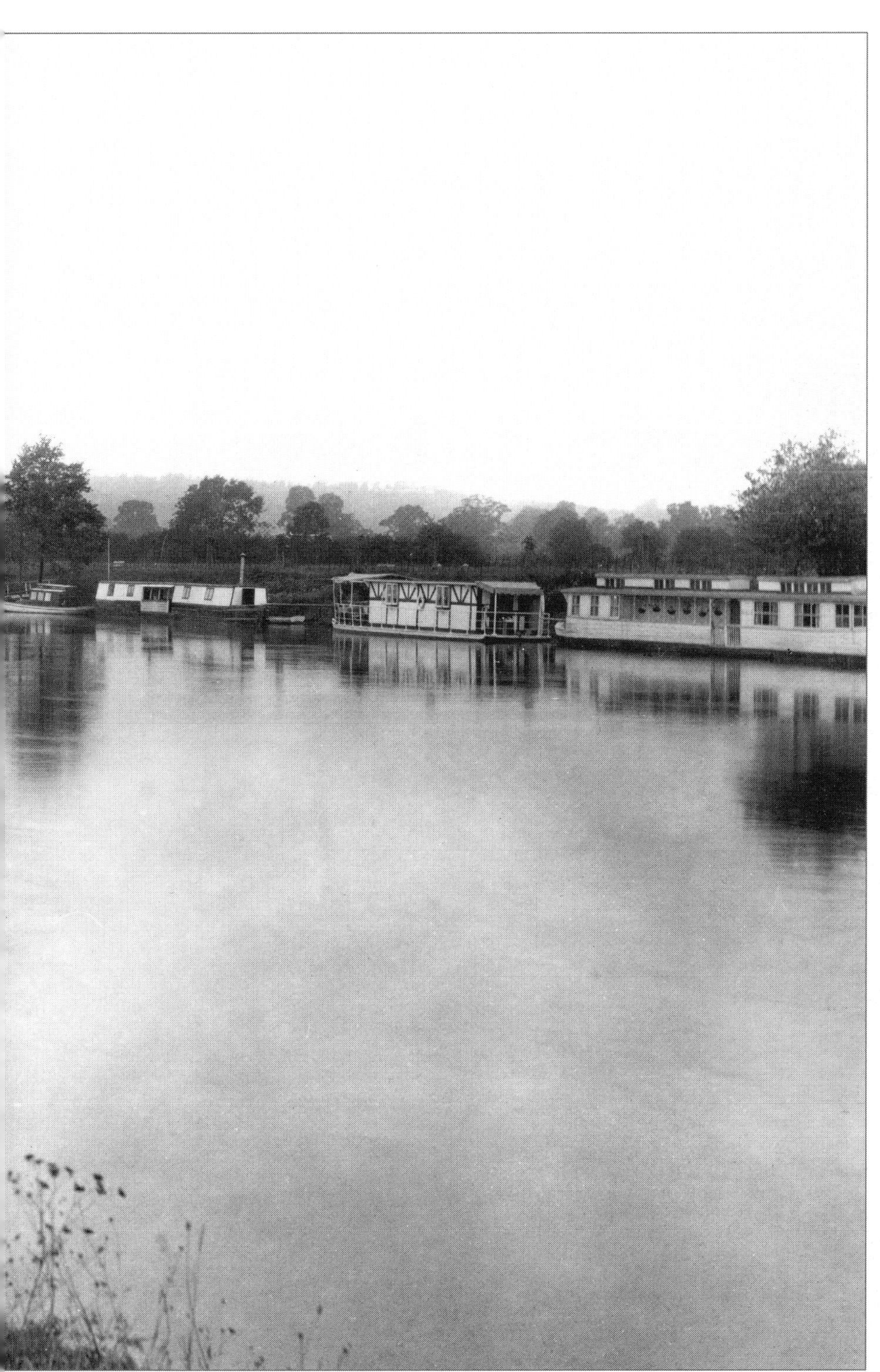

**STOURPORT-ON-SEVERN**
*Houseboats on the Severn 1931* 84628

Some of these houseboats are still lived in. Others have been adapted or destroyed, as they were in poor condition. In the Stourport basin, in dry dock by the big wharf, boats can be refurbished; the basin, reached by the canal through locks, was built to accommodate and service longboats with a full industrial schedule.

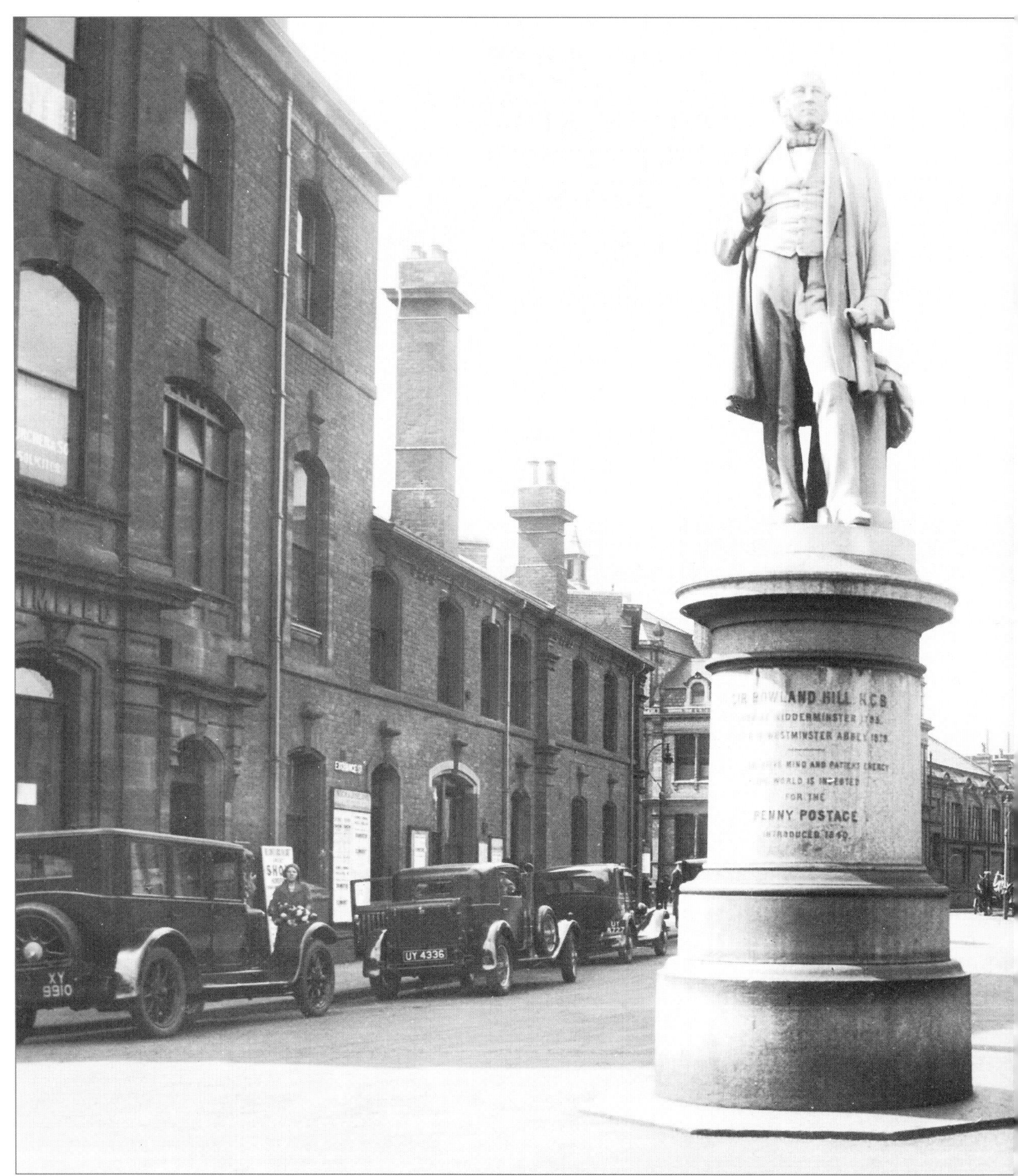
XY
9910
UY 4336
FOR THE
PENNY POSTAGE
SIR ROWLAND HILL K.C.B

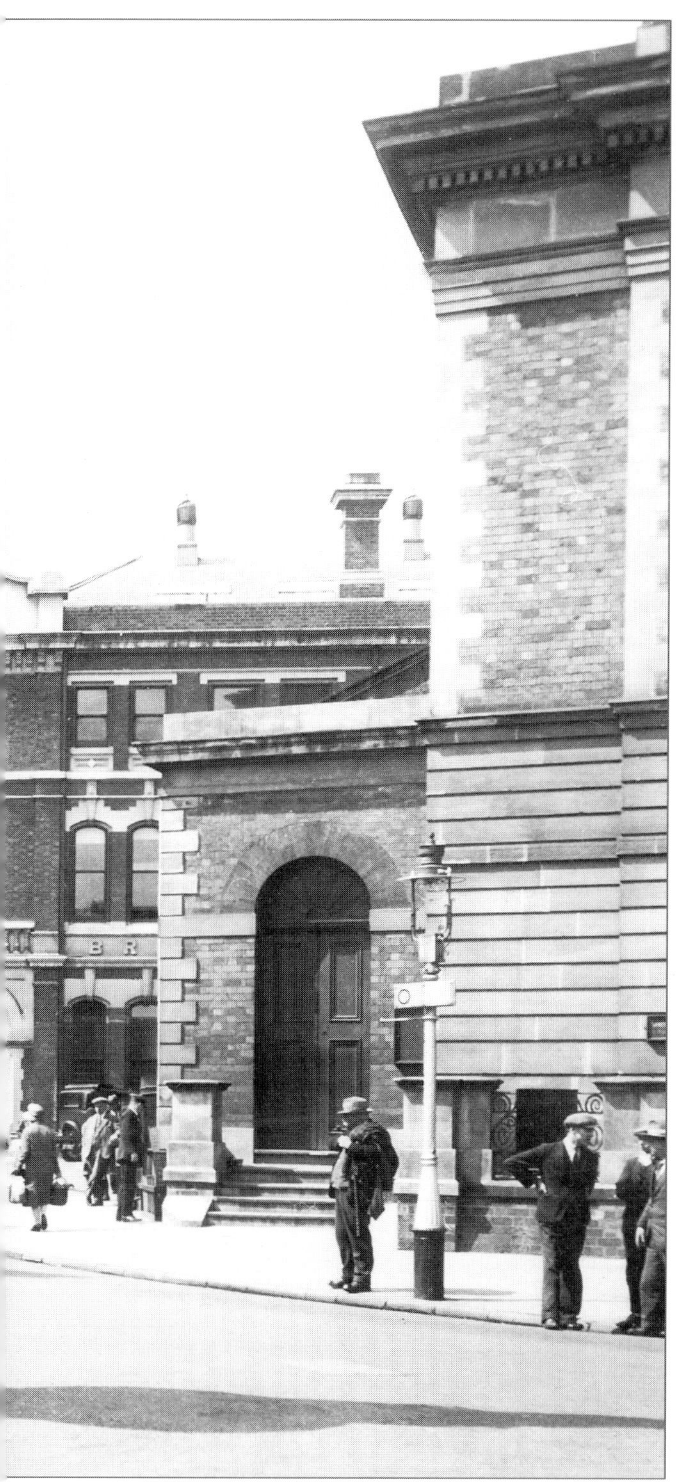

# KIDDERMINSTER

**KIDDERMINSTER**
*The Sir Rowland Hill Statue 1931* 84612

Sir Rowland Hill (1795-1879) was born in Kidderminster. He was the founder of the modern postage system; the first original Penny Black stamps appeared in 1840. In 1854 he became first secretary to the Post Office. It had been expensive to send letters by mail coach, and beyond what most people could afford, so Rowland Hill's promotion of the penny post was much appreciated. This photograph shows the statue sited in Exchange Street.

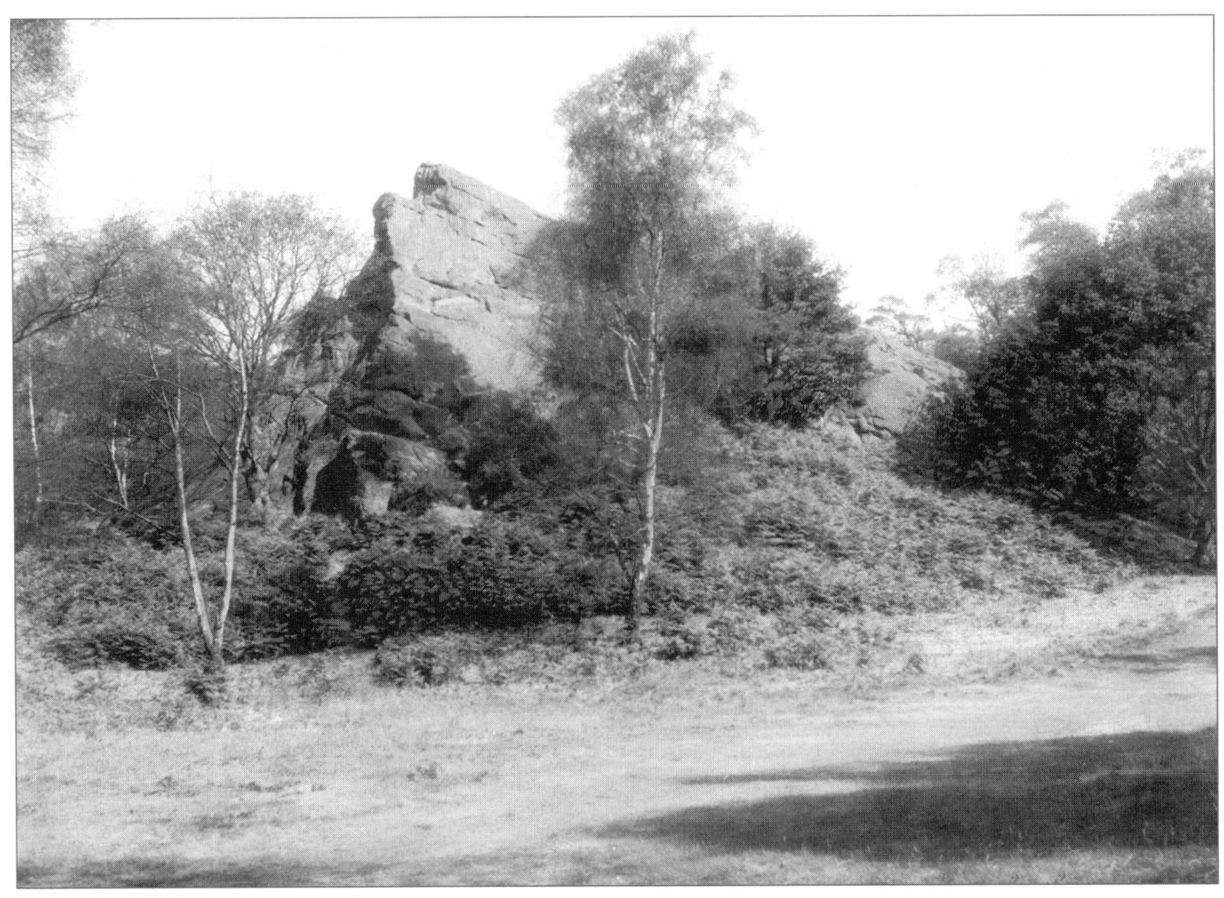

**KIDDERMINSTER**
*Peckett Rock, Habberley Valley c1960* K16054

Nature lovers taking the North or South Walk from the Visitor Centre in Habberley Valley will have a treat. Wyre Forest Leisure Council advise: 'Head towards the right of Peckett Rock, a magnificent Triassic sandstone outcrop that was formed 195 million years ago.' Birch, oak, ash, sweet chestnut, bilberry and wild flowers await. Ridgeston Rock, covered with pink bell heather, is a glorious sight as well.

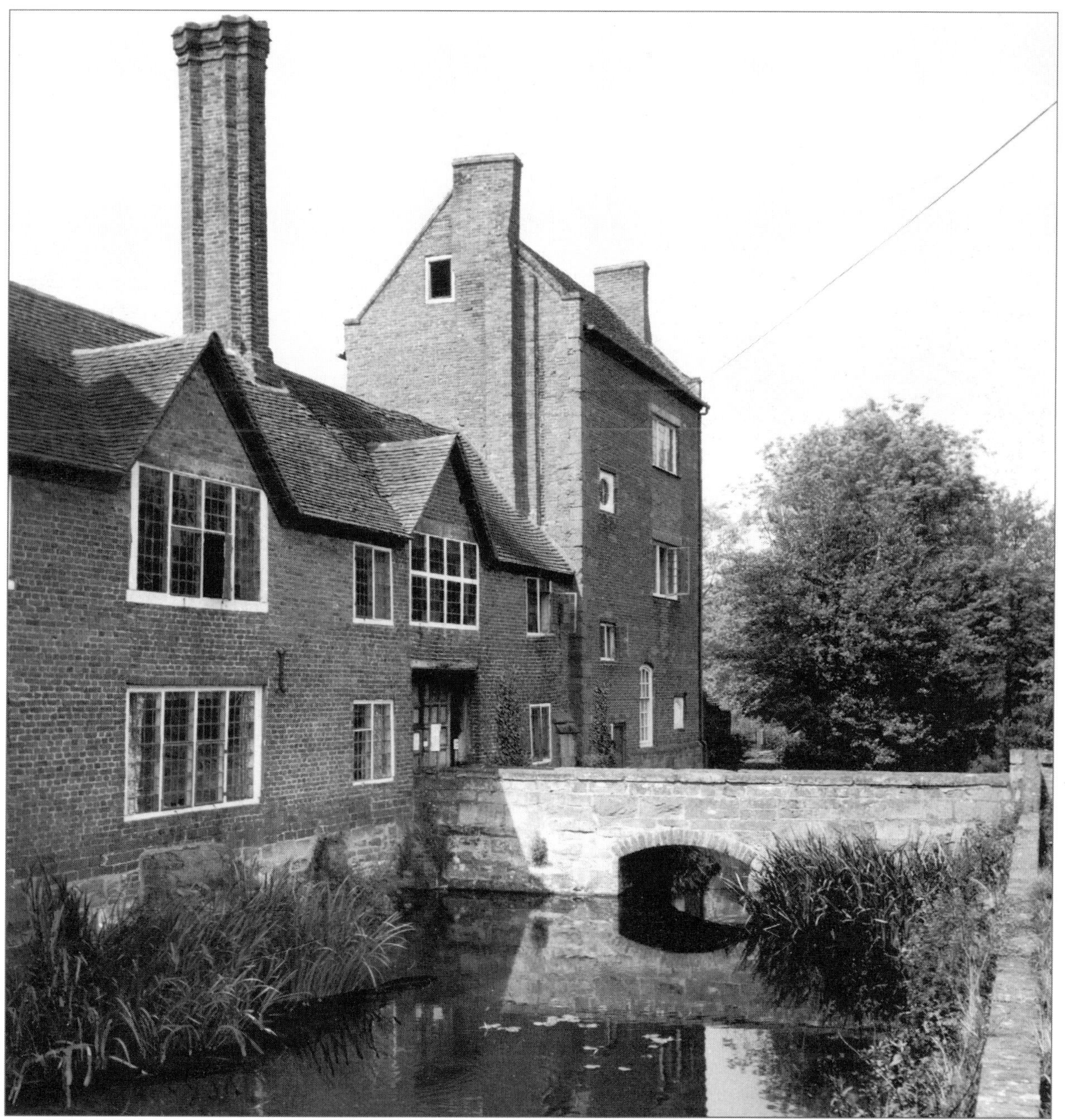

**KIDDERMINSTER,** *Harvington Hall c1960* K16067

Harvington Hall near Chaddesley Corbett lies 3 miles south east of Kidderminster. It was originally a 14th-century timber-framed house, the home of the Pakingtons, an old Roman Catholic family; there were once five avenues approaching it, but they were cut down before 1800. By 1920 it was a ruin smothered in ivy and choked with debris. Being of great interest and importance, restoration and weather-proofing was carried out in around 1930. The restored splendid mediaeval house now holds banquets for the Richard III Society.

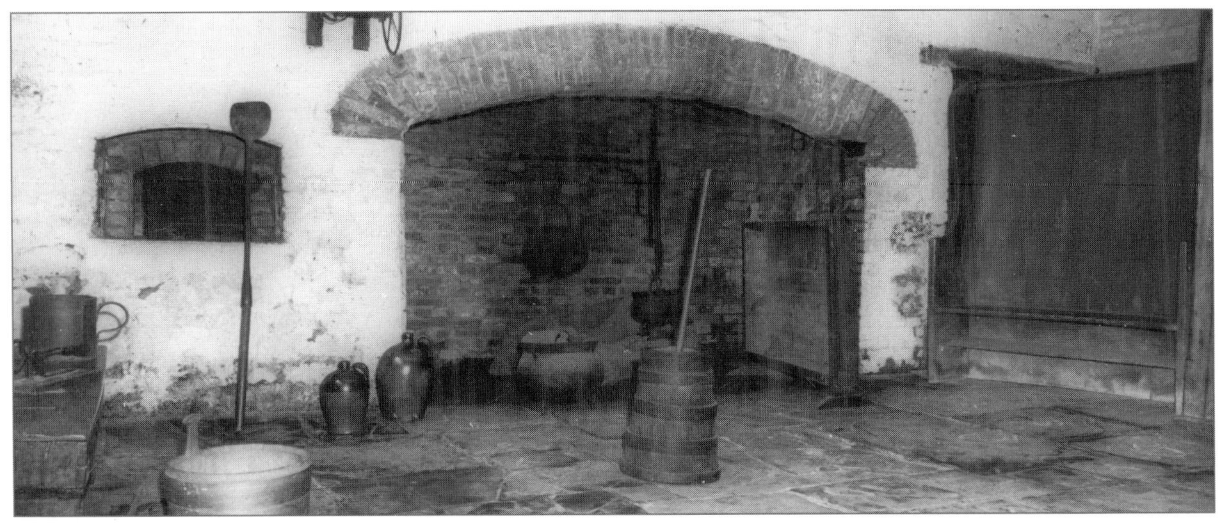

**KIDDERMINSTER,** *Harvington Hall, the Kitchen c1965* K16088

The huge fireplace in the kitchen of Harvington Hall is of particular interest because behind the Elizabethan bread oven (left) is a hiding place. The building of priest holes began in about 1580, when a network of great Catholic houses was built up where Jesuit priests could hide. At Harvington there are four of these priest holes. Nicholas (Little John) Owen, servant of Father Henry Garnett, Jesuit Superior in England, was the maker of some of them. He himself was eventually hunted down in a priest hole of his own making.

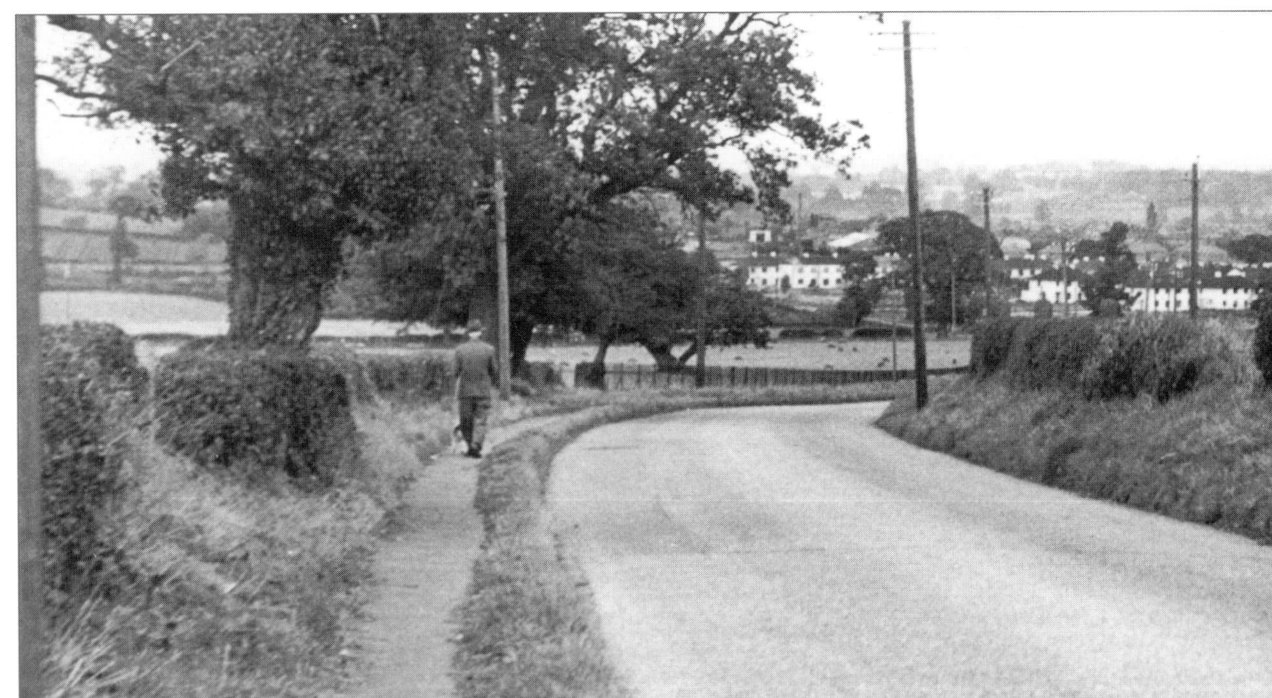

**KIDDERMINSTER**
*Harvington Hall, a Hiding Place, South Bedroom c1965* K16089

The installation of hiding places in great houses had to be kept secret; usually the work was undertaken when ostensibly a major architectural project was in hand. The priest-holes at Harvington are said to be the finest surviving series in the country - most are ingeniously placed near the great staircase.

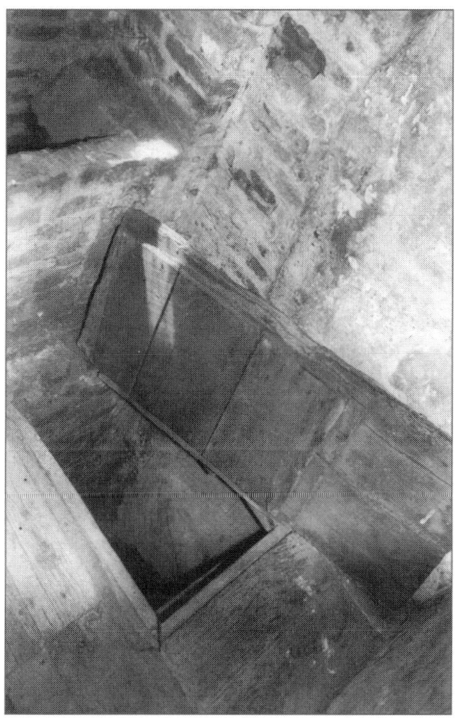

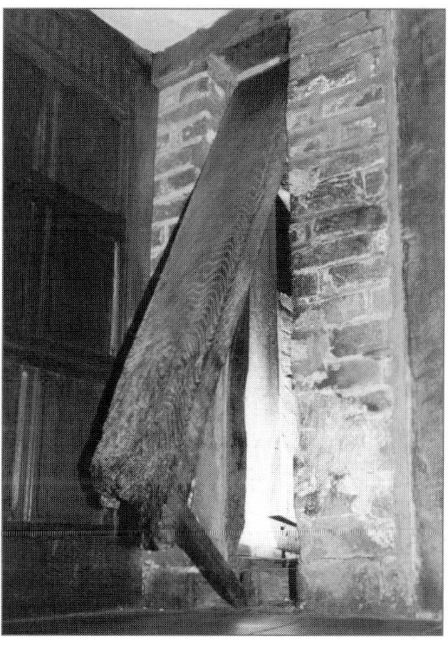

**KIDDERMINSTER**
*Harvington Hall, Swinging Beam Hide, Dr Dodd's Library 2004*
K16701

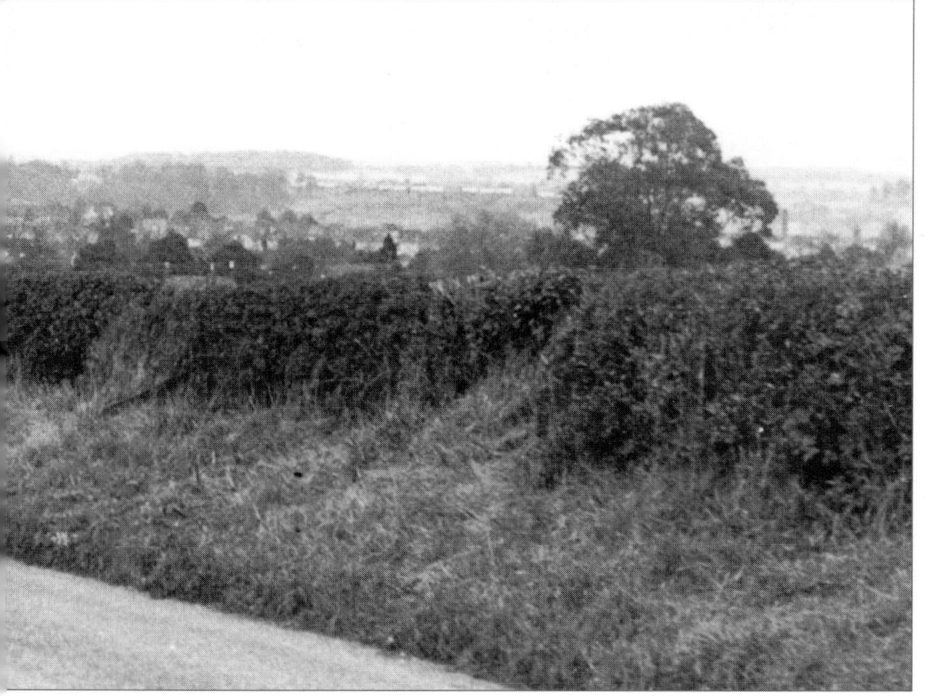

**KIDDERMINSTER**
*The Habberley Valley c1955* K16020

The Habberley Valley circular walk of 2½ miles passes Peckett Rock and Jacob's Ladder. After Eastham's Farm a picturesque tributary of the River Stour can be followed, which eventually flows towards Kidderminster. Carved into the sandstone cliff is a group of rock houses. The low doorways are still to be seen, but occupancy ceased in c1940. The Countryside Agency, sponsored by English Nature, have way-marked the circular walk.

▼ **KIDDERMINSTER,** *Habberley Reservoir c1965* K16090

Before John Brinton provided the means for a public park, Habberley Valley, approached by an unsurfaced track off Habberley Road, was a natural choice where townspeople could picnic and assemble. Kidderminster Brass Band entertained, and massed choirs sang lustily, weather permitting.

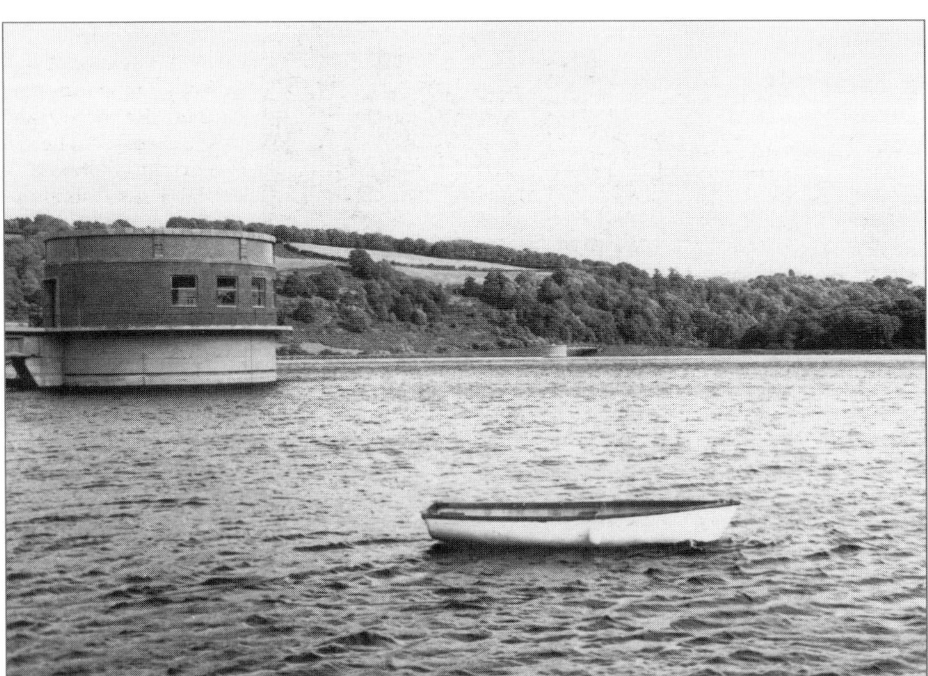

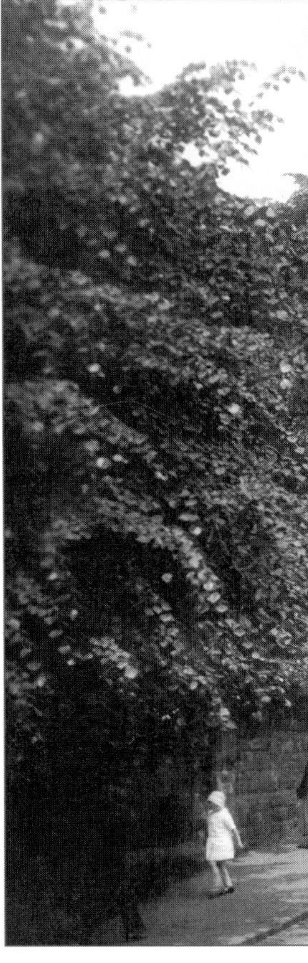

► **KIDDERMINSTER**
*Vicar Street 1931* 84606

Vicar Street is now much changed. The old vicarage was demolished and the town hall was built on the site - the land was purchased for £900 from William Brinton. In this view an old-style omnibus is driving off to the left, having passed Lloyds Bank. Across the street is a branch of Woolworth's; Amies's shoe shop next door adjoins Johnson's ladies' outfitters - their shop window is crammed with goods. Kidderminster's buildings are mainly 19th-century, and alterations are still going on.

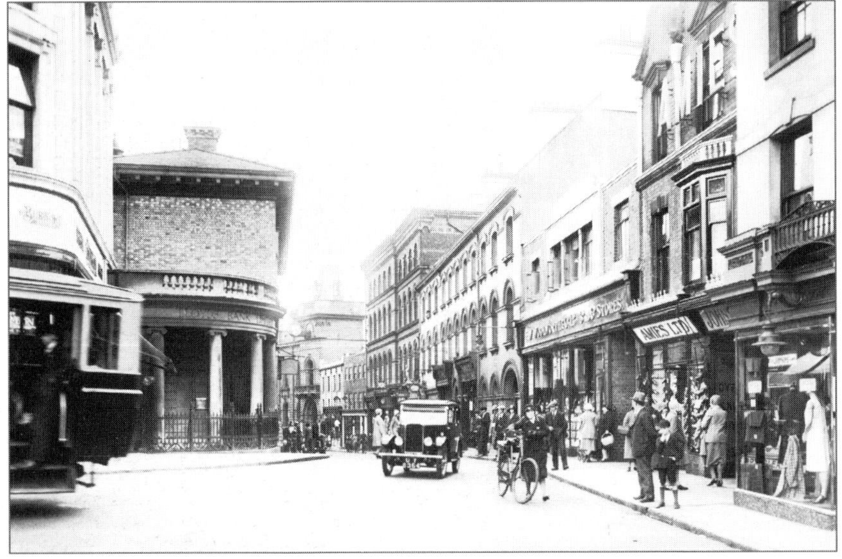

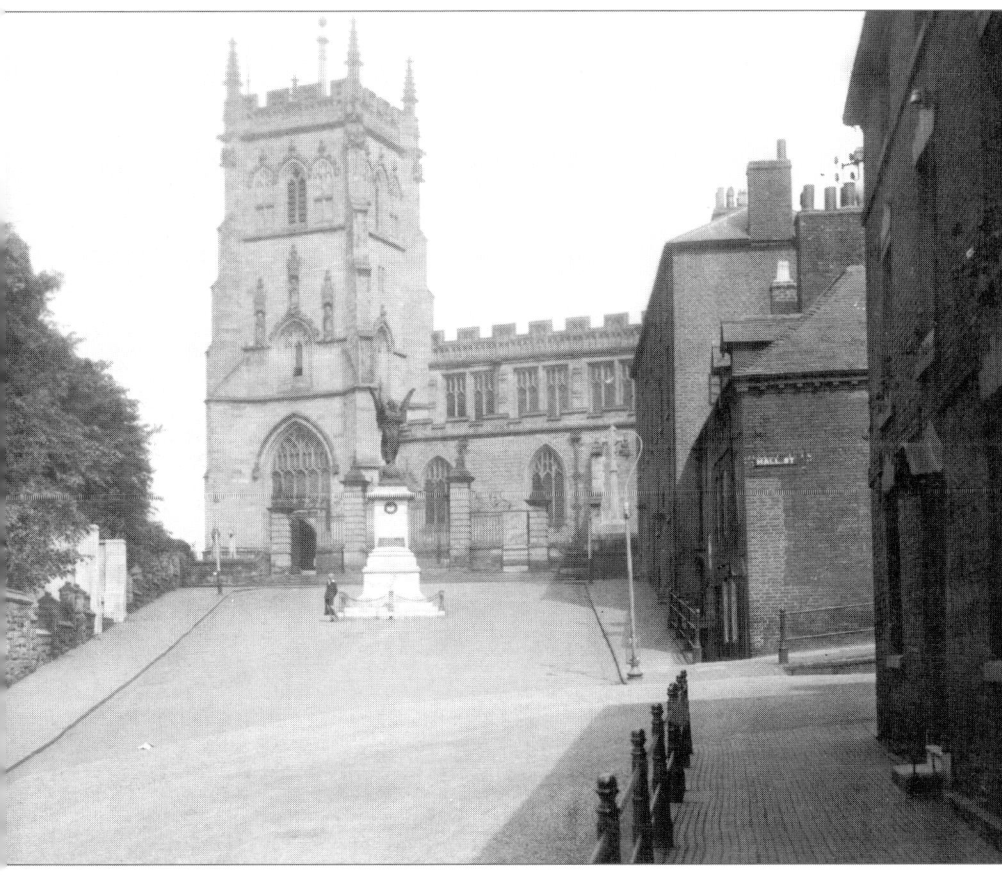


**KIDDERMINSTER**
*Church Street*
*1931* 84611

High on a hill above the River Stour, St Mary and All Saints' Church is all that remains of the medieval town. A well-known vicar here in the 1850s was the Rev T L Claughton; he encouraged the Habberley Choral Society and the brass band to sing and play in Habberley Valley, which had a splendid acoustic for massed voices and instruments. The church has two treasures: an Elizabethan cup, once used at the Mayor's banquets, and a Florentine processional cross.

**KIDDERMINSTER**
*Broadwaters c1955*
K16022

Broadwaters occupies a site where an ancient monastery once stood - it was destroyed by invading Danes. Broadwaters Park stream flows towards the town. It is culverted under the main road, and collects in a large lake, which lies between Broadwaters Lane and the estate of houses. Now it is a valuable habitat for wild birds, but before piped water came, this pool was a better water supply than some of the town wells.

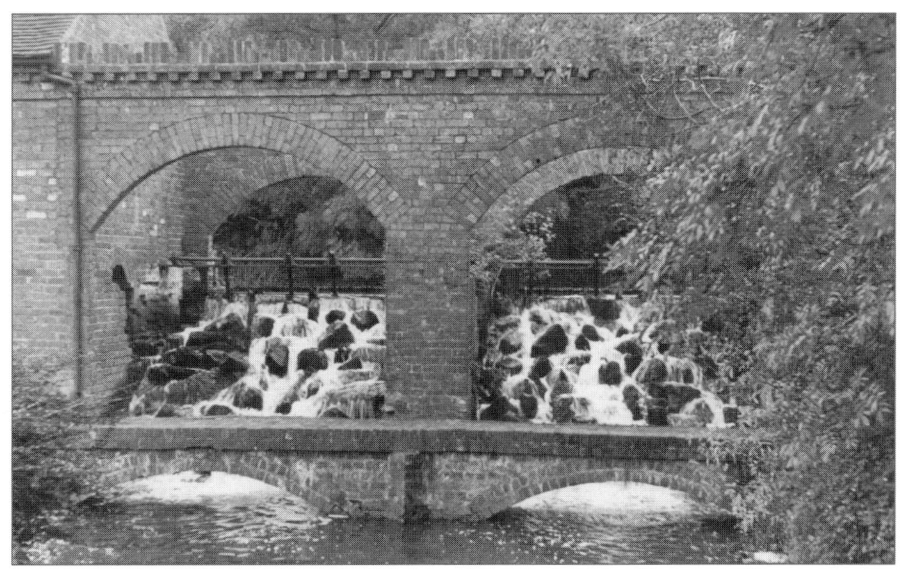

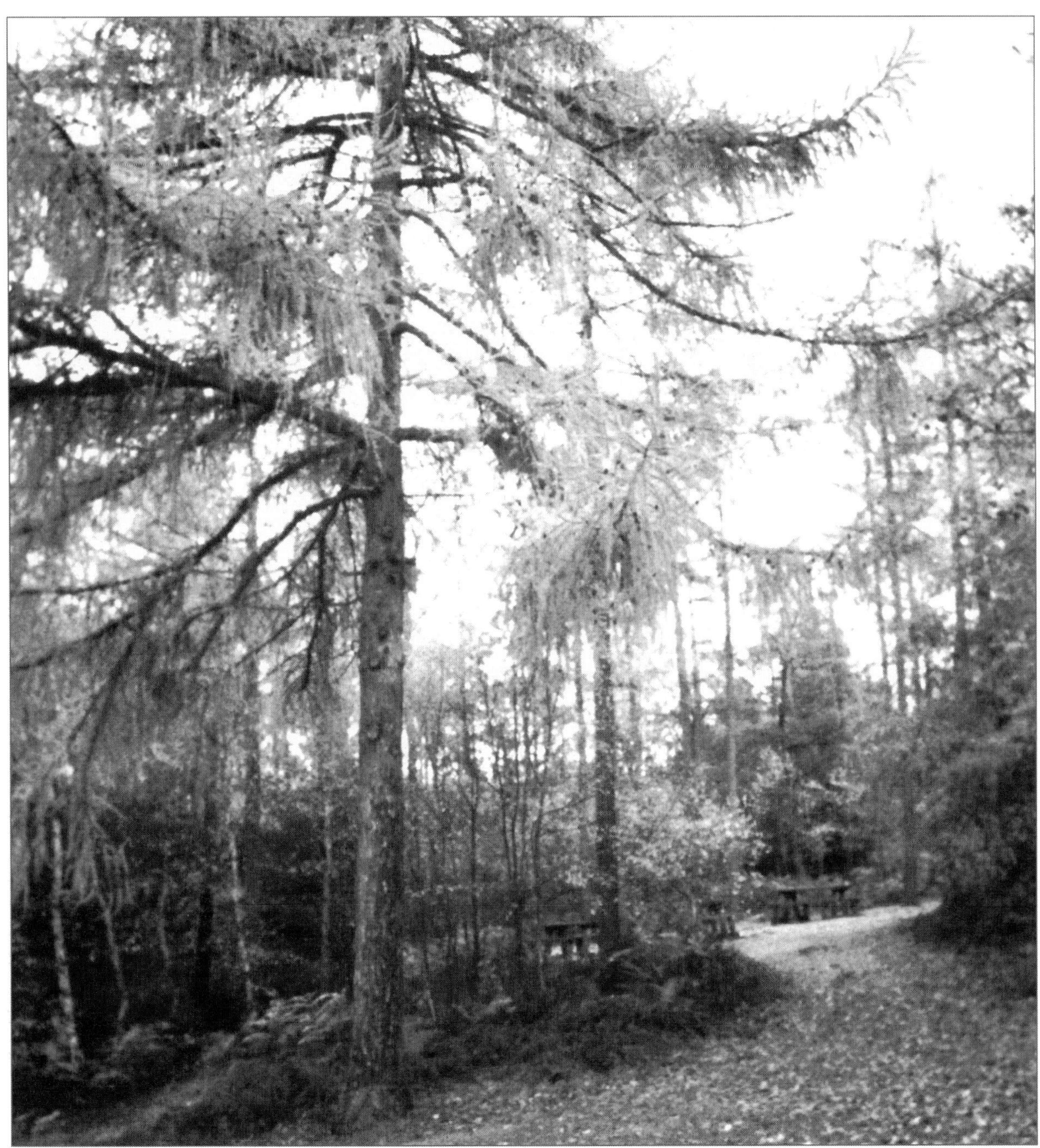

**WYRE FOREST** *2003* W643001

Within the forest there are specimen stands of Scots pine, red cedar, Lawson's cypress and larch. Alongside the streams, alder, blackthorn, and guelder rose with its creamy flowers followed by brilliant scarlet berries, all flourish near Button Oak. One ancient oak with 72 branches was eventually burned down.

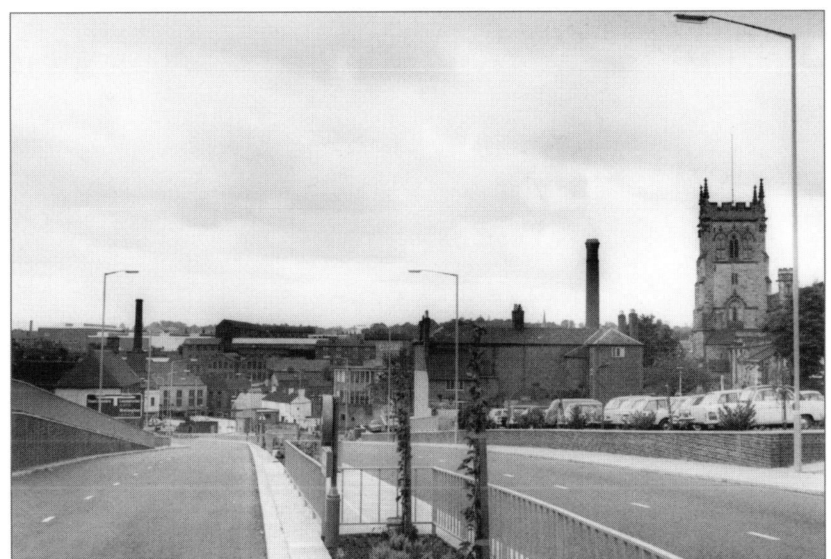

**KIDDERMINSTER**
*The Ring Road c1970* K16109

The new ring road brought relief from traffic congestion in the town centre, particularly Vicar Street and the High Street, which became pedestrian areas. Increasing traffic made it necessary to build yet another bridge over the River Severn at Blackstone incorporating the Bewdley by-pass, and this involved the demolition of landmarks at both Bewdley and Kidderminster. On the right is the church of St Mary and All Saints; Sir Edward Blount was a benefactor to the church, and to King Charles I Grammar School as well.

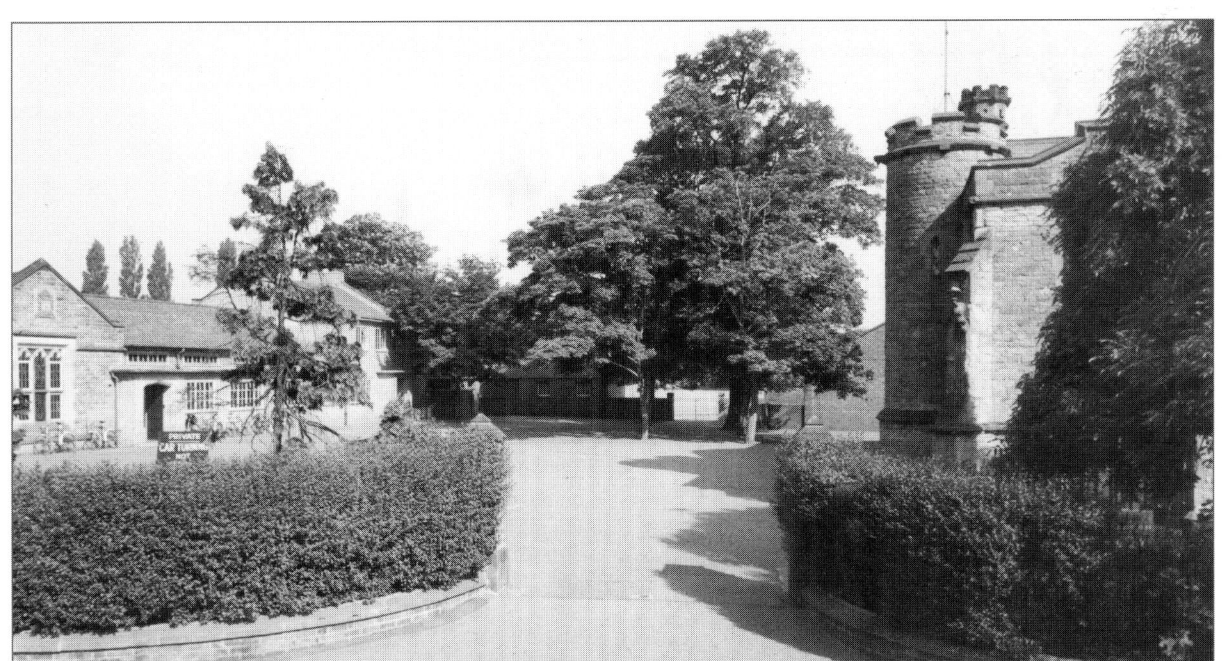

**KIDDERMINSTER,** *The Grammar School c1960* K16049

In c1570 a deed conveying lands to the school was made by Henry Benton, High Bailiff of Kidderminster. When he granted the Kidderminster charter, King Charles I ordered that the grammar school should bear his name. Schoolmasters' houses built in the 18th century were later demolished to make room for gardens and houses on Church Street. In 1847, 51 acres of land owned by the school at Greenhill Farm were exchanged for Woodfield House and its estate. A new school with playing fields and a gymnasium could then be built. Accommodation was provided for boarders. Founded in 1637, Charles I's Free Grammar School now lives on as King Charles High School, Chester Road.

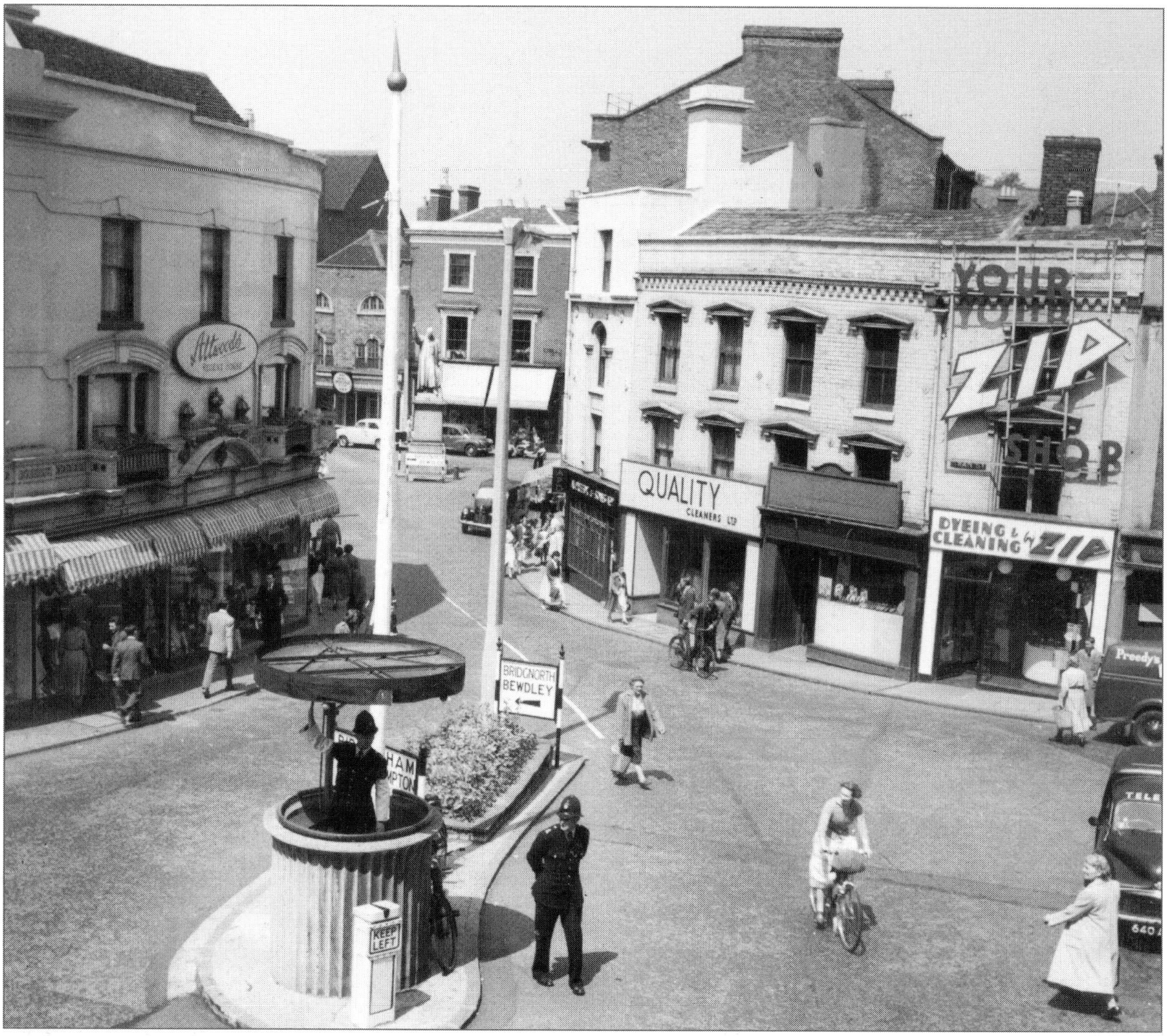

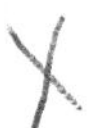

**KIDDERMINSTER**
*Policeman on Point Duty c1960* K16026

We can see Attwoods Regent House (left), the Baxter statue in the distant Bull Ring, and Quality Cleaners and Zip Cleaners (centre and right), but the centre of interest is the policeman. The original wood stand in the Bull Ring was removed by the police in 1945, to be replaced with this fluted concrete stand and canopy, sited at the corner of Vicar Street and High Street giving access to the Bull Ring. Christened 'the pulpit', it was used by visiting bishops for open-air preaching during a service to mark the 1948 Lambeth Conference. New traffic regulations made the pulpit redundant, and it was removed in October 1962.

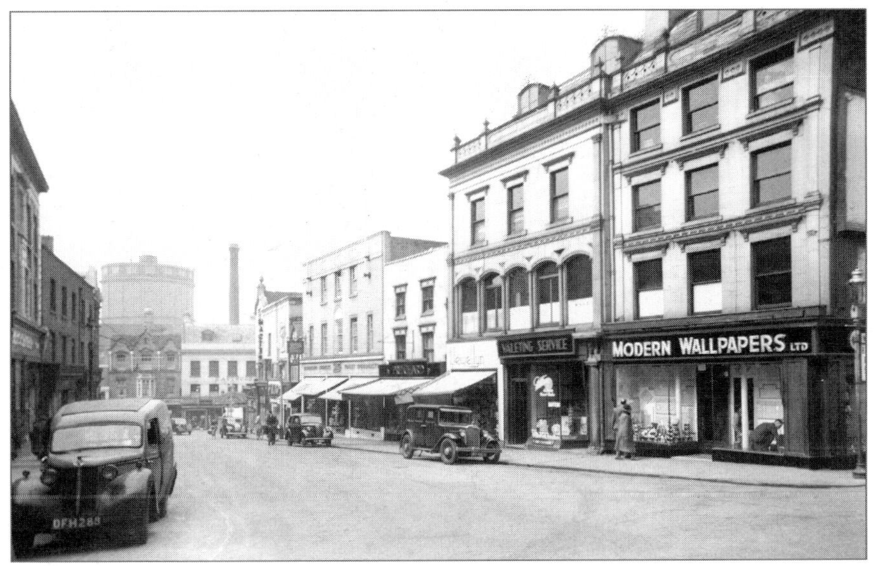


**KIDDERMINSTER**
*High Street c1955* K16008

On the right-hand side of the High Street, working from the distant end by the tall chimney, the shops we can see are H Attwood, Masters, Boots the chemists, Pritchard's and Llewellyn's, followed by a dry cleaner's and Modern Wallpapers Ltd. The traffic situation has changed, for now only pedestrians can pass from the head of the High Street into Coventry Street. On this corner is the Swan Centre and car park. The Bull Ring end of the High Street was where the Guildhall stood until 1878, when it was demolished.

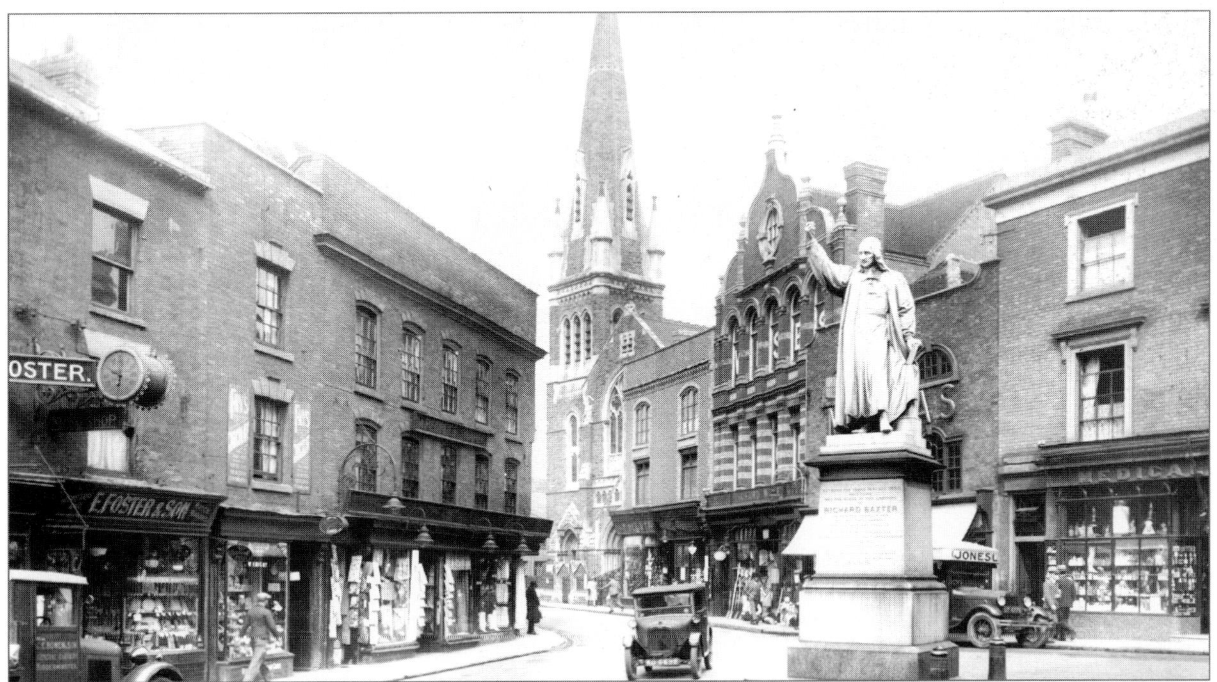


**KIDDERMINSTER,** *The Bull Ring 1931* 84609

From the left are Fosters, a watchmaker's and jeweller's, W Knight, a confectioner's and the People's Draper. Opposite are an ironmonger's and Blunt's Emporium. Pride of place is given to Richard Baxter's statue. He was vicar of Kidderminster from 1641 to 1660. In 1872 A H Greaves proposed a memorial statue, and under Joseph Naylor's chairmanship subscriptions were raised. The 26-year-old Worcestershire sculptor Thomas Brock, pupil of the famous J H Foley, was chosen to carry out the work.

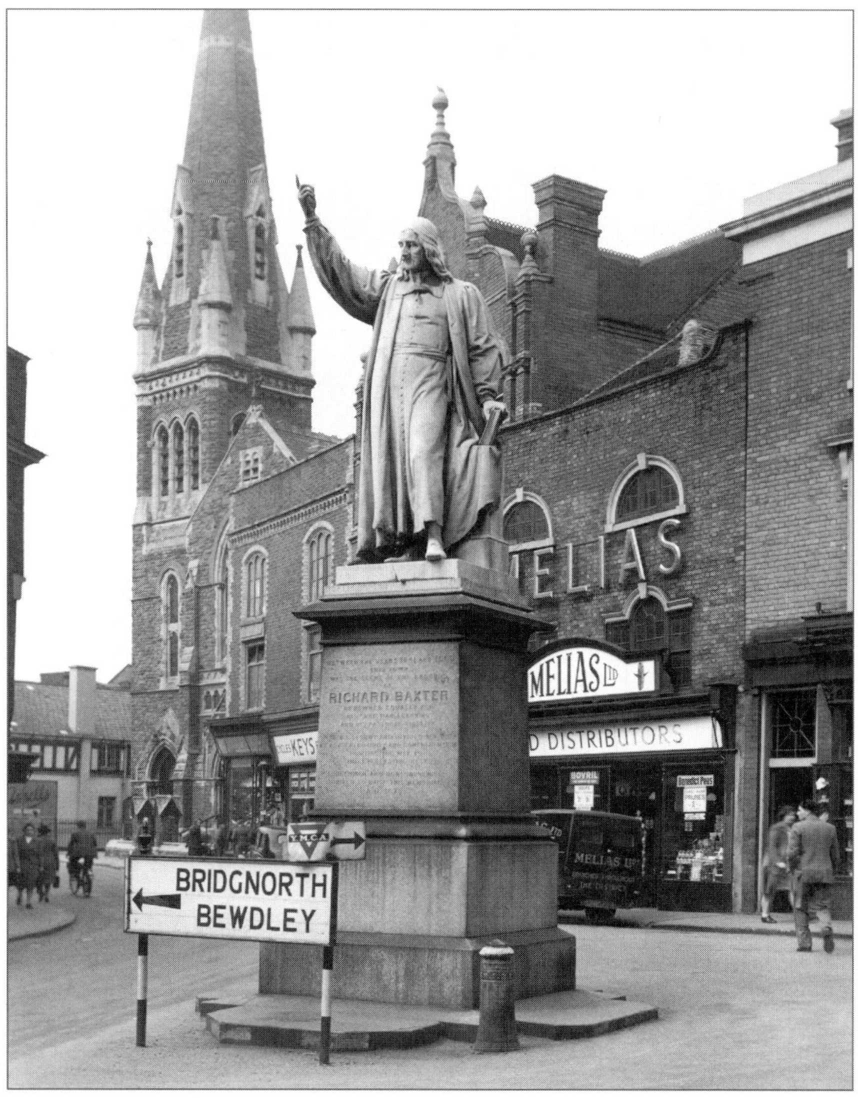


**KIDDERMINSTER,** *The Baxter Statue c1955* K16011

The completed statue was unveiled on a sunny day, Wednesday, 28 July 1875. Factories, shops and schools were closed. Crowds witnessed Councillor Naylor present the statue to the Mayor and Corporation. A platform adjacent to the statue had been erected in the Bull Ring, and the officials, having assembled in the Town Hall, processed down Vicar Street. Fixed on a pedestal of Cornish granite, the 10ft-high statue of Sicilian marble is inscribed: 'Between the years 1641 and 1660 this town was the scene of the labours of Richard Baxter, renowned equally for his Christian learning and his pastoral fidelity. In a stormy and divided age he advocated unity and comprehension, pointing the way to the everlasting rest. Churchmen and nonconformists united to raise this memorial.' When the ring road was built in 1967, the statue was taken from the Bull Ring to a site adjoining the parish church. Note Richard's hand pointing upwards to 'the everlasting rest'.

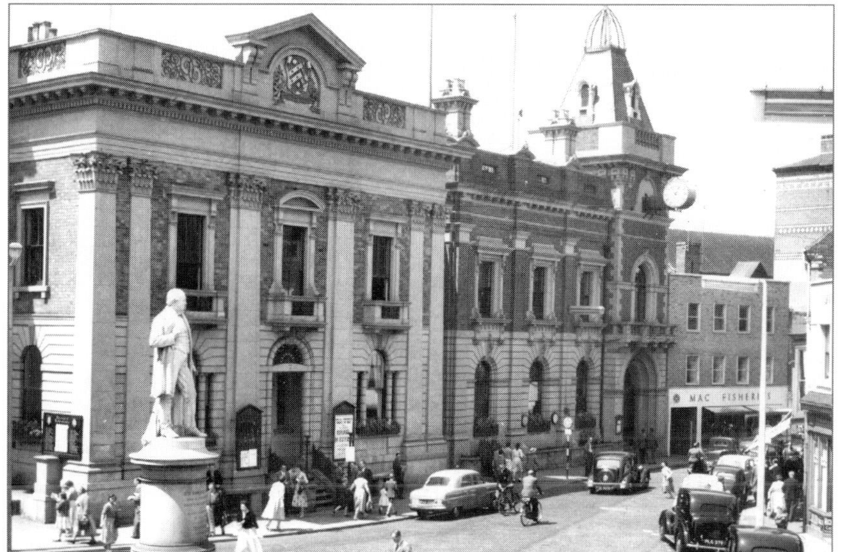


**KIDDERMINSTER**
*The Town Hall c1960* K16034

This excellent photograph shows the Town Hall; on the wall outside a poster advertises a performance of Handel's *Israel in Egypt*. On the left is the statue of Sir Rowland Hill, surveying a fair sized crowd and a line of motor cars outside Mac Fisheries shop and the pub opposite. Shortly after the unveiling of Richard Baxter's statue, Mr Phipps of the Vine Inn stated that Sir Rowland Hill should also be honoured, and in 1876 a committee was formed. before the big event, 5000 medals were struck and distributed to Kidderminster school children.

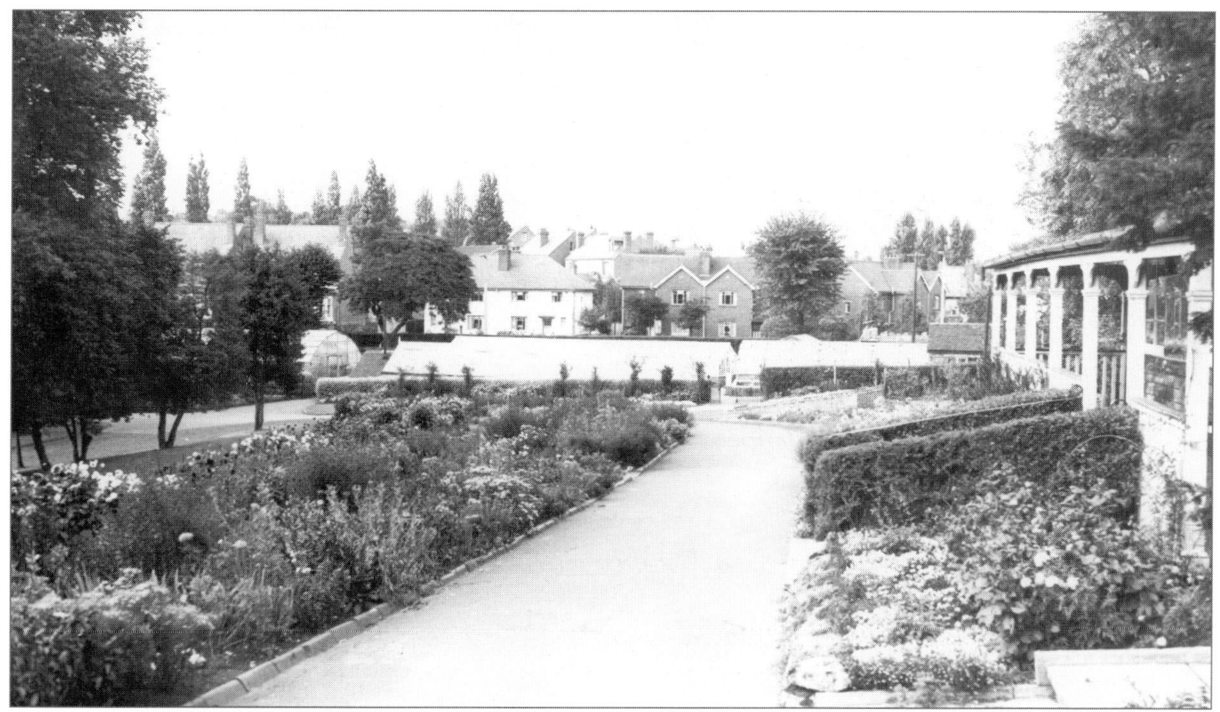

**KIDDERMINSTER,** *Brinton Park c1965* K16099

Stourport Road, Park Lane, Sutton Road and Talbot Street surrounded Brinton Park; this 24-acre site, formerly Sutton Common, was presented to the town by John Brinton in 1887. John Brinton (1827-1914) was a native of Kidderminster - the Brinton family had carpet weaving interests here. An additional 6 acres in Sutton Road became available in 1905, and these were purchased by the Council to extend the park's boundaries.

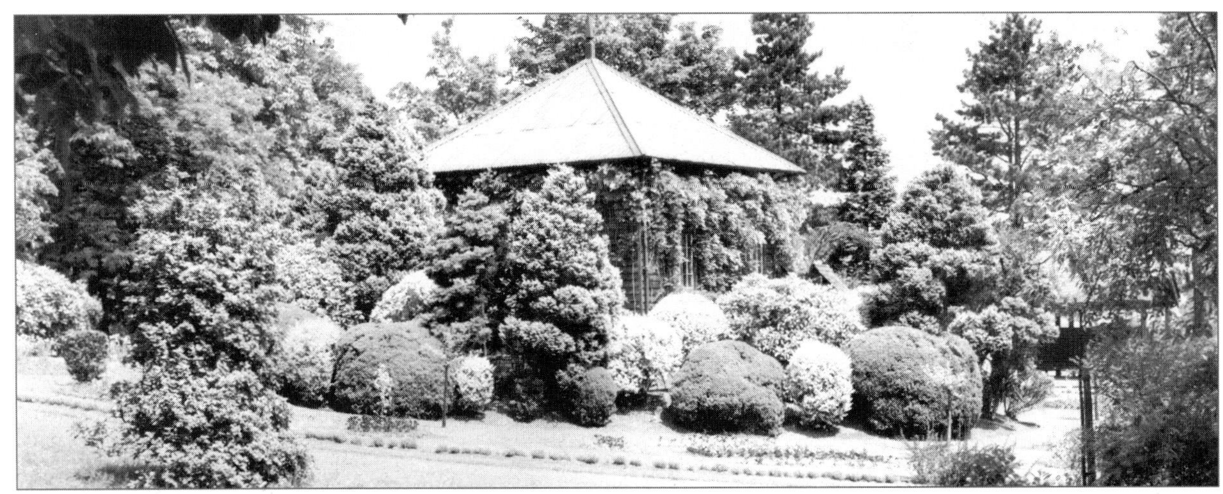

**KIDDERMINSTER,** *Brinton Park c1957* K16043

A memorial to John Brinton, a drinking fountain made of glazed Doulton ware, was unveiled on 14 June 1902 in Brinton Park; it bears the borough motto and coat of arms and the inscription: 'To keep his memory green in his native town which he ardently loved, admiring friends have raised this memorial.' At the peace celebrations in 1919 after the First World War, 2,200 servicemen were given a dinner here in two large marquees. The parish church bells rang throughout the afternoon and evening festivities. Alderman May, the mayor, Major Knight and Major H Tomkinson presided over the planting of commemorative oak trees, and an evening bonfire rounded off the day.

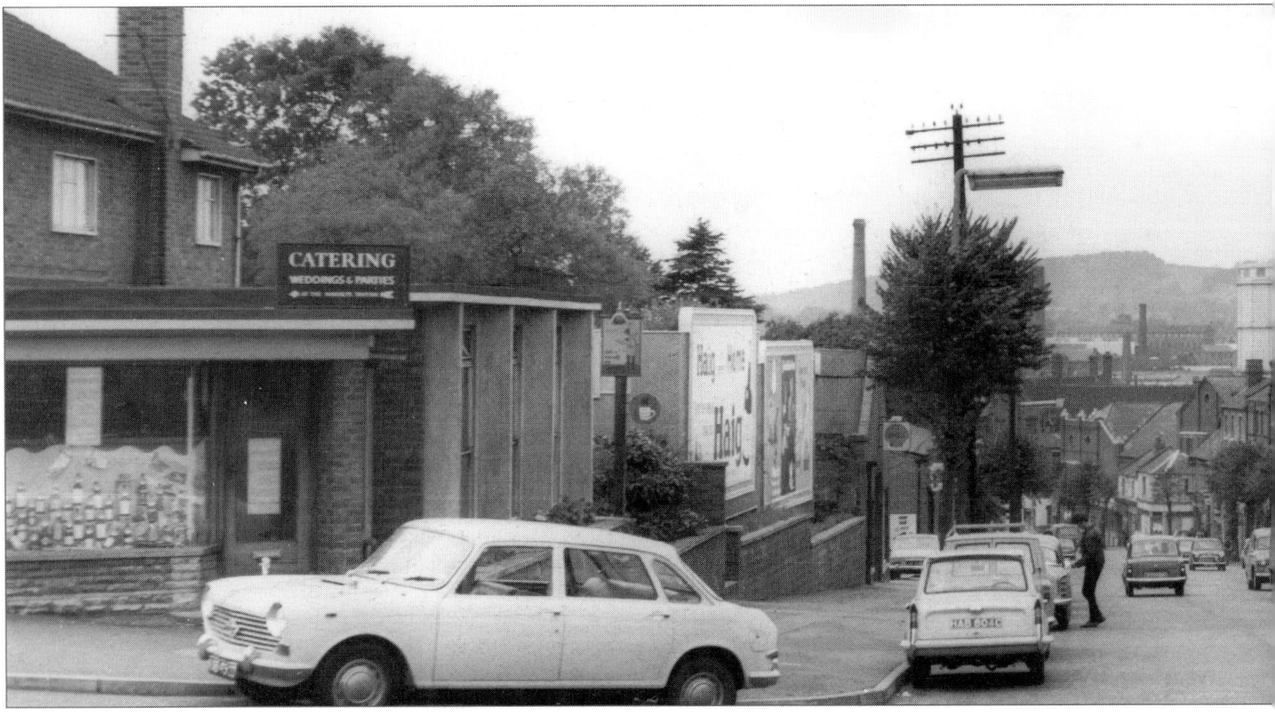

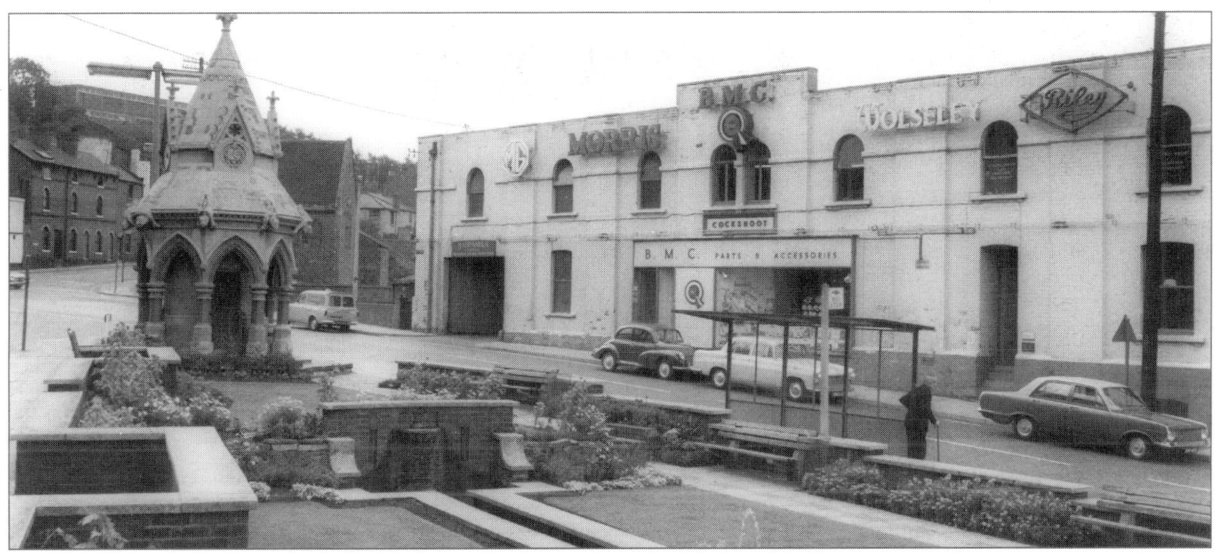


**KIDDERMINSTER,** *Clock Tower Gardens c1965* K16101

At the bottom of Comberton Hill stands the clock tower, erected on the site of a toll house in 1873. John Brinton, who became the first Freeman of Kidderminster in 1904, presented the clock tower, a fountain and these gardens to the town. Opposite is Cockshoot's garage.

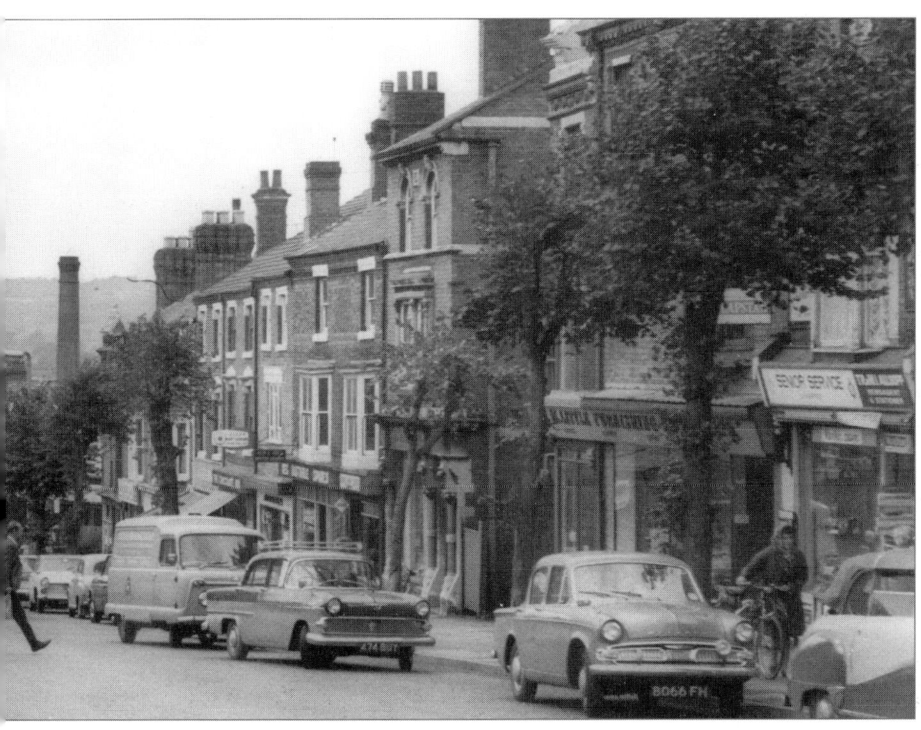

◄ **KIDDERMINSTER**
*Station Hill c1965* K16097

This is also known as Comberton Hill. The station approach is off to the left beyond the hoardings. The Oxford, Worcester and Wolverhampton railway opened on 1 May 1852, and amalgamated in 1863 with the Great Western Railway. The restored Severn Valley Steam Railway is a great tourist attraction - it ran its first public train on 23 May 1970 between Bridgnorth and Hampton Loade. At Kidderminster the Carriage Shed project was completed in 2000 to protect a unique collection of railway carriages.

**KIDDERMINSTER**
*Coronation Gardens c1960*
K16047

Here we have a closer view of the gardens and the fountain. From the clock tower two of the town's major roads branch off left (Oxford Street) and right (Worcester Street), leading into Vicar Street. This triangle of land as far as Mount Pleasant is known as the Worcester Cross area. The tall building (left) is an example of the robust mid 19th-century architecture still to be found in Kidderminster.

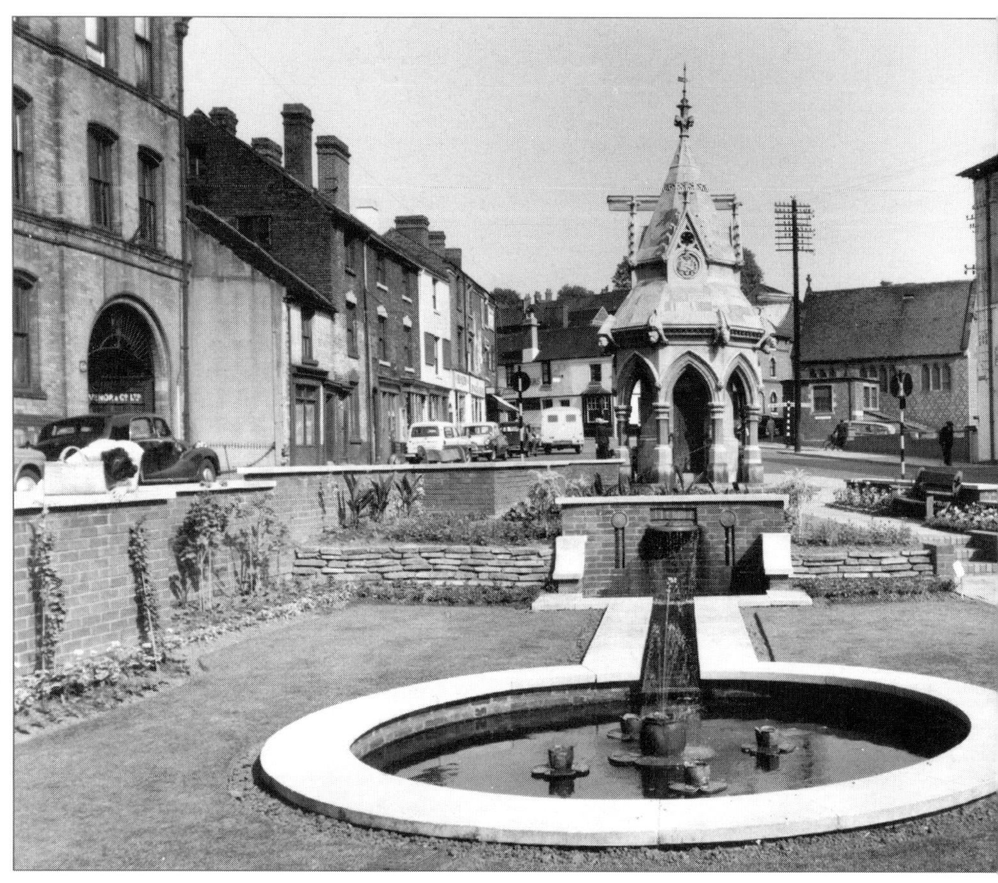

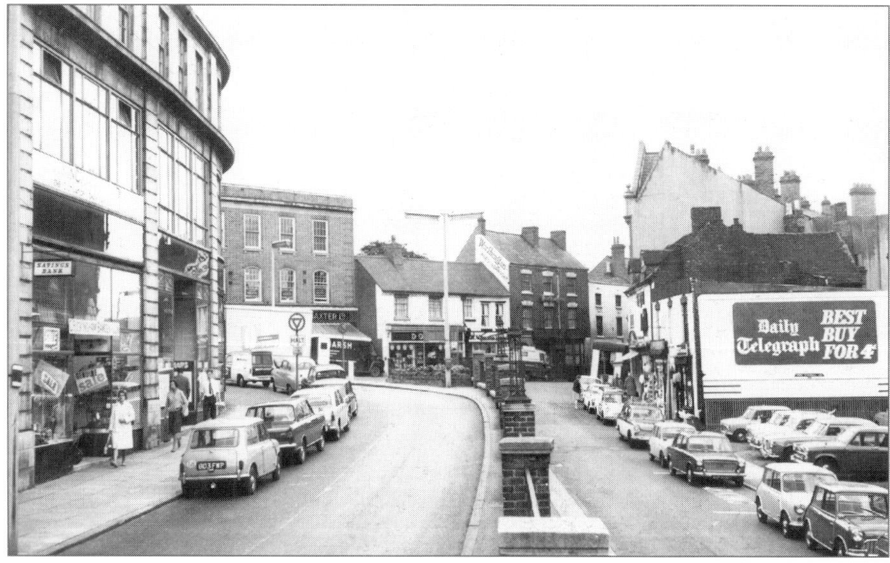


**KIDDERMINSTER**
*Blackwell Street c1965*
K16108

Blackwell Street, marked on Doharty's map of 1763 as Black Star Street, is where Rowland Hill was born in 1795. His home became the Traveller's Rest inn, but it was demolished when the Tower Building Telephone Exchange was built in 1934. The Nelson Inn in Blackwell Street held cockfighting bouts in the 18th and 19th centuries. The two street levels we see here have gone, along with an elegant Victorian gas lamp.

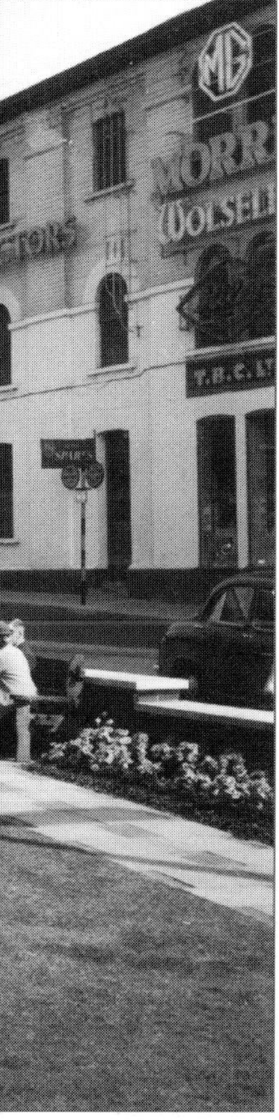


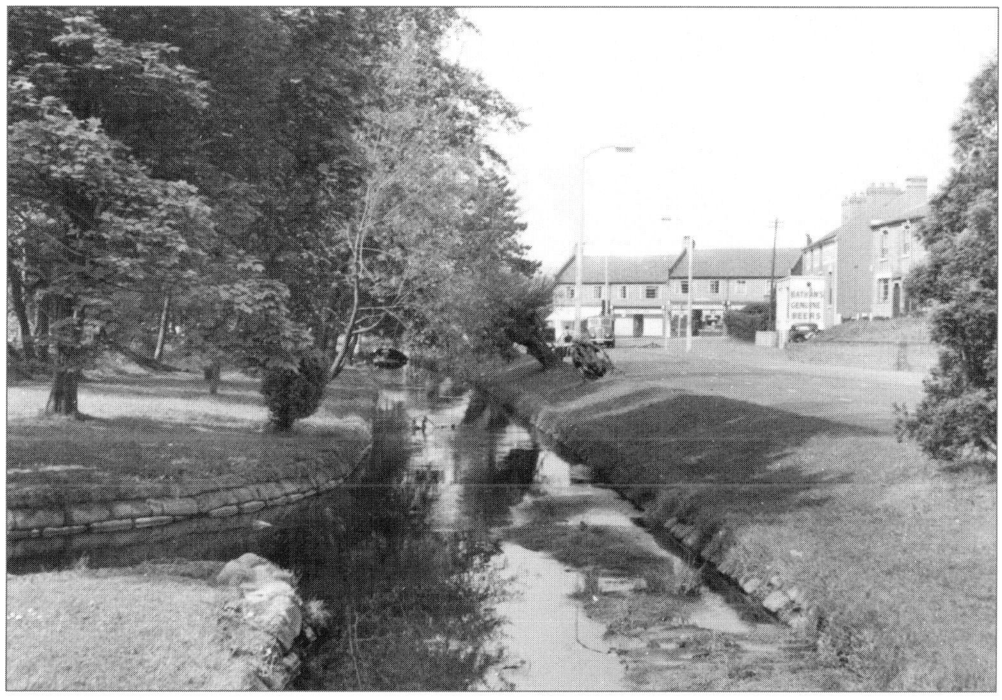

▲ **KIDDERMINSTER,** *Broadwaters c1960* K16069

In 1933 a house clearance and house building scheme was developed at Broadwaters. What was Broadwaters Lane led from the town centre as a continuation of the Horse Fair to meet the main road, where it became Chester Road. After the battle of Worcester, King Charles is said to have travelled along Chester Lane.

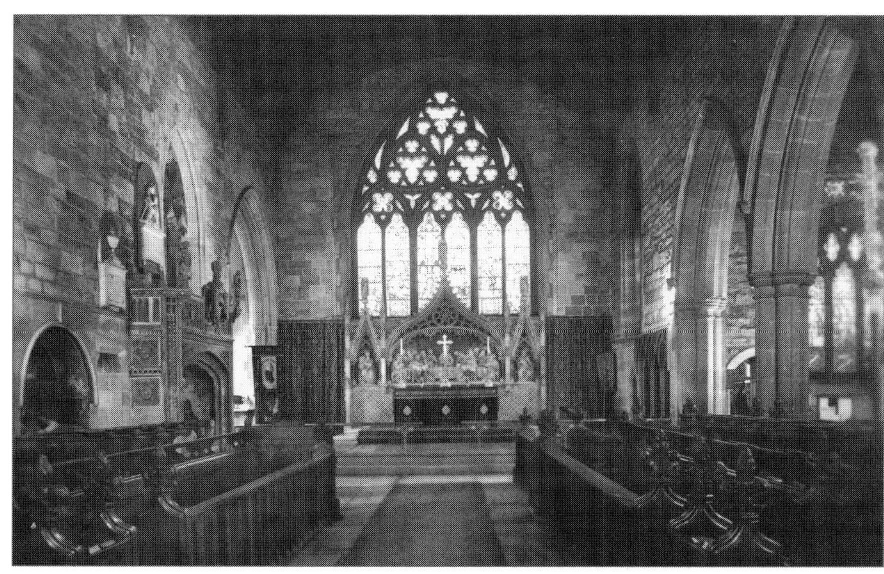

◄ **KIDDERMINSTER** *The Parish Church, the Interior 1931* 84617

The earliest part of the church is the chancel, which may once have been the chantry of the Blessed Virgin Mary - the east end is still known as the chantry. It was once separate from the main church, but the late 18th-century vestry joined it to the main building. The 84ft-high tower dates from c1450. In Richard Baxter's ministry there were five galleries, but by 1847 these were reduced to two.

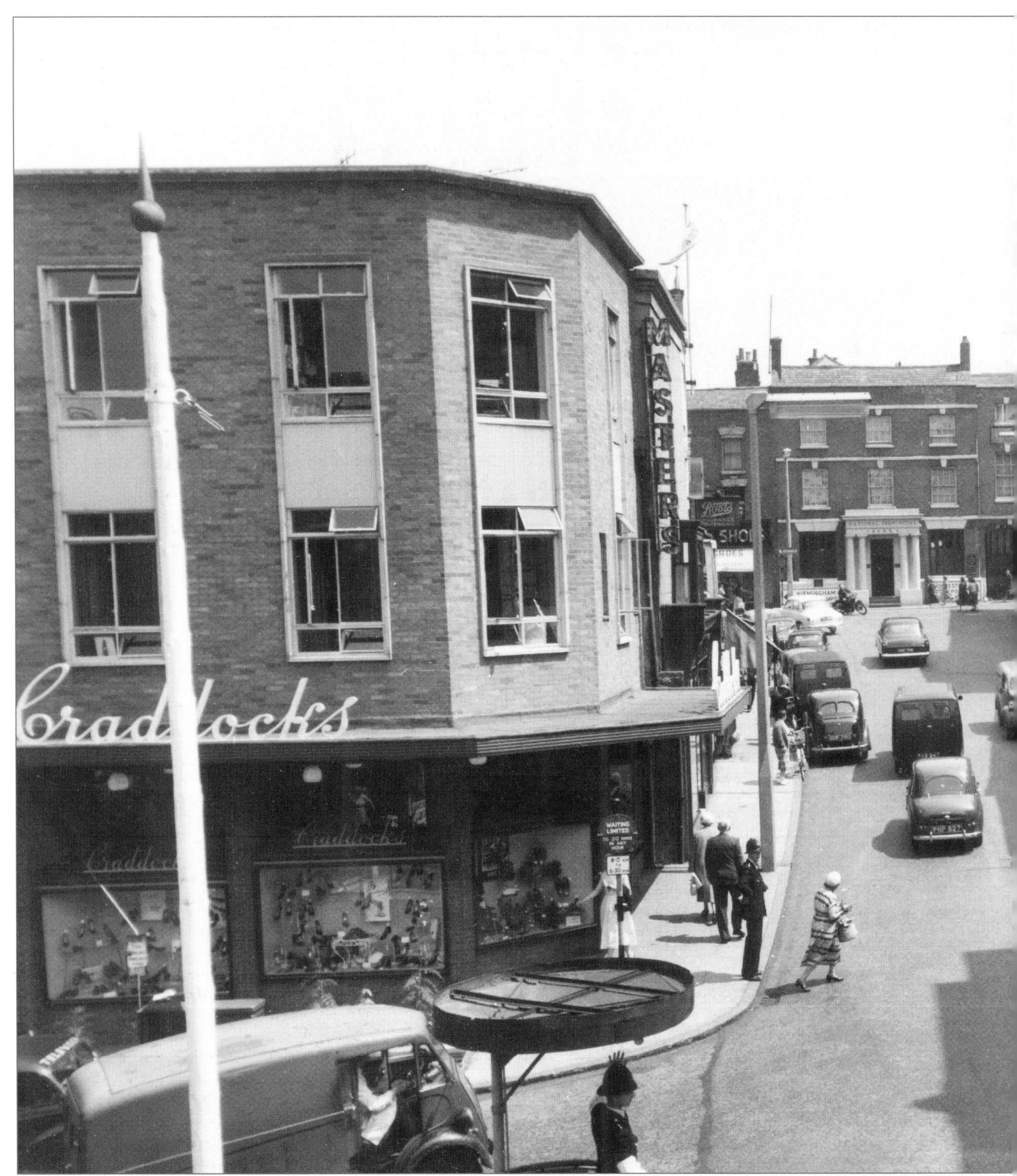
MASTERS
WAITING LIMITED

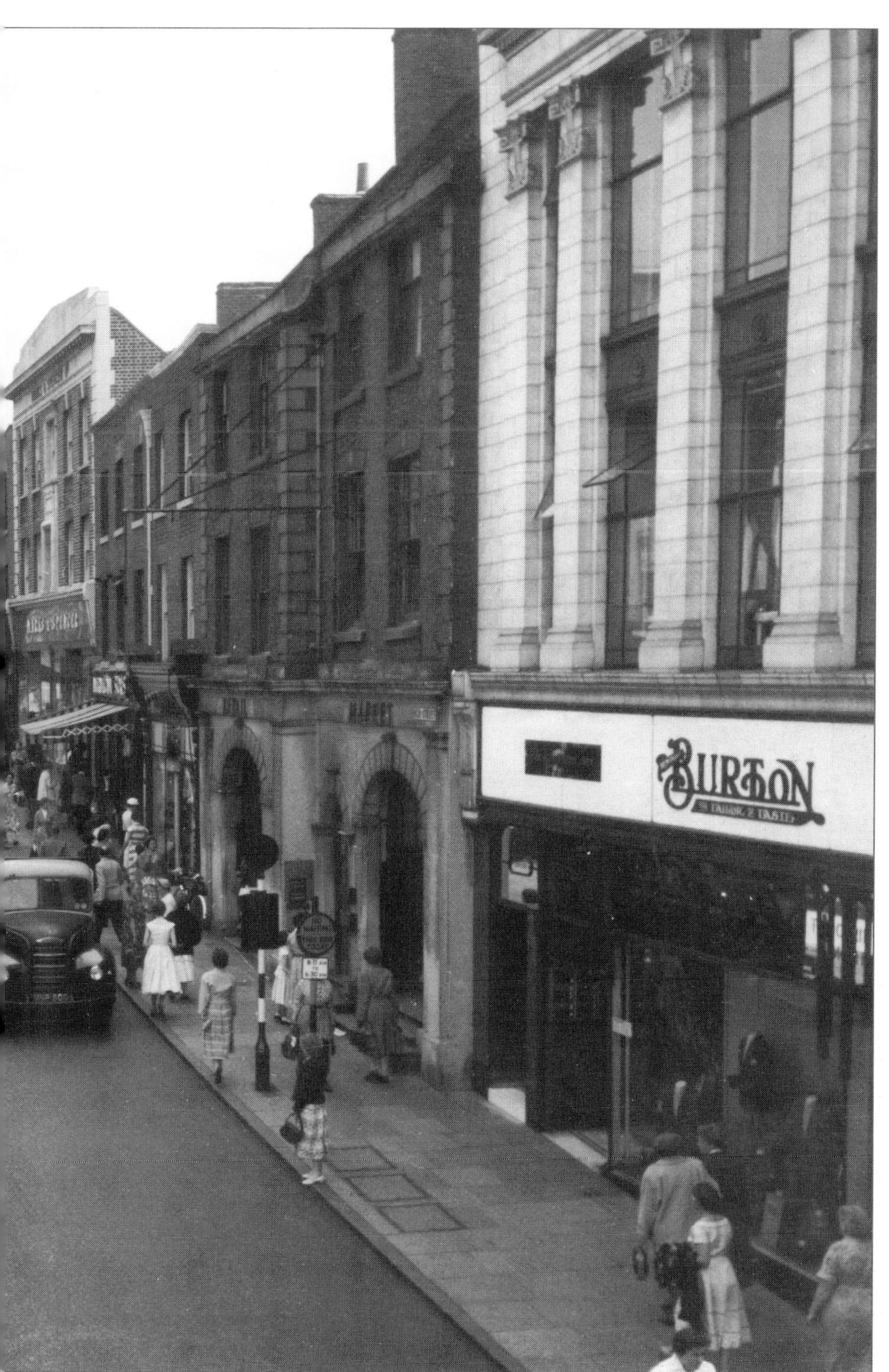


**KIDDERMINSTER**
*High Street c1960*
K16027

Craddock's outfitter's (left) was a household name on the High Street. Next door is Masters, then Boots the chemists and a shoe shop. At the top of the street is the National Provincial Bank. To the right is Burton's, once a well known chain of men's outfitters, the Market, and then Marks & Spencer in a typical art-deco building. As fashions change, so do shop names, but this busy scene is even busier nearly 50 years on. In its heyday, the High Street was lined with prosperous shops like Fehrenbach's, a baker's and confectioner's, where David Lloyd George took tea on 28 September 1911.

# SEVERN BROWN TROUT

3 cleaned trout, traditionally with head and tail left on
sea salt, freshly ground pepper
150ml/quarter pint cider
good squeeze of lemon
1 teaspoon chopped parsley in a cup of diluted tarragon vinegar

Pat trout dry and place in a dish, tailed and headed if required. The ovenproof dish should then receive the seasoning, cider, lemon juice and herbs in vinegar. Cover and bake for 25 minutes at 180C. Baste, then place nuts of butter all over the fish and replace in oven without lid to brown thoroughly, about another 7 minutes. In the 18th century, river trout was also made into pies.

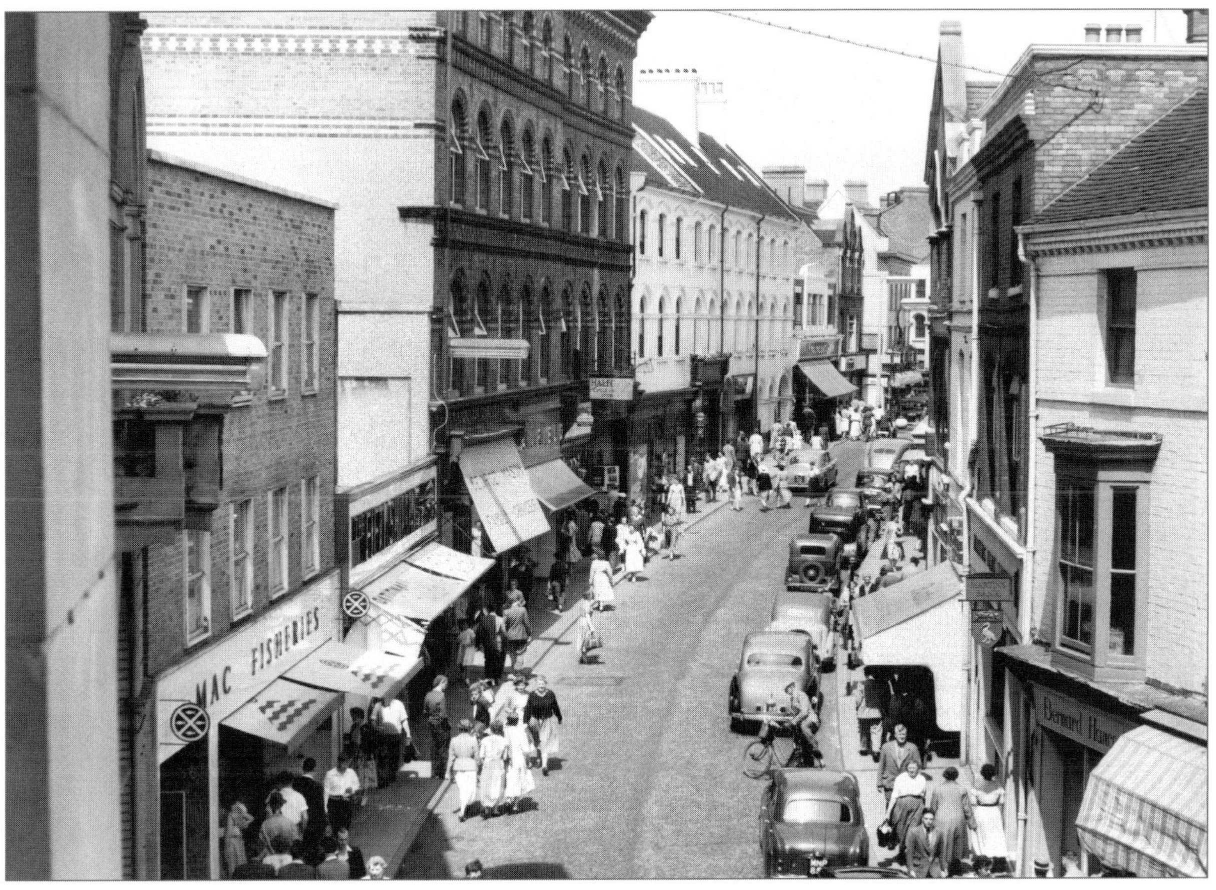


**KIDDERMINSTER**
*Vicar Street c1960* K16033

Included in this busy scene are crowds of shoppers, parked cars in a long line, and a solitary cyclist. On the immediate left is Mac Fisheries, which once had a branch in every town, George Mason, a grocer's, and Halfords, who kept spare parts for bicycles and motor cars. Martins Bank is on the right. Sun blinds of the canopy type are less seen today. The police station was in Vicar Street from the 1870s until the new one was built on the site of Blakebrook House.

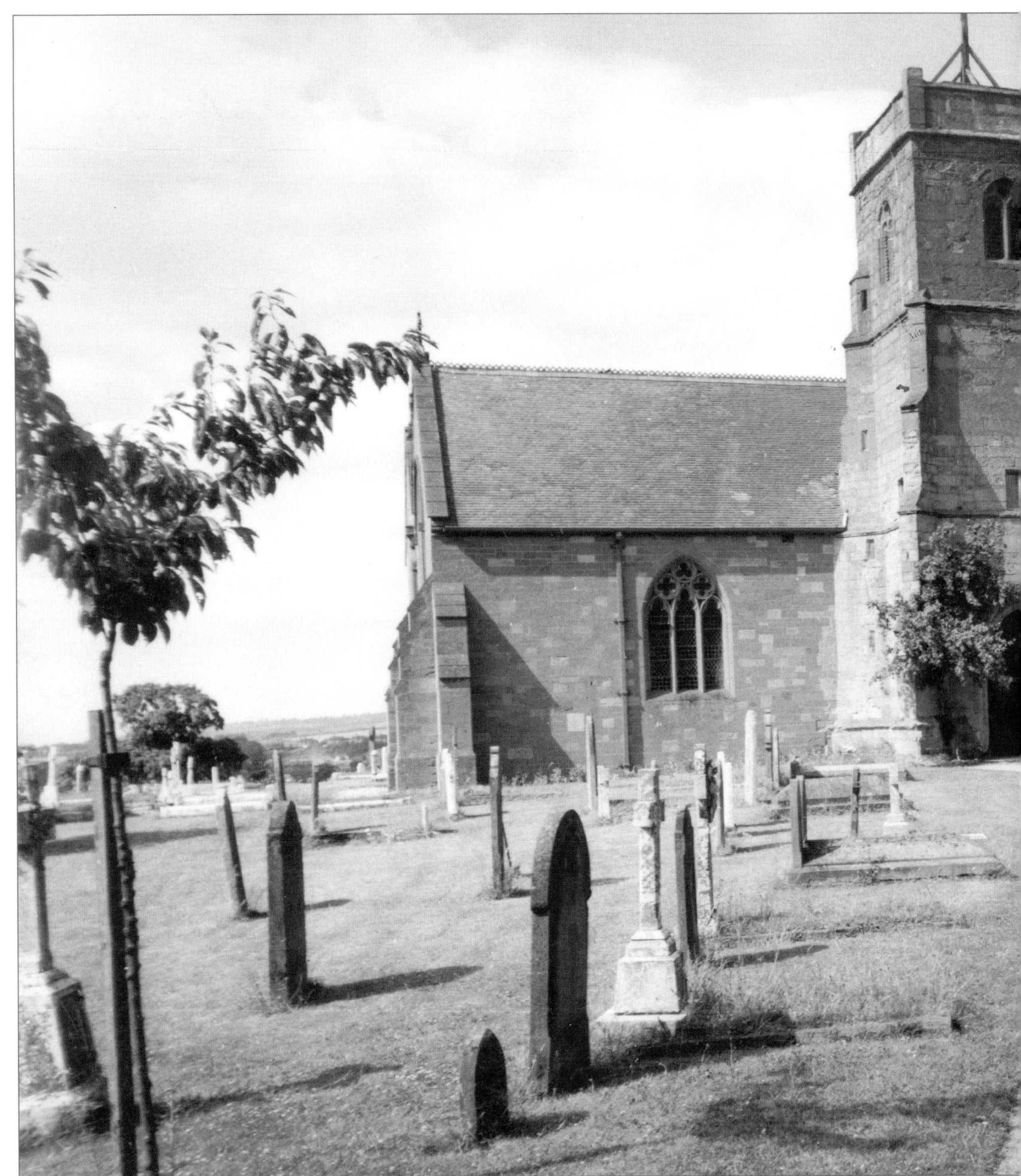

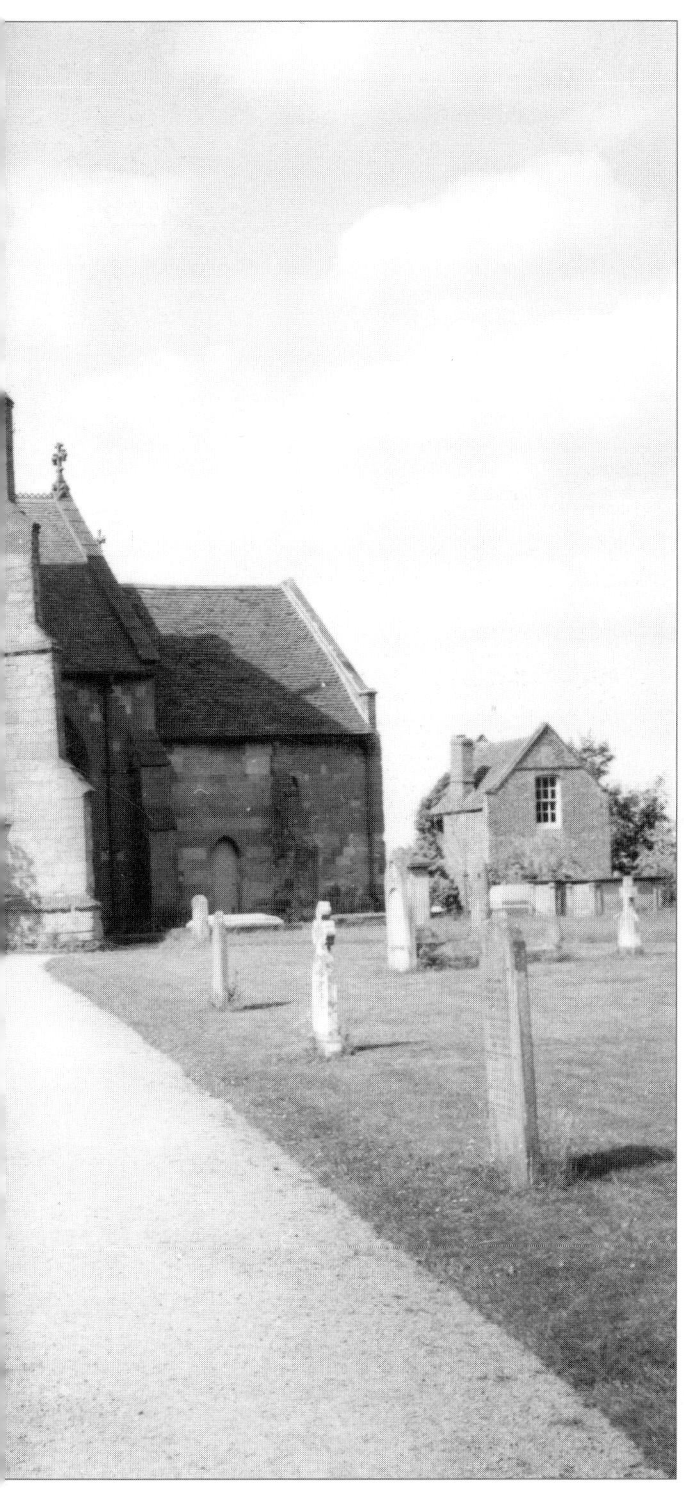

# THE VILLAGES

**ARELEY KINGS,** *The Church c1965* A367060

St Bartholomew's parish church stands on a magnificent site above the Severn. There has been a church here for 800 years, and St Bartholomew's still has some Norman features. Changes came about in Georgian and especially in Victorian times, when a rood screen and a staircase were demolished. At the base of the tower in the ringing chamber a notice states: 'The new peal of 6 bells was completed 1867 at an expense of 350 pounds.' The bell founders were Mears of London and Blews of Birmingham. The new peal came when John P Hastings was rector, coinciding with a rise in the population as the completion of canal work brought more trade to Stourport. To the right of the tower is the Layamon window, a stained glass memorial to 'a priest of Ernley (Arley) who wrote in vernacular speech the deeds of the English' in the 12th century.

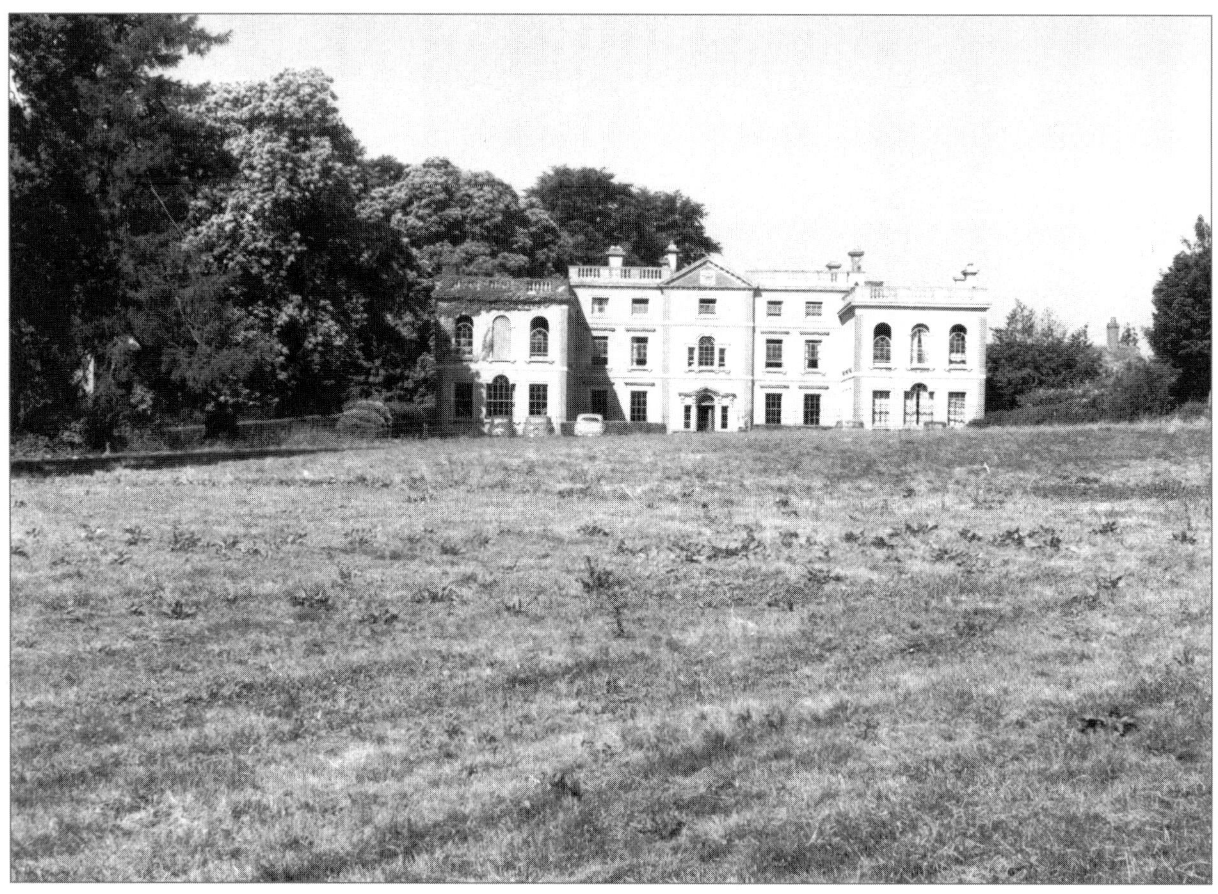

**ABBERLEY**
*The Elms Hotel c1960* A255042

This lovely Queen Anne mansion near the village of Abberley was built in 1710 by the architect Gilbert White, a pupil of Sir Christopher Wren. Elms once lined the drive, but these, like hundreds of others, succumbed to Dutch elm disease. They have been replaced with lime trees. Admiral Malin occupied the house in 1854, but its ownership changed when a local racehorse dealer, Sir Richard Brooke, took over; he transformed the mansion by adding two wings and building historic fireplaces into the fabric. Various hoteliers have owned the house since 1946, but when Lord and Lady Vaughan of Buckland bought the Elms in 1999 it returned to private ownership. However, it carries on as an internationally famous hotel, with award-winning cuisine and an excellent wine cellar.

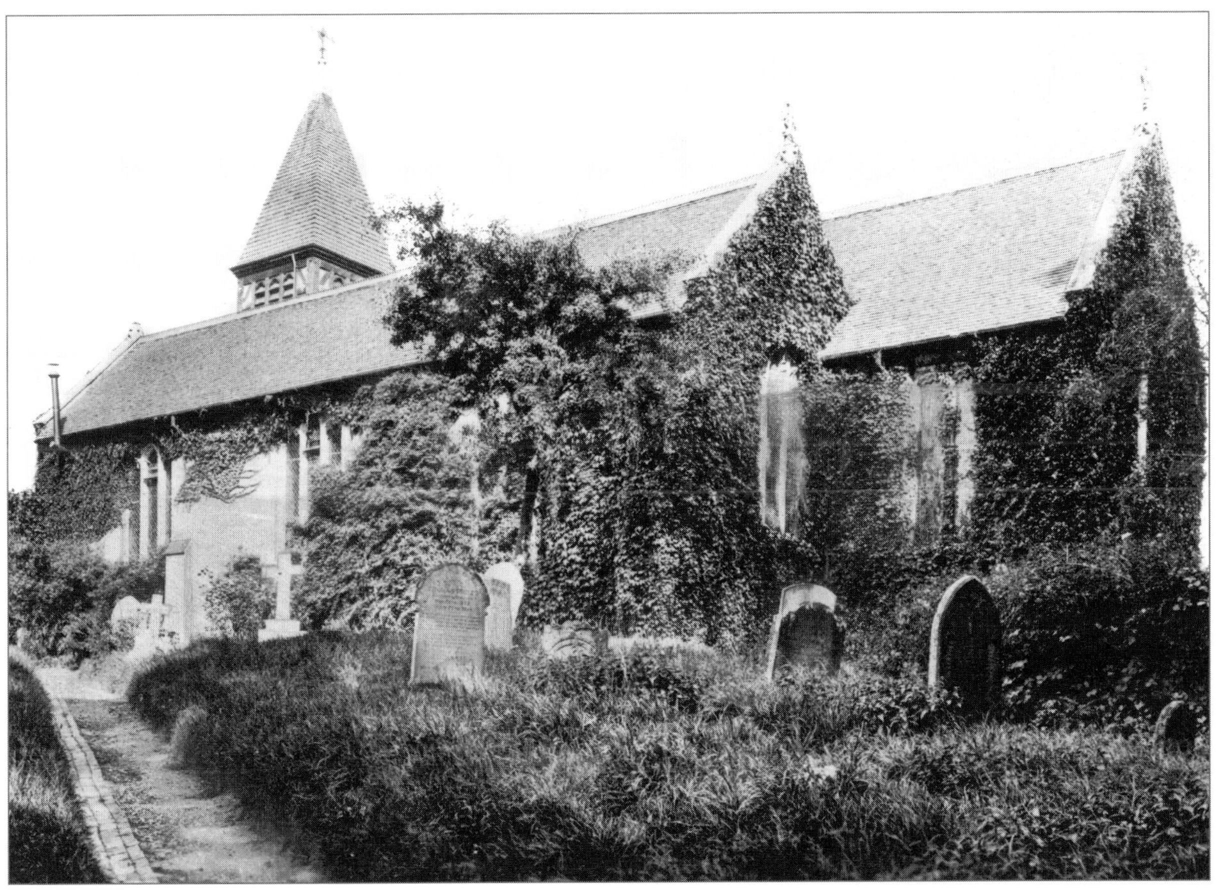

**RIBBESFORD**
*The Church c1940* R269307

The church of St Leonard's at Ribbesford, where the Rev George Macdonald was buried in the 19th century, has an interesting connection. The vicar had four daughters, Agnes, Georgina, Alice and Louisa. Alice married John Lockwood Kipling, and their son was the author Rudyard Kipling. Louisa married Alfred Baldwin, head of the great engineering firm, and their son, born in High Street, Bewdley, was Stanley Baldwin, who became Prime Minister. Georgina married the painter Sir Edward Burne-Jones, who created the wonderful stained glass windows of Wilden Church near Stourport. Agnes and Louisa were married on the same day; Agnes married the painter Edward Poynter, who became president of the Royal Academy. The sisters had a panoply of talented friends, not least William Morris, who designed the beautiful altar cloth, worked on for years by lady embroiderers. It hangs in a frame near the altar at Wilden church.

## RIBBESFORD

*The Lido Café c1965* R269006

Flanked by thick forest the Lido Café was well situated and this pleasant spot was popular with walkers and cyclists especially after World War II. It was to be found on the back road passing Areley Kings and Stony Bottom but no sign of the café remains. The Wyre Forest Society and the Ramblers' Association, aware of possible damage to wildlife and woodland, must constantly be on guard against schemes that could mar the environment. In November 2003 the creation of a route, part of a national cycle network, which could have impinged on the Wyre Forest was mooted. Fierce opposition was voiced and the idea of a cycle track has since been dropped by Wyre Forest District Council.

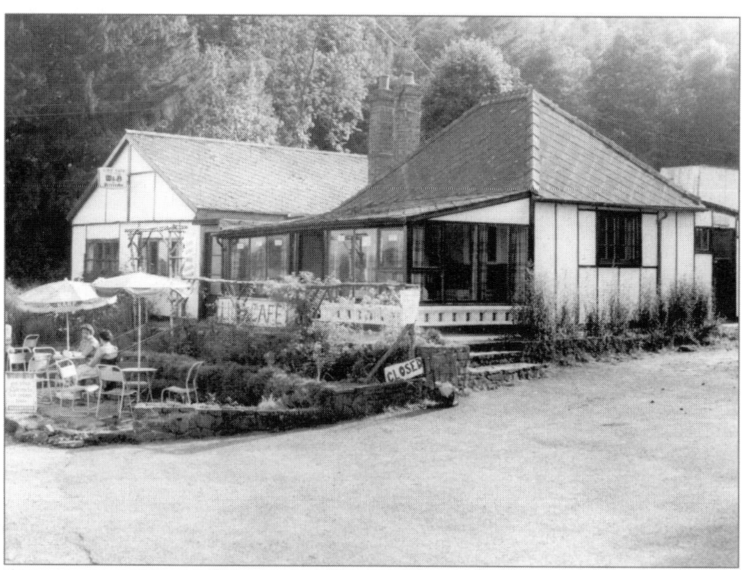


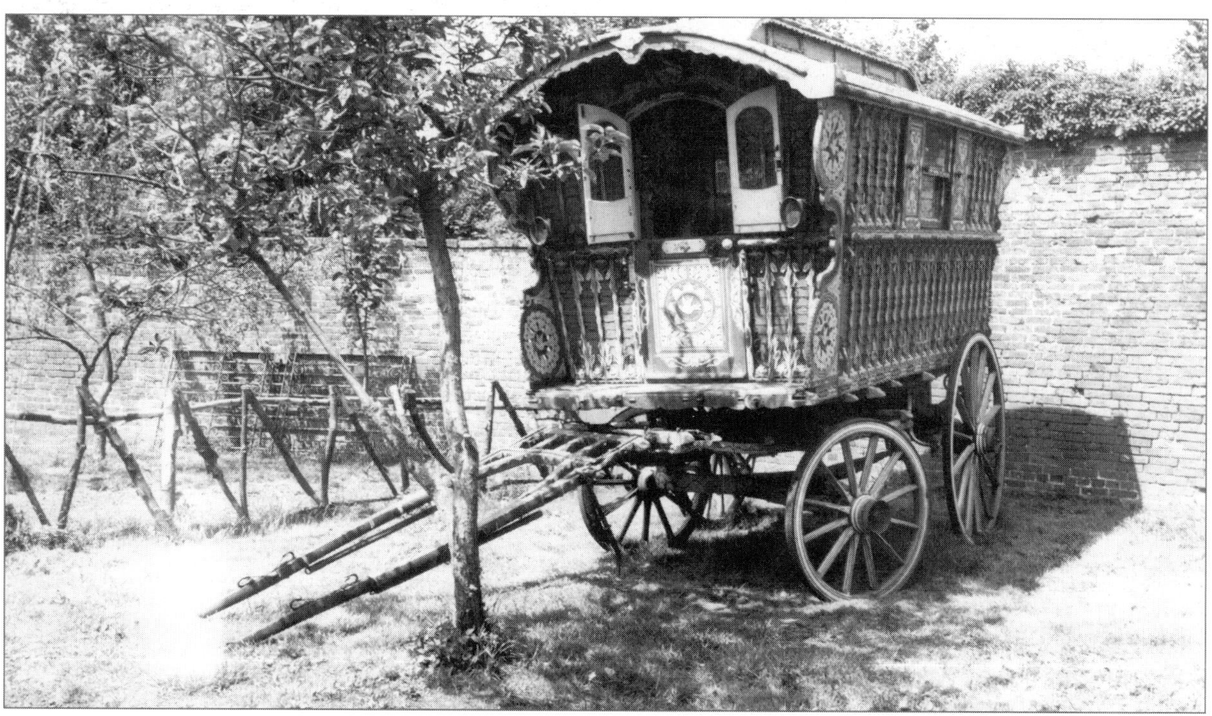

**HARTLEBURY,** *A Gypsy Caravan, Worcester County Museum c1960* H376008

Hartlebury Castle has been the home of the bishops of Worcester for over a thousand years. Today, Worcestershire County Museum is housed in the north wing. In the orchard there is a display of traditional gypsy caravans, many of which once wound their way along the lanes of Midland counties. So expensive was the gold leaf and paint in their refurbishment, that the caravans are now protected with a glass canopy.

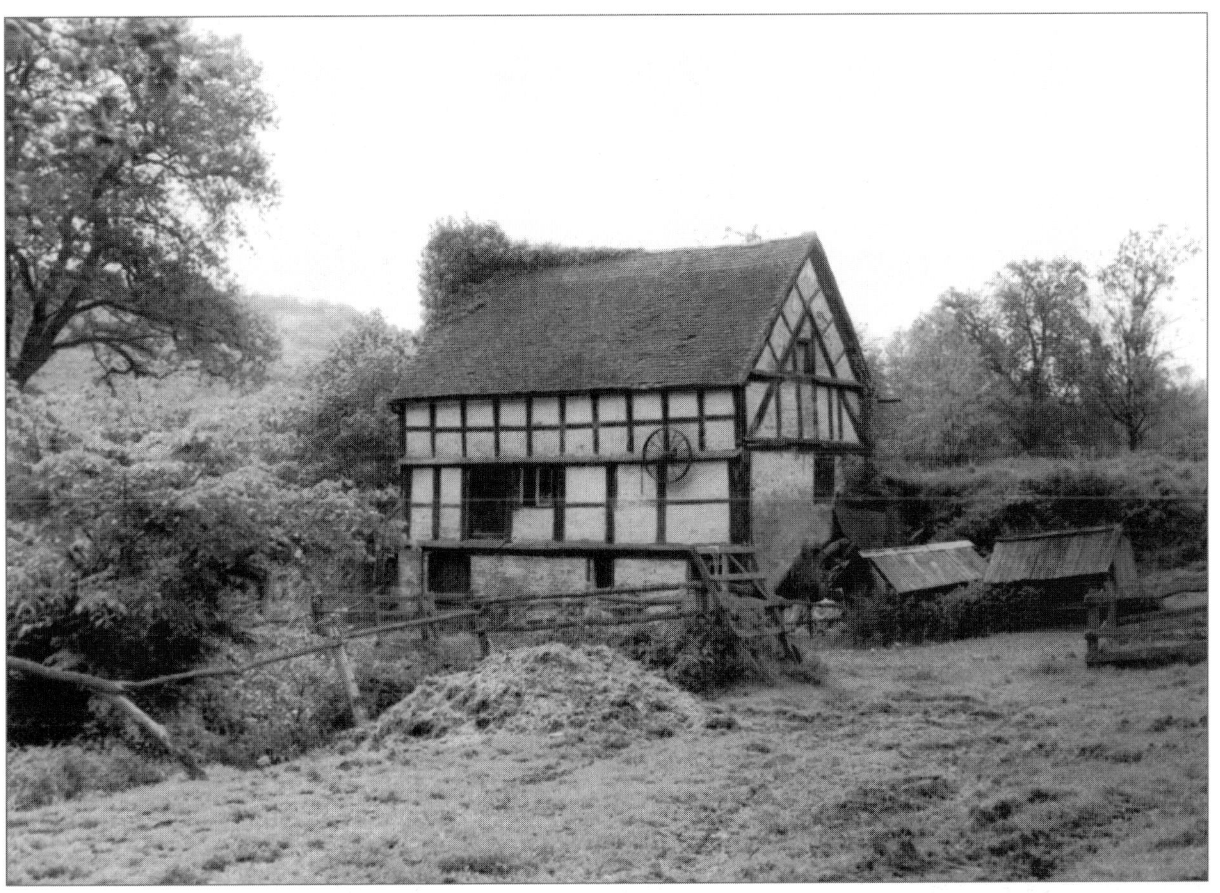

**ASTLEY BURF,** *Astley Mill c1955* A366009

There was a water mill on this site at the time of the *Domesday Book*. A mill on this site was inhabited by monks in the 14th century, when it was known as Prior Allen's Mill or Prior's Mill. The mill we see here was workable until 1940, when a great flood damaged machinery. Indeed, it may have been then that the sliding gate at the front, stamped 'Stourport Foundry 1827', was swept away. The building remained derelict, with the leat and tailrace blocked, the penstock collapsed, the sluice gate broken, and the crown wheel rotten - so were all the buckets on the wheel. Rebuilding started in 1976; before then, the mill had been used as a farm store. There remains much interest in this historic building, which is now the home of Mr and Mrs M Heywood, who have restored it most beautifully and sympathetically. The photograph shows the broken mill wheel (centre), the sluice gates and the large mill pool (right). Behind the mill (left) is the weir, with a 20-foot drop to the lower pool. All the area at the front of the photograph is covered now by gardens.

**ASTLEY BURF,**
*Rosary Lodge, Witley Court c1955* A366013

Witley Court, Great Witley was the home of Lord Ward, Earl of Dudley; it was built in the flamboyant style of India's New Delhi when the British Empire was at its peak. Through this lodge gate passed the luminaries of the day to the many house parties held at Witley Court - the Prince of Wales (the future Edward VII) frequently came. Entertainment was lavish. Dame Nellie Melba, the opera diva, had the head chef's creation named after her when she visited: Peach Melba was born. The earl owned coal mines, which was just as well - all the open fires in the vast establishment needed to burn a lot of coal to ensure the guests' comfort. The present owner, Mr Woodman, has much restoration work in progress. Blocks of honey-gold stone to match the original colour lie waiting with the mason's hammer. Rosary Lodge is a listed building, and its character must be preserved. It is now known as Stourport Lodge.

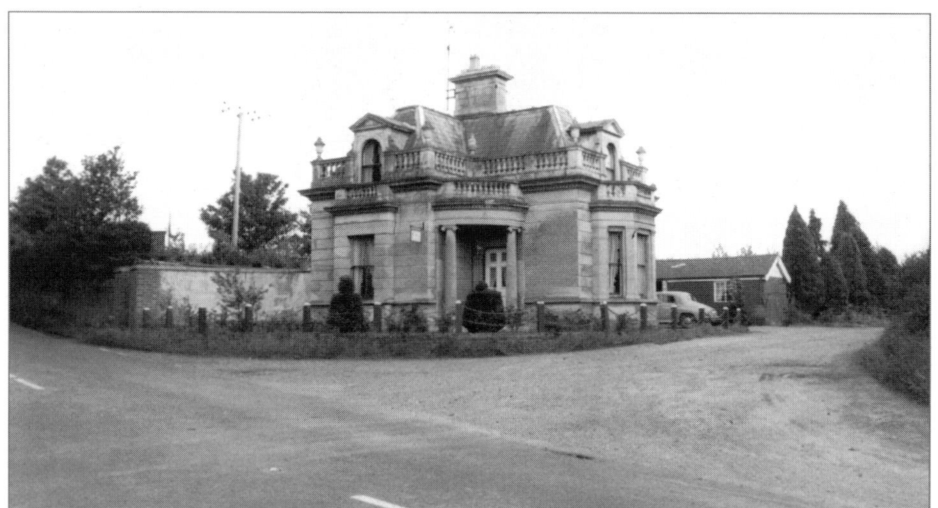

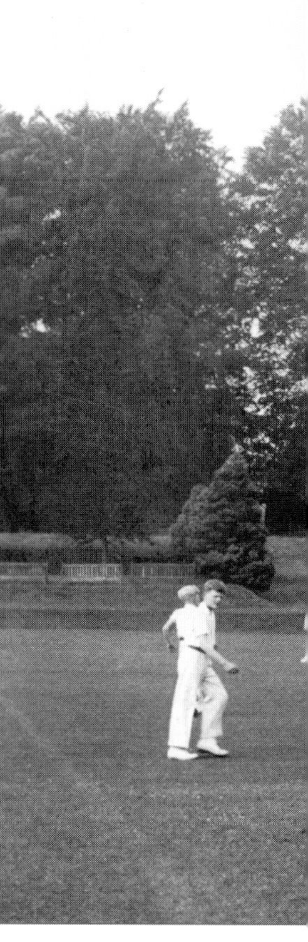

**ABBERLEY**
*The Tower 1911* 64057

This clock tower sited between Abberley village and Woodbury Hills is known locally as Jones's Folly after the enthusiastic squire, John Joseph Jones, who built it in 1880 upon Merritt's Hill. Palman and Fotheringham completed the structure in 1884; their bill was for £7,980. The building contains a carillon of 16 bells and a clock by J B Joyce of Whitchurch (the same firm services it today). The clock tower was inhabited by the Home Guard during World War II, as it commands a view of 6 counties.

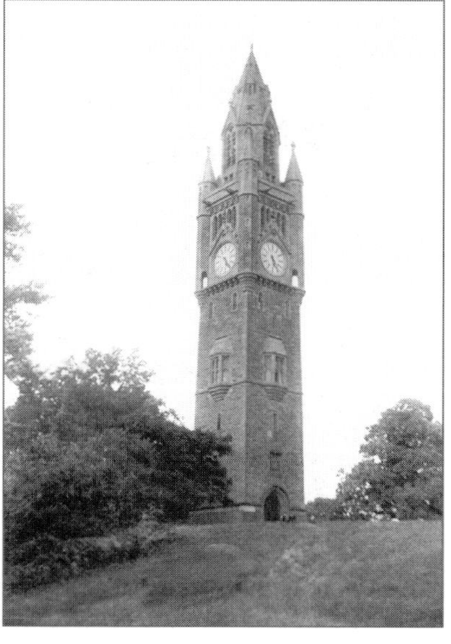

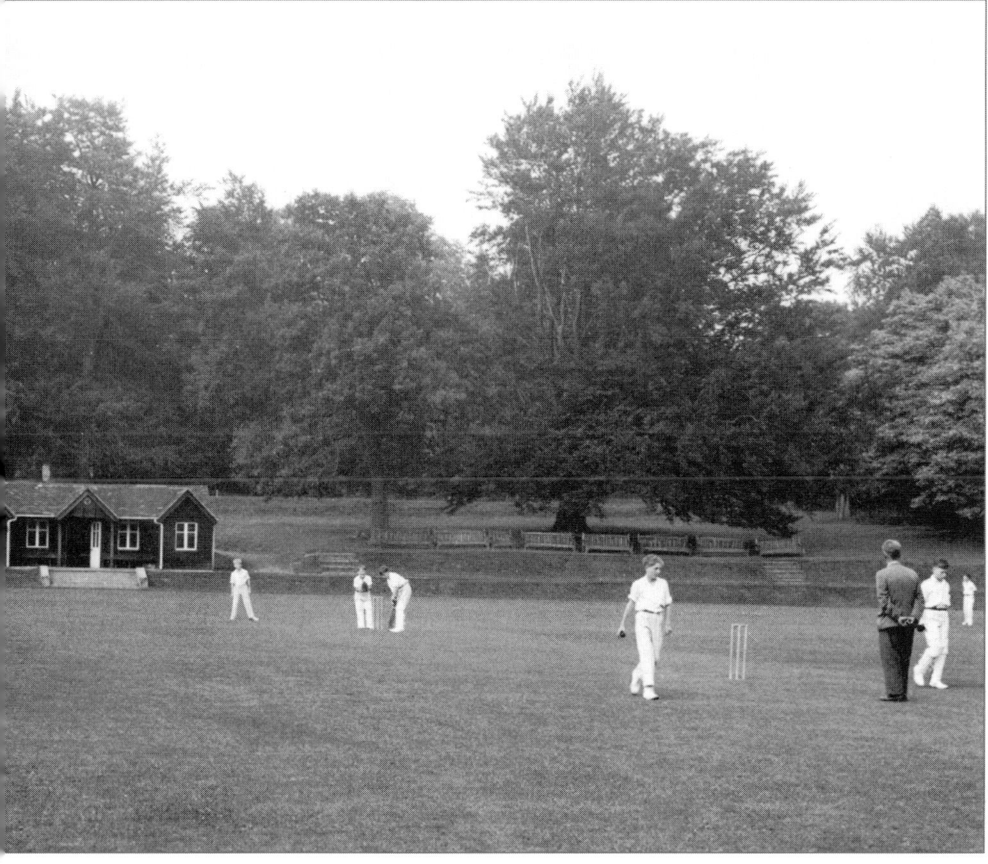

◄ **ABBERLEY** *The Cricket Field c1955* A255032

The cricket field, backed by mature trees, is a beautiful setting for a school playing field. The 1950 fathers' match, held annually at Abberley Hall School, was long remembered. Father spectators 'nobly stood in continuous rain for 2 hours while the boys collected 114 runs for the loss of 3 wickets.' The village of Abberley, with pastureland and spacious meadows stretching to the horizon, remains a typically English scene.

► **ABBERLEY** *The Hall c1955* A255011

The house was originally Abberley Lodge. In 1844 a Birmingham banker employed S W Daukes to rebuild the house in Italianate style. On Christmas Day 1845 it burned down, but it was refurbished by the banker's widow, Mrs Moilliet. By 1870 the estate passed to the Jones family; further improvements were made, including rockeries, gardens, grottoes, and a portico. 1916 saw Abberley Hall, with all its furniture and fittings, acquired as a boys' school.

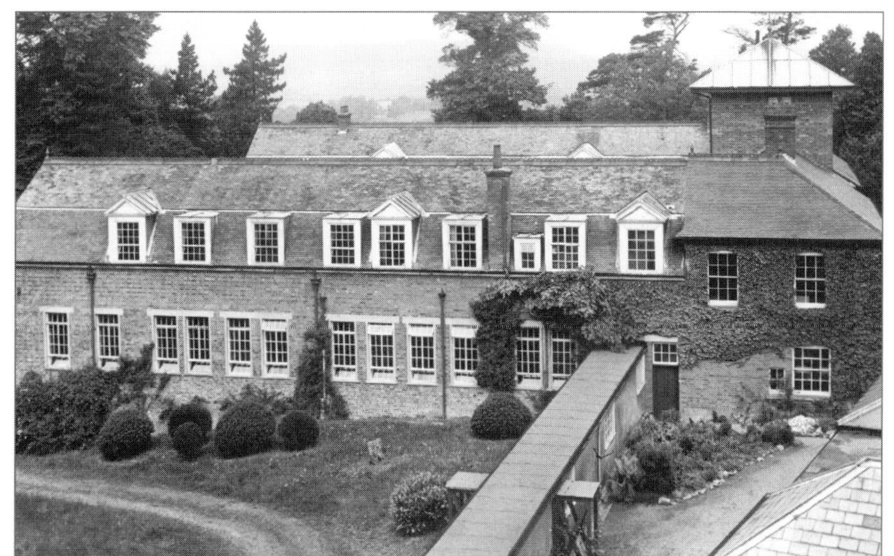

▼ **ABBERLEY,** *The Hall, a Dormitory c1950* A255004

Mr A M Kilby purchased Abberley Hall as a haven for the boys of Lindisfarne School, Blackheath, London on 26 September 1916. The school also acquired a valuable library of books and part of the estate for £10,000. In Joseph Jones's time, when the stable block was remodelled, a rare example of a country house theatre was built, which still survives. The Patrol Challenge Cup, awarded annually, involves dormitory inspection by the Patrol members.

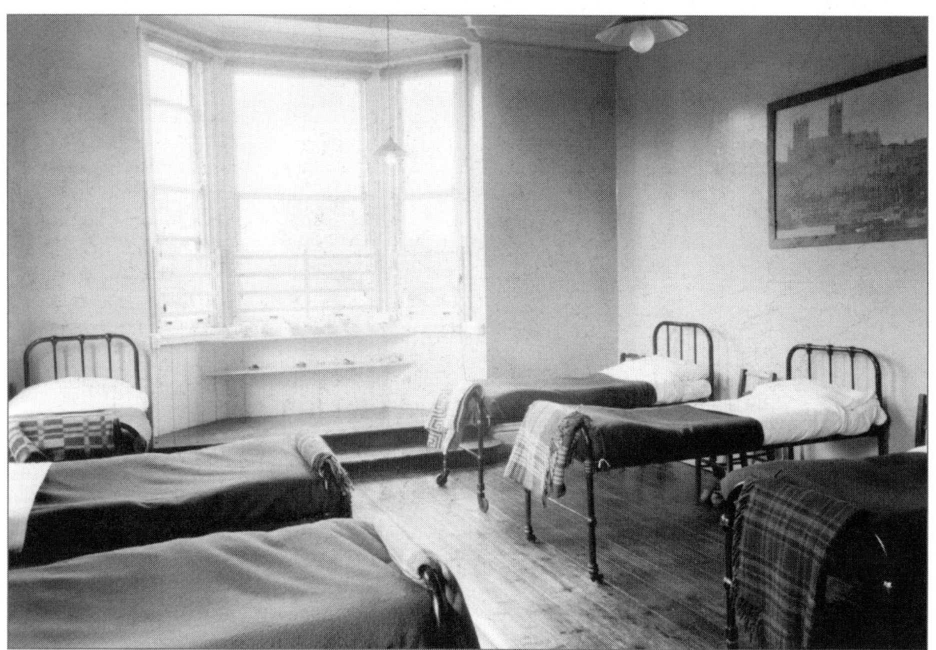

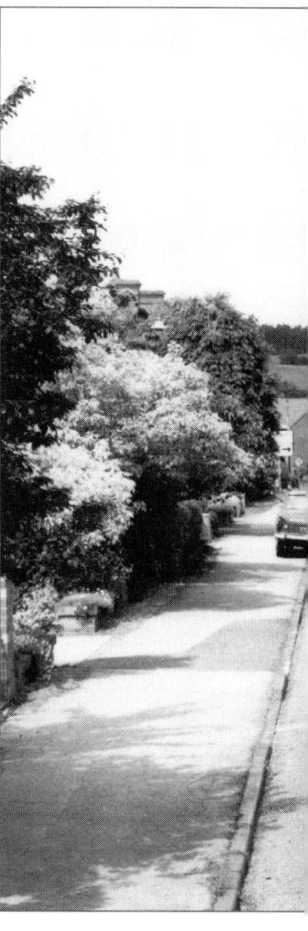

► **BELBROUGHTON**
*Church Road c1960*
B418002

This large village near Clent has Georgian and Tudor architecture and sandstone walls. The church on a hill commands the scene; it has a 14th-century tower and a slender spire, with a newer nave and chancel designed by the Victorian architect G F Bodley. In 1854 Belbroughton was a hamlet with an inn, 4 farms, and a blacksmith; Blakedown Common and Harberrow common lay beyond, until they were claimed under the Enclosure system.

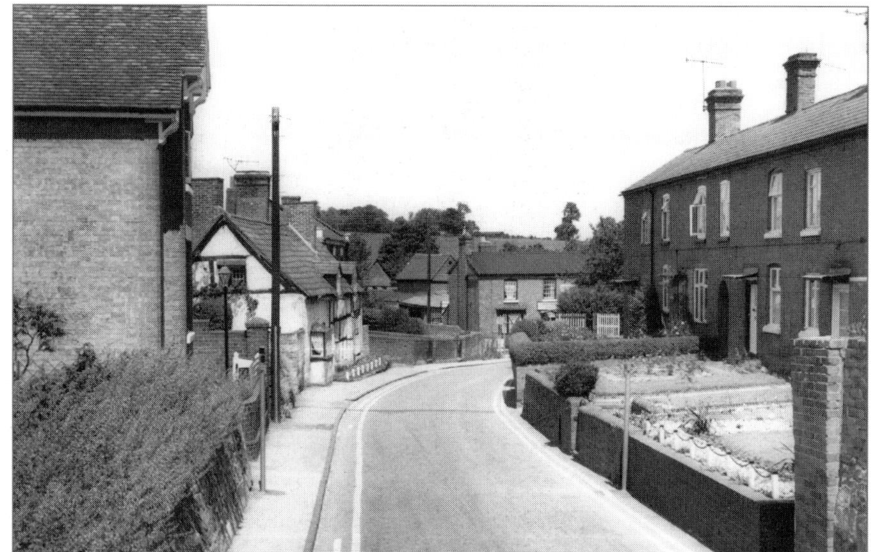

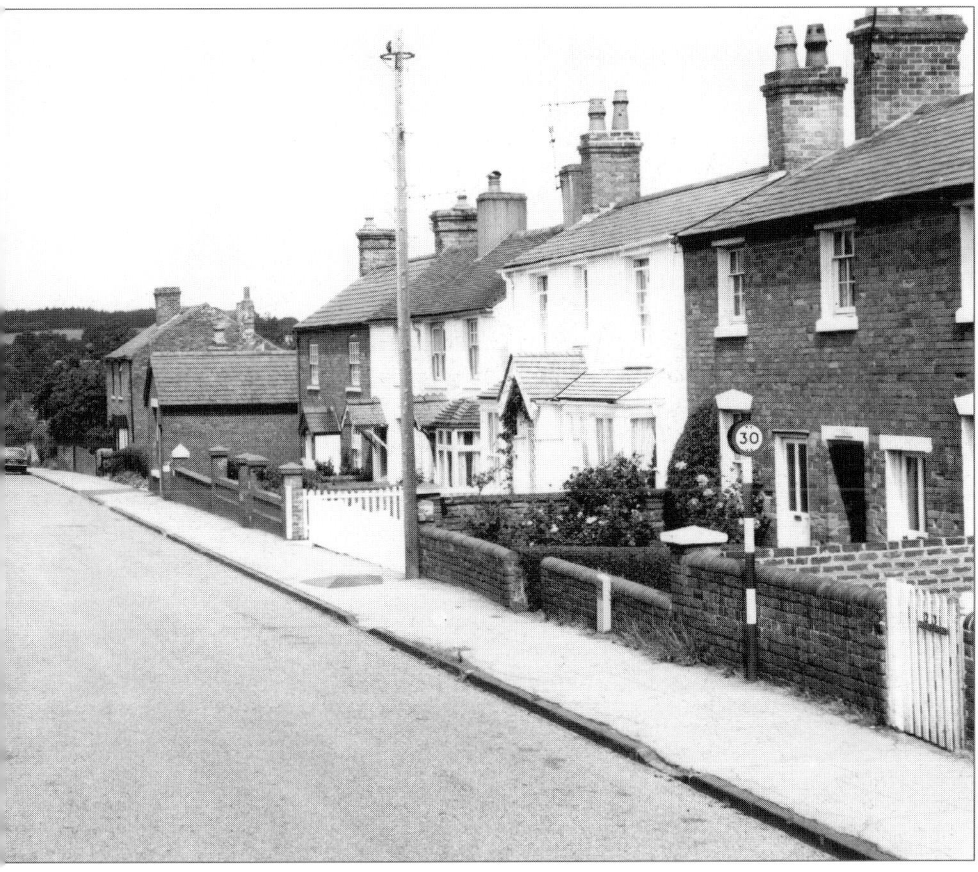


◄ **BLAKEDOWN**
*Belbroughton Road c1965* B419007

On the right at the end is what was the toll house until 1877. It became a grocer's, but the toll gate was left propped up by the roadside! Solomon Rutter was the village grocer from 1895 to c1940. Later, the village had an antiques shop, a post office, and Mr Wormington's butcher's shop. The railway arrived in 1852, when there was a saw mill, blade mill and foundry in full production not far from the turnpike toll house.

► **BELBROUGHTON**
*High Street c1965*
B418006

On the right, outside the post office selling Park Drive cigarettes, there is an old-style red telephone box, and beyond it two village shops. Even a quiet village of this type has had recourse to road markings for the traffic increasingly passing through. A solitary boy on a bicycle passes the village shop.

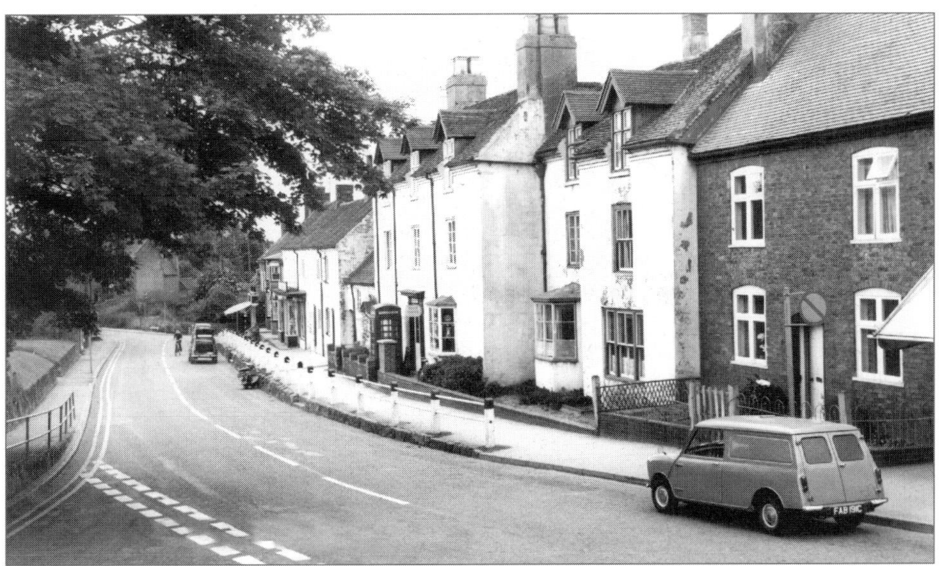

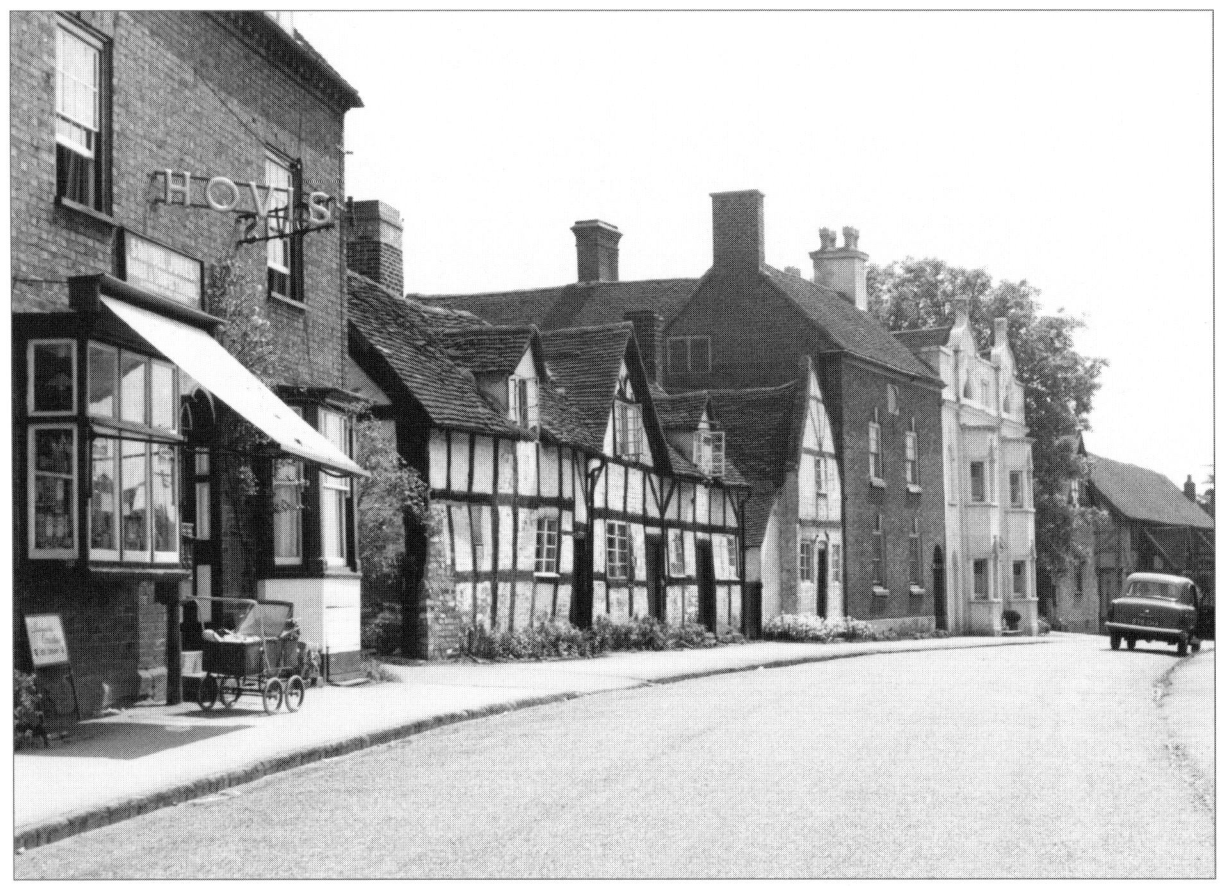


**CHADDESLEY CORBETT,** *The Village c1955* C328015

Off the Kidderminster to Bromsgrove road, this village street shows a pleasing mingle of red brick, Georgian and half-timbered work. Samuel Jukes, baker and confectioner, with his gold-coloured Hovis bread sign (they appeared all over in the fifties) was still baking bread when he was 80, but he was killed in a tragic accident when the bake house collapsed around him. Immediately next door is the post office (left and off the picture). Next door is a private house, The Old Bakery. Next again, the half-timbered structure is Beam's End. The house with the plaque was School House, home of the headmaster until 1965. Beyond the trees, after what was always the doctor's house, is the inn sign of the Talbot. In between Old Bakery and School House is an ancient cruck-framed cottage, since demolished.

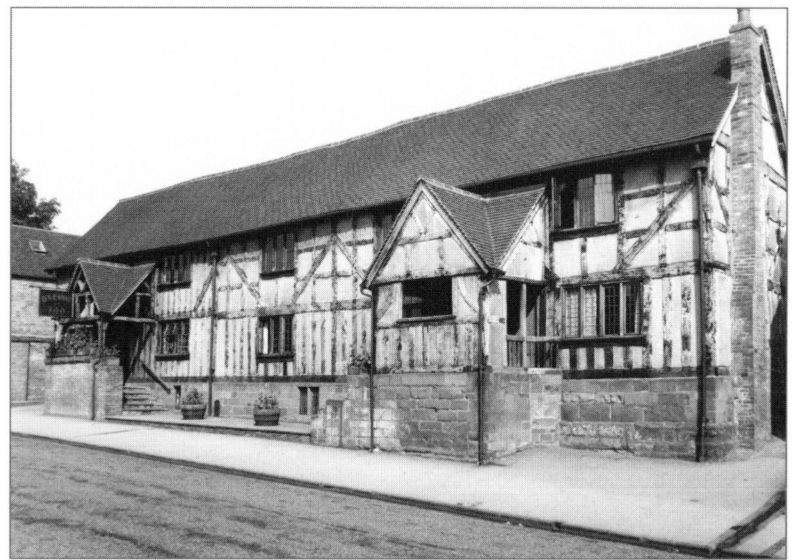

**CHADDESLEY CORBETT**
*The Talbot Inn c1957* C328016

Travelling brewers used to prepare ale in the brew house at the back of the ancient Talbot Inn. Facing the half-timbered inn (which dates from c1600, and owned then by the Talbot family), is the church, with some Norman fabric, but 18th-century tower and spire. The Norman font is carved with plait work and five dragons with unicorn horns; they encircle the massive font so that they bite each other's tails. Thomas and Margaret Forest with their 11 children are depicted in brass. The church is dedicated to St Cassian, the only one in England of that name. Cassian was born in Alexandria in the 5th century, and was bishop of an African diocese.

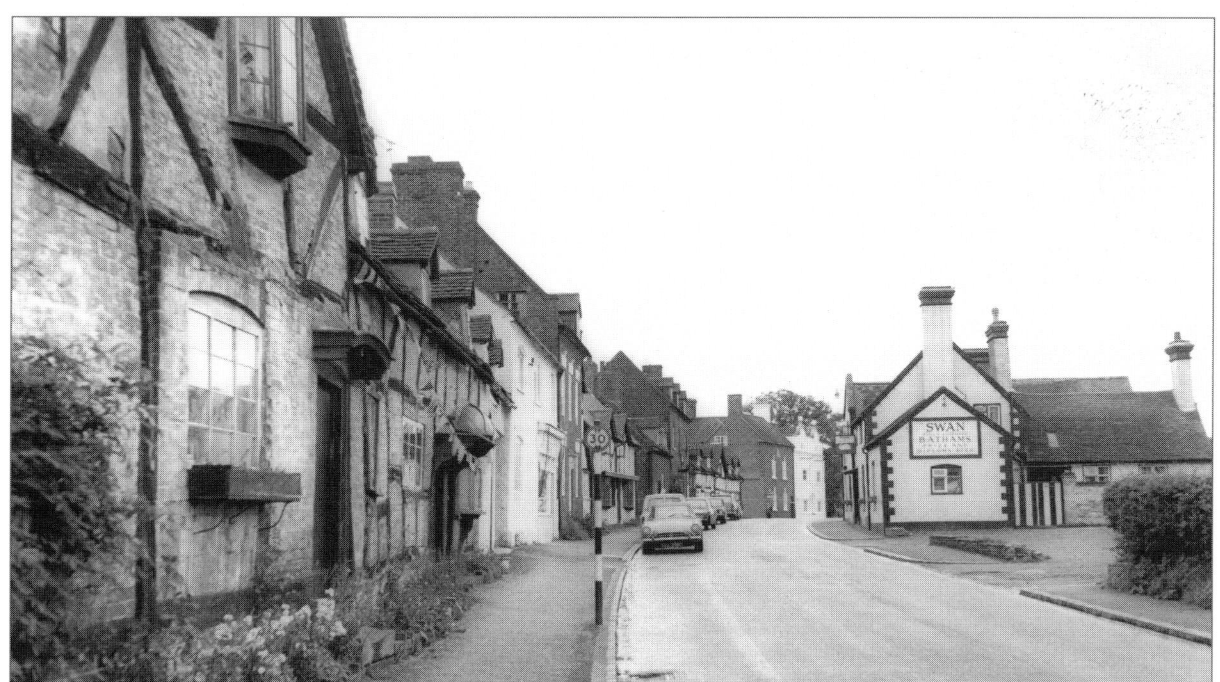


**CHADDESLEY CORBETT,** *Lower Village c1965* C328021

Batch Cottages (near left) are said by Pevsner to be the best timber-framed houses in Lower Village. The doorway with the half cupola was a barber's shop. Beyond was Bank's the butcher's and a malt house. Just out of view on this same side is tall Harkaway House, refurbished from the old workhouse. The Swan (right), supplied by Bathams, was one of many inns that held cock fighting. The Valentia at Arley had a skittle alley and the occasional ox-roast, where they sold steaming portions to villagers wanting a hot dinner.

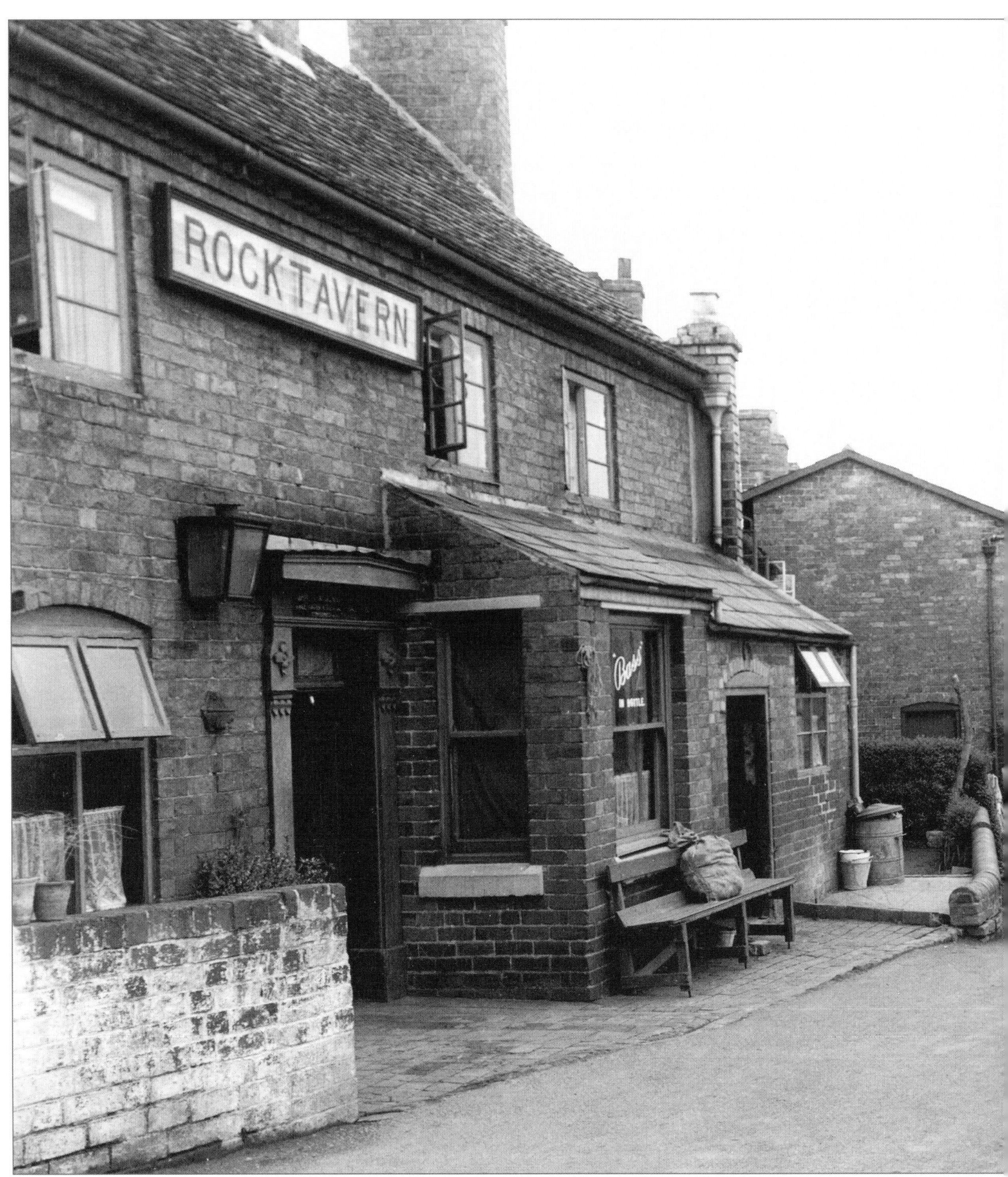
ROCK TAVERN
Bass
IN BOTTLE

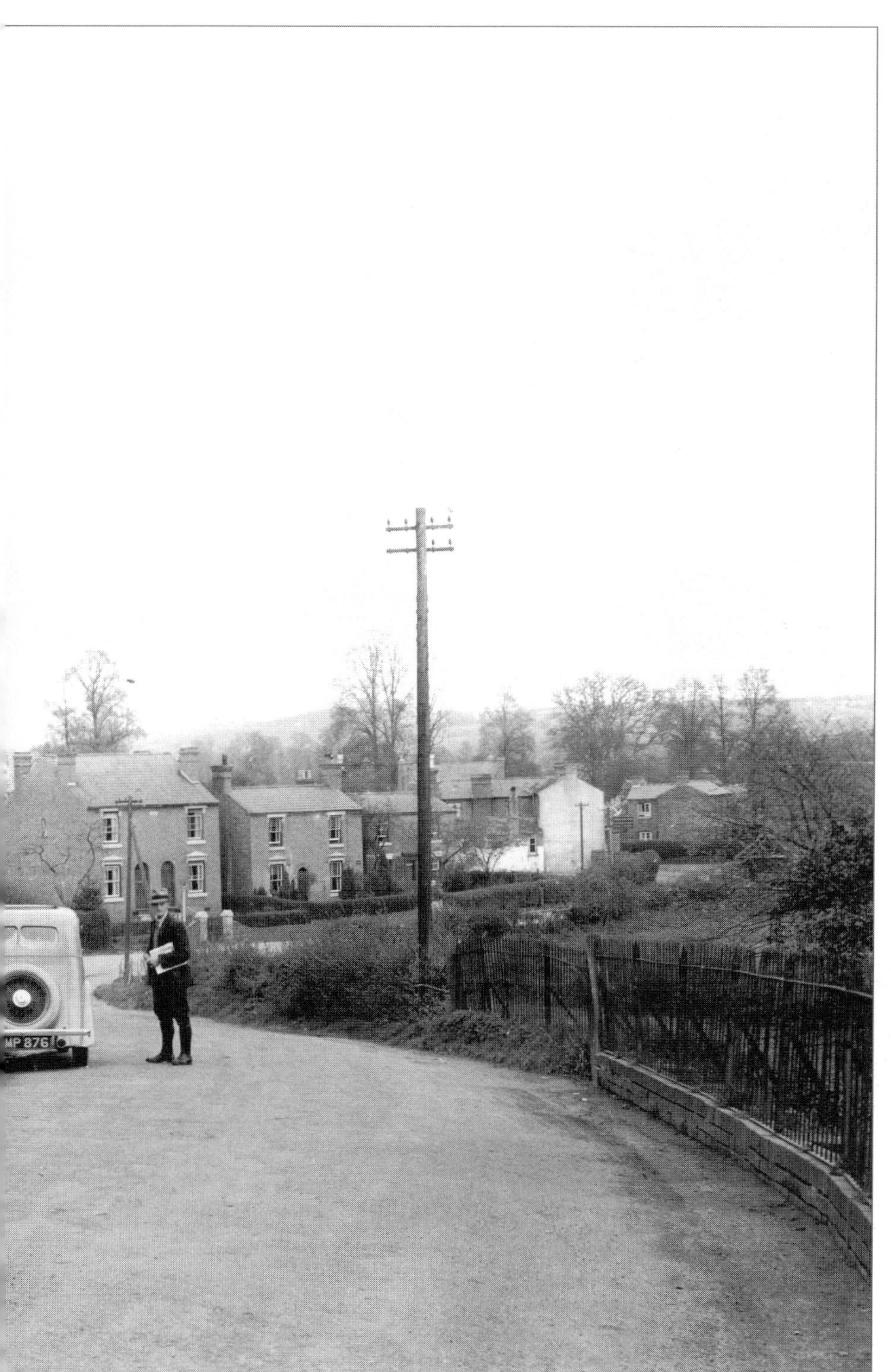


**CAUNSALL**
*The Rock Tavern c1950*
C761008

Many one-roomed beer houses opened after the Beer House Act of 1830, which allowed any householder to sell beer on payment of 2 guineas. Thomas Hyde and his family left Cookley to open a beer house called the Britannia, but they later changed the name to the Rock Tavern. In 1905 J Tunnington was landlord; that year a great send off was organised for him by a score of Rock patrons, including C Pitt, John Birch, J Fox, C Cartwright and George Edge.

**CAUNSALL**
*The Village c1950* C761013

The road from Rock Tavern led to Cookley Iron Works; then it climbed to Bridge Road beyond the canal and the River Stour, leading on to Sebright Place in Cookley Square. Caunsall Road passed the Anchor Inn, where Fred Wills, who lived at Rose Cottage, brewed the beer - it varied in taste, but was always 'strong and full of flavour'! The Anchor was popular with bargees from the canal boats. Tim Clarke, whose barge was the *Edris*, won the May Day competition for the best dressed barge horse one year.

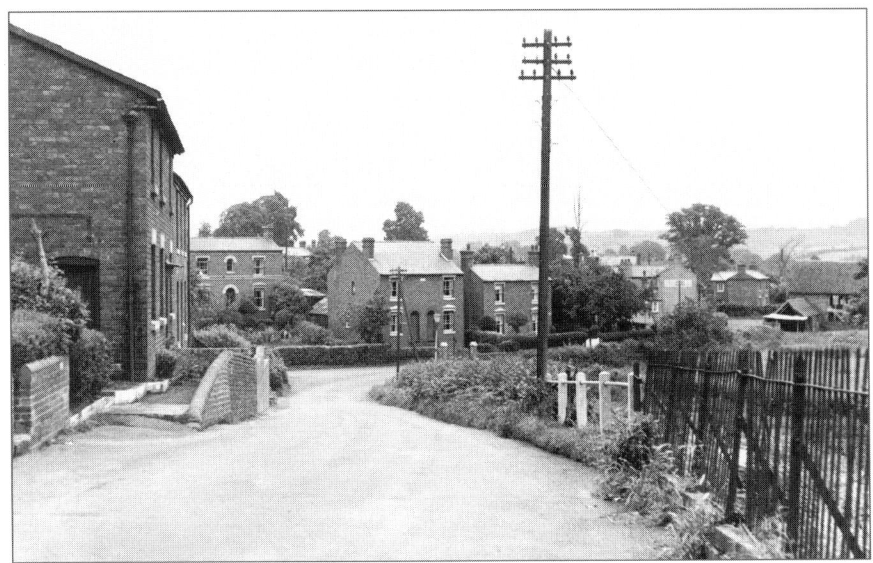

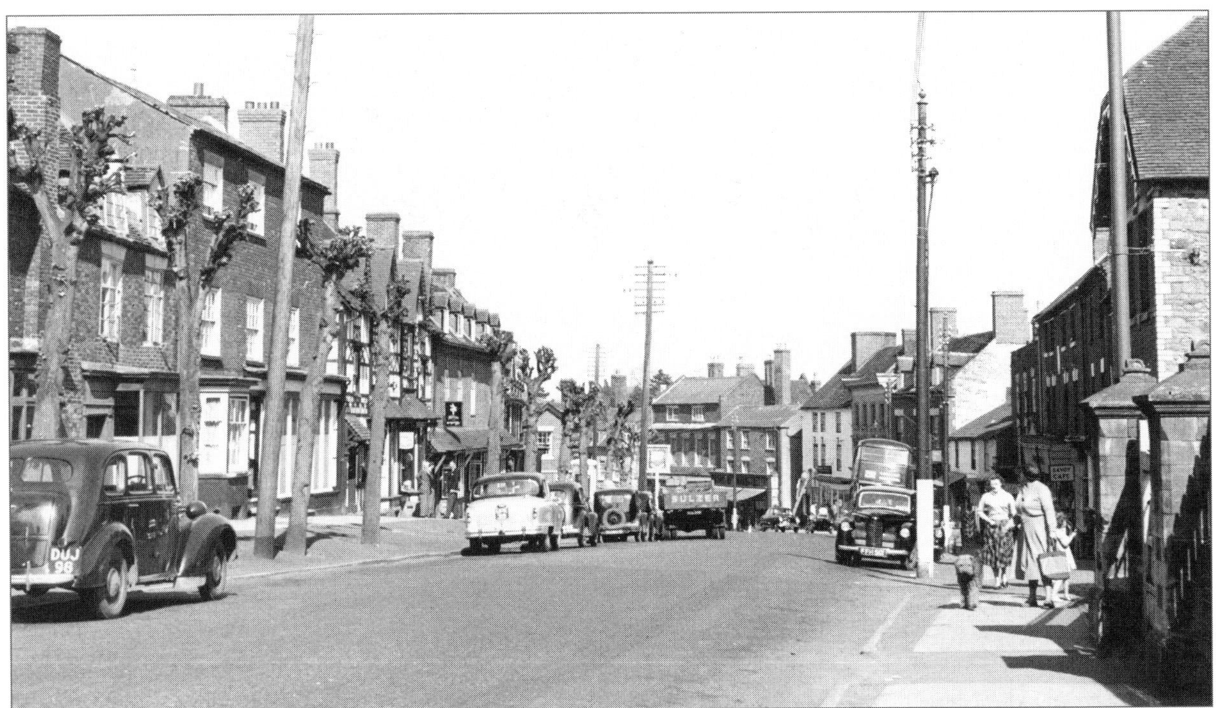


**CLEOBURY MORTIMER,** *High Street c1955* C506039

The Savoy Café is on the right, and further down hill across the road Mazda lamps are for sale close to the inn sign. A double-decker bus, probably from Kidderminster, is across from the delivery wagon marked Sulzer (centre). A line of trees (left) has had to be pollarded; they were planted long before motorised traffic was thought of, and their branches were a threat to safety.

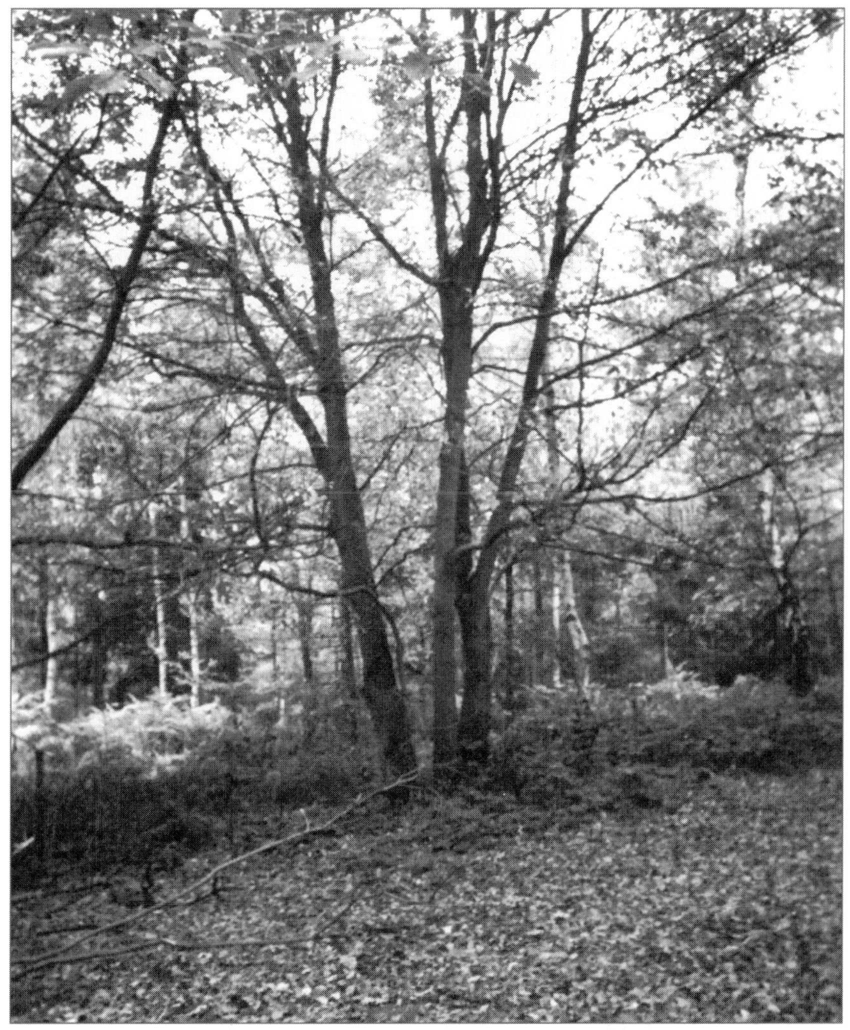

**WYRE FOREST** *2003* W643003

The most famous tree of Wyre Forest is perhaps the Whitty Pear, 50ft high, a descendant of the specimen presented by Robert Woodward of Arley Castle. At Cleobury Mortimer there is another giant of Wyre Forest, the Mawley Oak. Common oak, silver birch, sweet chestnut and buckthorn, loved by the Brimstone butterfly, abound, along with Norway spruce. The Severn Valley Railway, championed by Sir Gerald Nabarro MP, once had a second line, which continued to Tenbury Wells through the Forest. It is thrilling to hear the whistle of a steam train echoing through the trees.

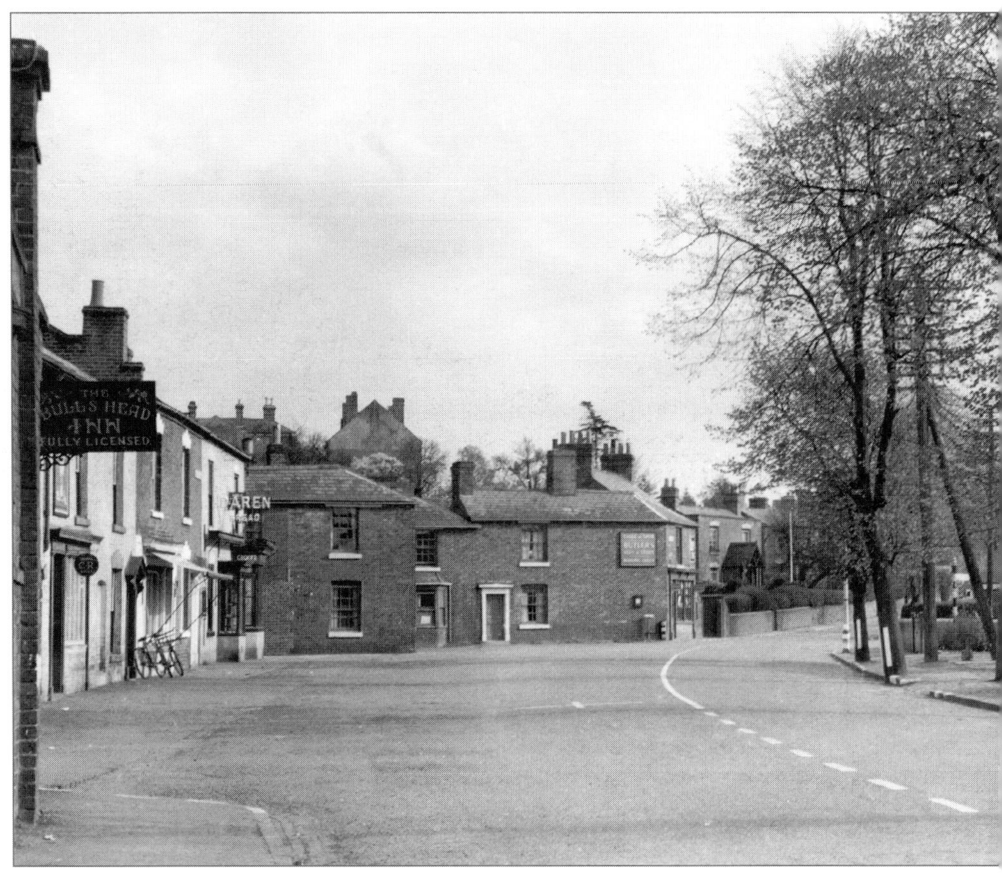


**COOKLEY**
*The Square c1950*
C333006

The Bull's Head Inn is to the immediate left; a 19th-century advertisement extolled the Bull's Head 'for its splendid cellars and caves in solid rock'. Another hostelry, the Eagle and Spur, is further along the Square (centre). A baker's shop founded in 1832 is in between, selling Daren bread. The trees on the right still bear their white markings to warn people in the years of the blackout during World War II. Seabright Fisheries behind the trees is now Seabright Sea Foods, selling fish, chips and pizzas.

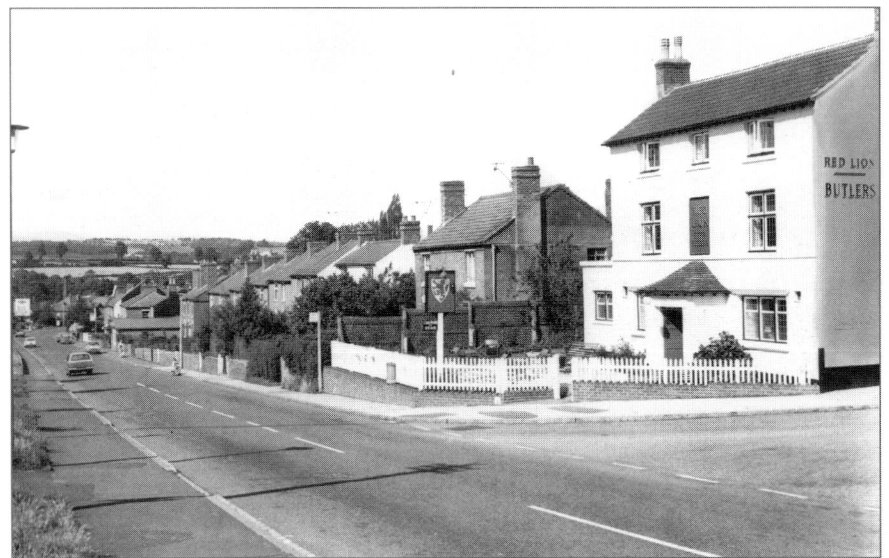


**COOKLEY**
*Castle Road c1965*
C333047

Castle Road leads to the Square. The chimney stack in the distance is that of Cookley Iron Works. The Red Lion public house (right) opened after 1830, along with the Eagle and Spur Inn. John Rowley ran the Bird in Hand in about 1860, but he changed its name to the Red Lion, perhaps because Lion Field is adjacent. The most important landowner in Cookley in 1650 was Sir Edward Sebright, who had a large estate with valuable sporting rights.

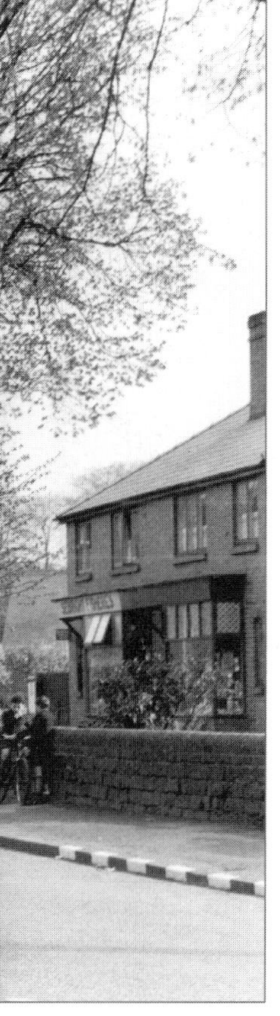

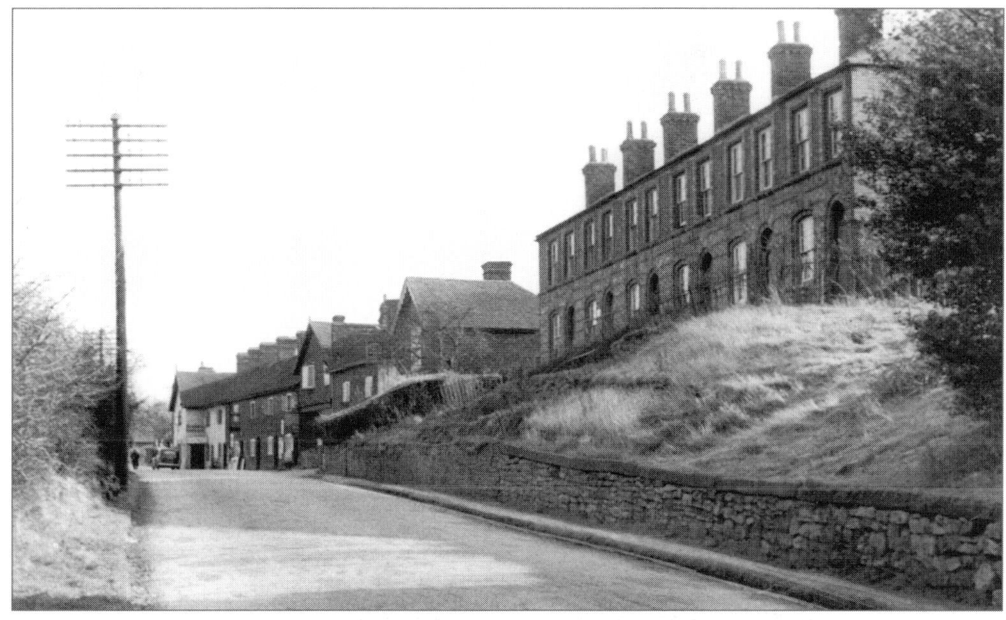

▲ **SHATTERFORD,** *The Village c1955* S384001

In the 1850s there were extensive coal workings at Shatterford, and this terraced row could have been built by the first mining company. At the end of the row was Shatterford post office, and Bellman's Cross Inn was at the other end. Pottery was made here from local clay; this brought more clay workers as well as mineworkers to the village, but later in the 19th century both industries were closed down, and Mr Lane used what was left of the clay works as a blacksmith's forge. On the Green at Shatterford was the ancient gospel oak where the first Christian missionaries preached the Gospel (Worcestershire is traditionally associated with the work of St Augustine).

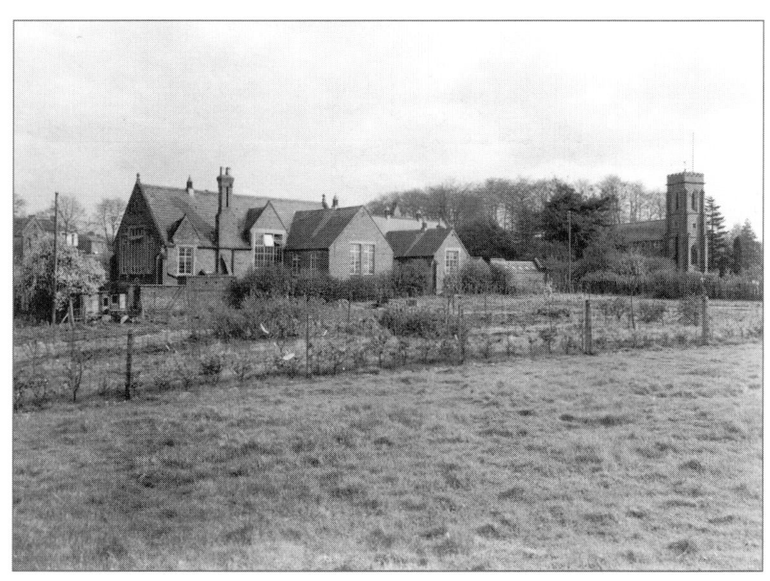

◄ **COOKLEY**
*The School and the Church c1950*
C333007

William Hancocks of Blakeshall Hall and his wife laid the foundation stone of Cookley church on 20 February 1849. From the Hancocks family in 1920 was the gift of a chair believed to have belonged to Richard Baxter. The Piper Family were also benefactors. They had between them several houses, and in the garden of each they planted a mulberry tree - school children from the village dance around the one at Shrubbery House. It was customary to ring the school bell when good work was done.

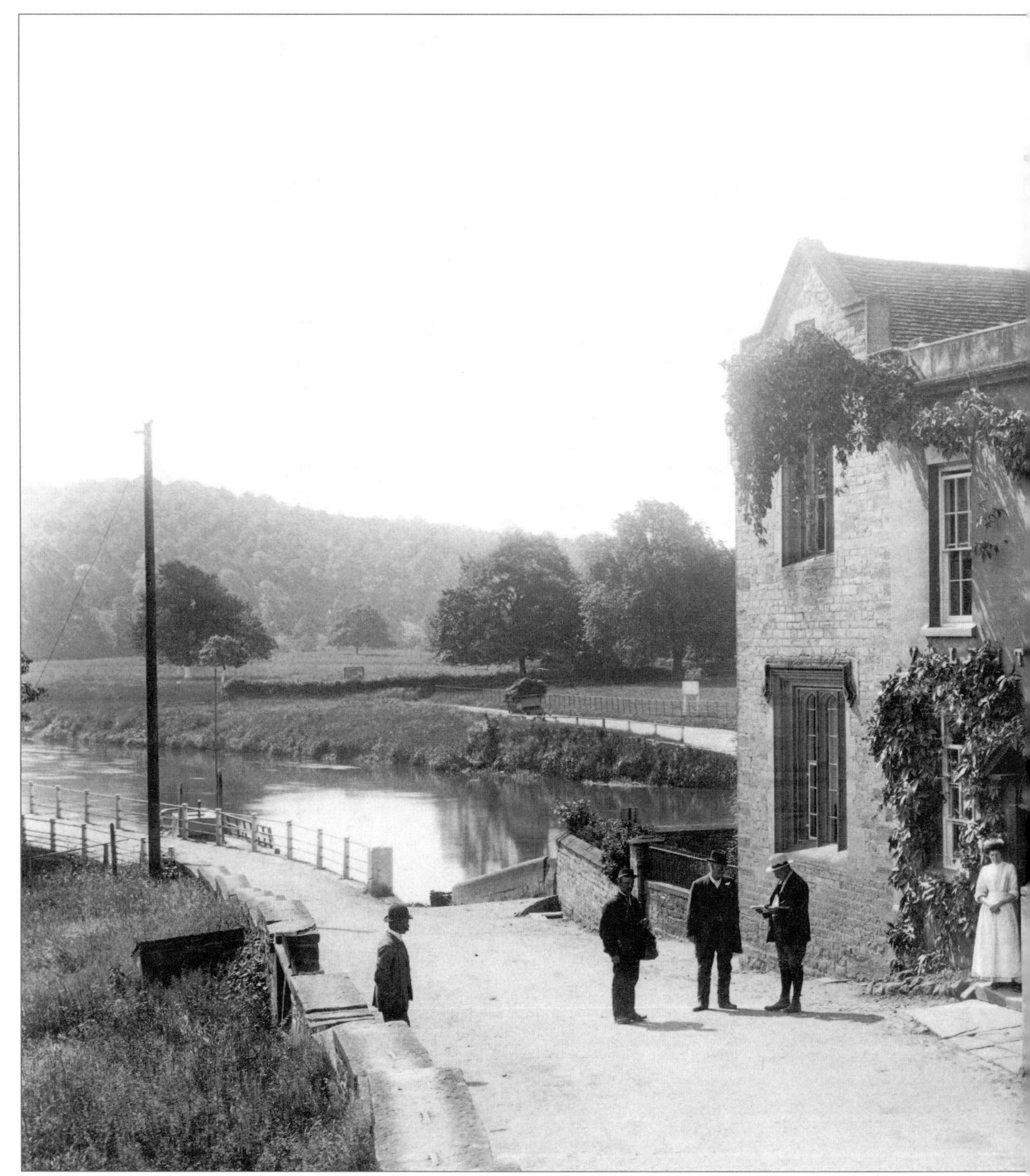

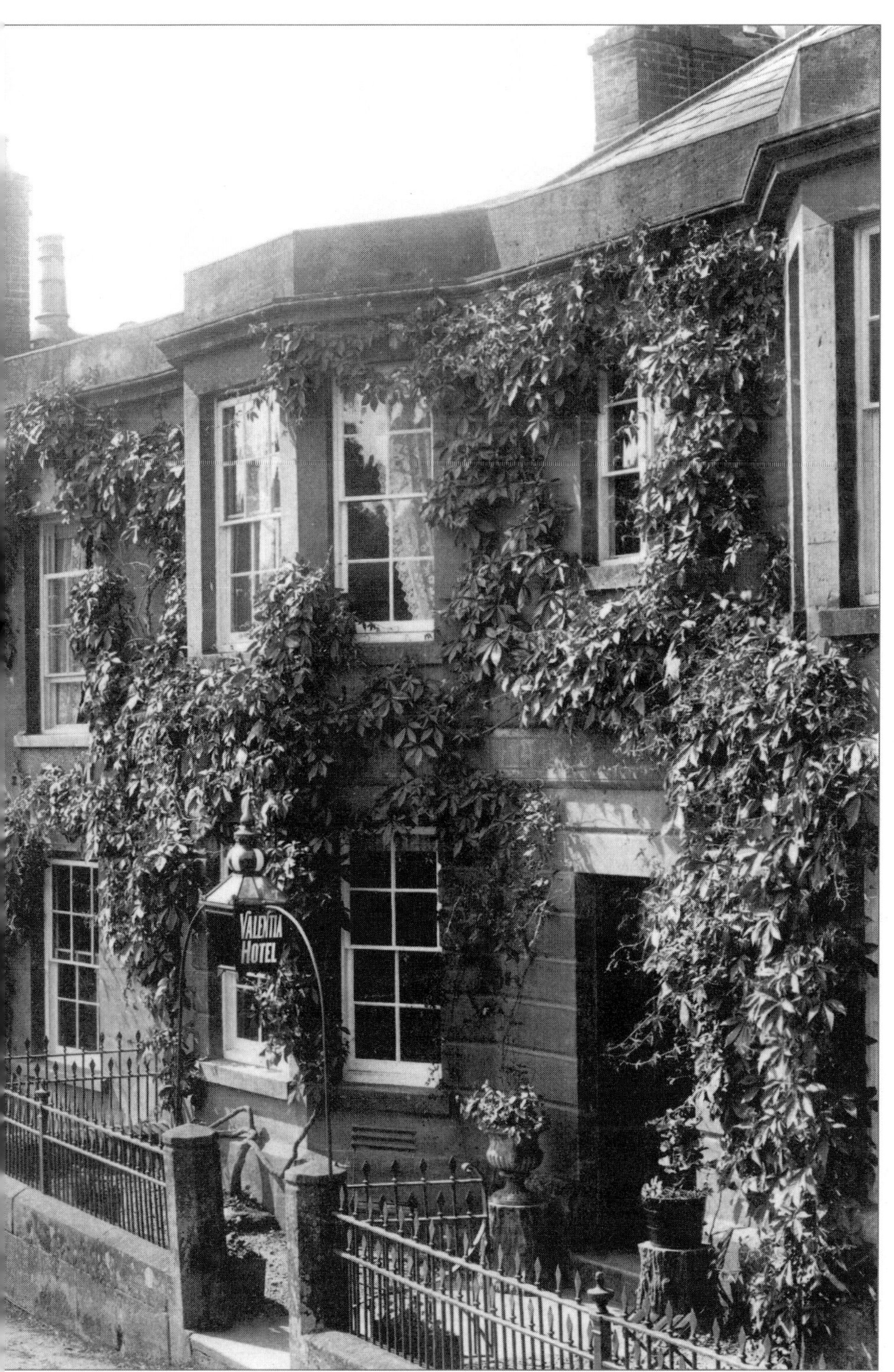


**UPPER ARLEY**
*The Valentia Hotel*
*1910* 62376

This building was originally a school; part of it was occupied by the Willcox brothers, who rented Hoxton's quarry from Lord Mountnorris. They had a thriving trade with stone-carrying barges on the River Severn. Lord Mountnorris wanted to buy their house, but Sam Willcox refused. A further annoyance was that some barges were fitted with old cannon, which were fired at every landing stage where they called! In 1910, next door was the red sandstone Halfren House. Behind the three men is Ferry Wharf. The Valentia Hotel has now been turned into individual houses.

▼ **UPPER ARLEY,** *Victoria Bridge and the River Severn c1950* A164009

In the background are Hawkbatch and Seckley Woods. Victoria Bridge, on the Severn Valley railway line from Bewdley to Bridgnorth, has a span of 200 feet; when it was built in 1862, it was considered the largest cast iron single arch bridge in the world. Far left of the bridge is Trimperley, with the Severn Trent reservoir and pumping station.

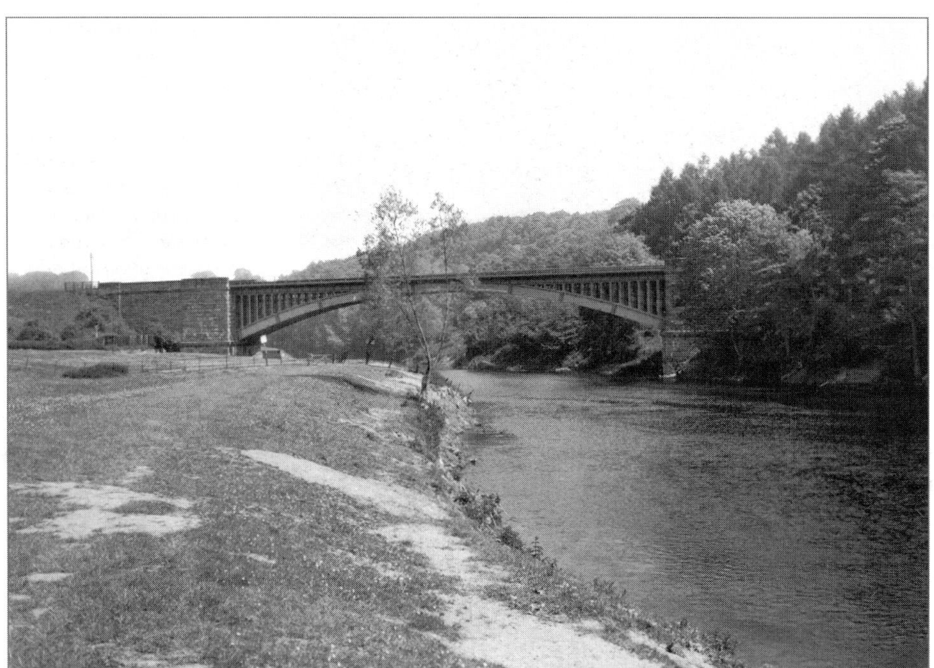

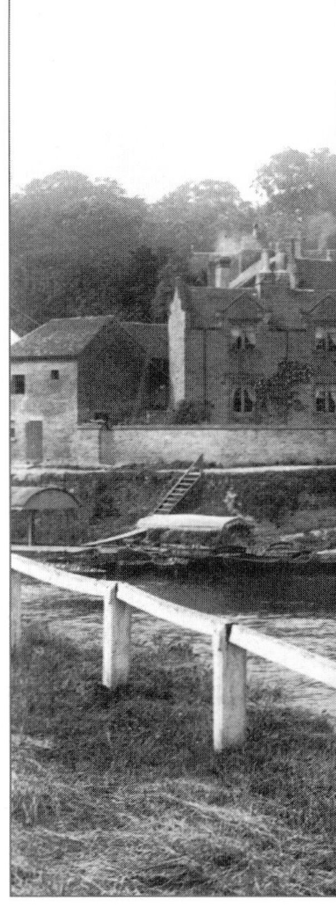

► **UPPER ARLEY**
*The Old Post Office c1957*
A164065

The Old Post Office was diagonally across from Halfren House (see No 62376 page 82-83). After 1957 it became a private house, with the walls coloured cream and the arch bricked up. Lower down on the right, what was the Glebe House is now called Shades of Green. On the left, a row of brick-built workmen's cottages climbs the hill leading to St Peter's Church, with the Old Bakehouse Teashop at the end of the row. The post office is now nearer to Arley C of E School and the footbridge.

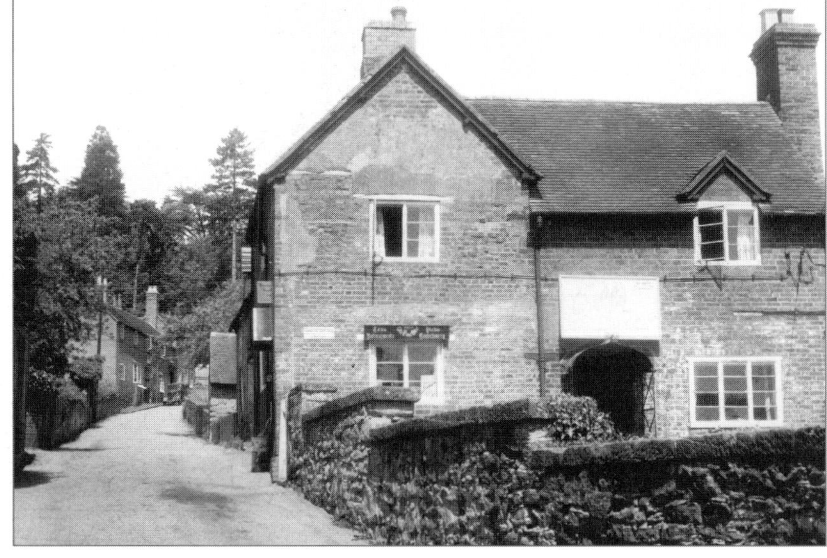

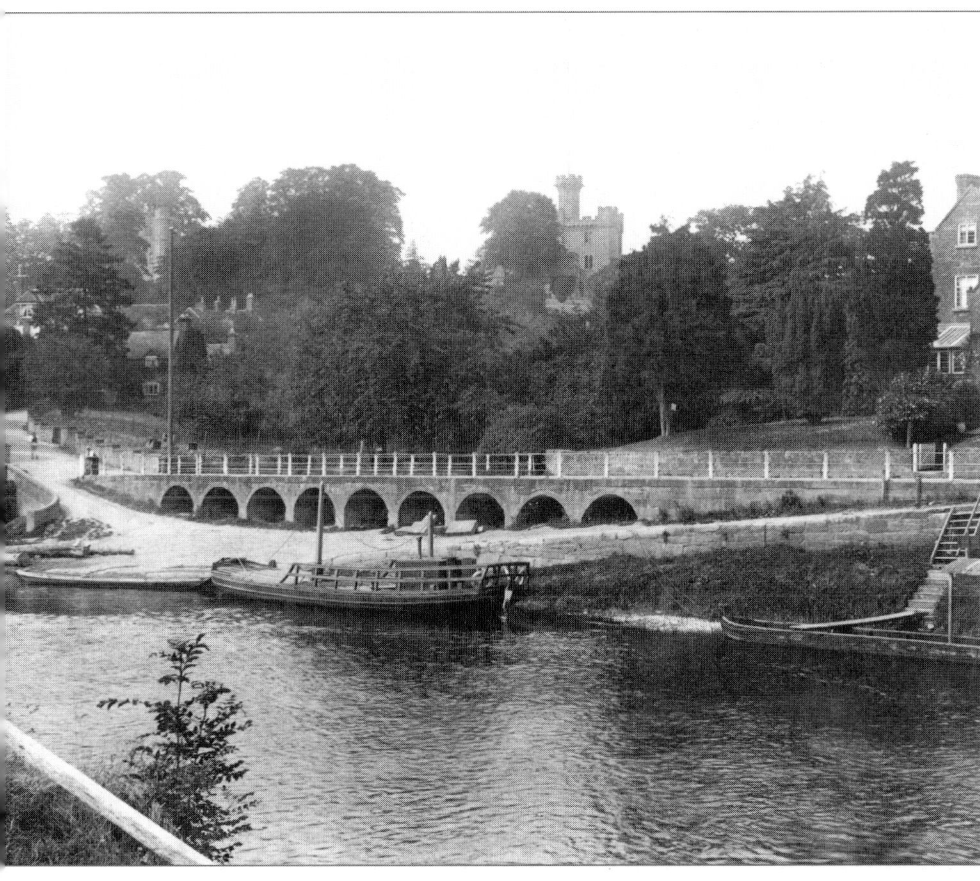

**UPPER ARLEY**
*The Ferry 1904*
51983

The ferry was replaced with a footbridge in 1972 to give access to the Severn Valley Line railway station and to connect both banks of the river. This view was taken from the road past the Harbour Inn. In the wooded background can be seen the Castle (centre right - now gone) and Arley Tower, which the disgruntled lord of the manor built to hide the Valentia Hotel. Hoxton's Quarry lies northward of the bridge at Stone Wharf. At the river's edge the village main street can be seen, supported on a series of stone arches.

**UPPER ARLEY**
*The Castle 1910* 62373

Built in the early 19th century by Lord Valentia, the Castle was bought by Mr R D Turner in 1959. By 1958 it had become a ruin, and it was demolished in 1962. Viscount Valentia was a colourful character who loved fireworks and spent hundreds of pounds on his hobby. His castle was originally the ancient manor house of the Lyttleton family, Arley Hall, and huge sums of money were spent in converting it to a medieval-style castle with four massive towers and a great hall. Although the Castle has gone, there remains an arboretum of trees wonderful to behold, especially in autumn.

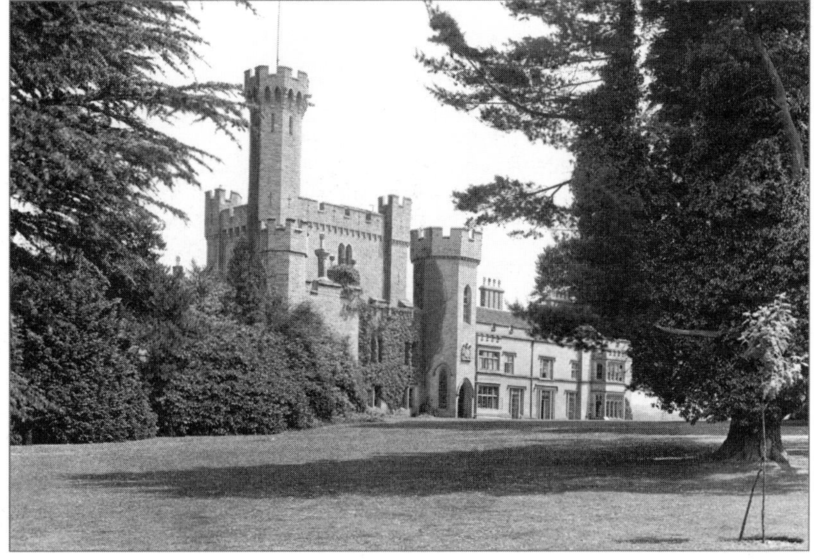

**BLAKEDOWN**
*The Golf Course c1965*
B419016

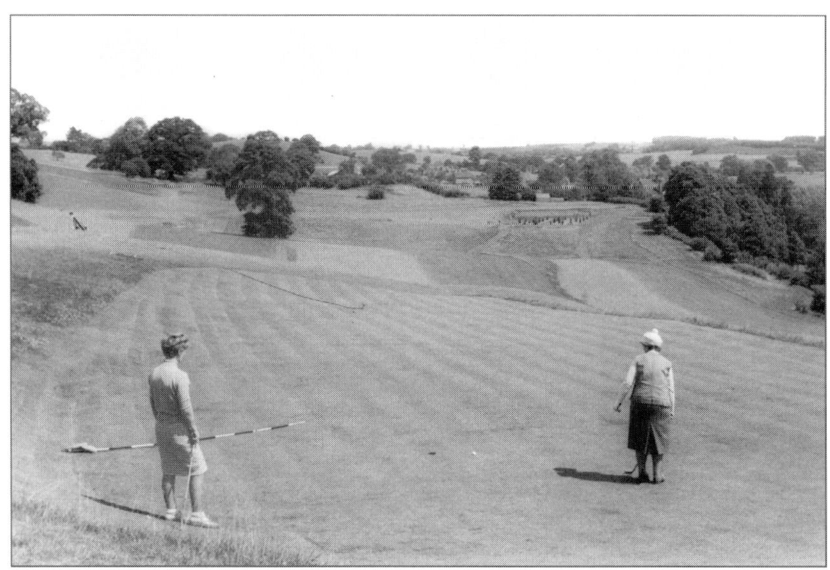

Mr Peter S Legatt's authoritative statement tells us that 'the sloping ground on the western side of Churchill Lane, enclosed by Waggon and Stonewaggon (or Cut Throat Lanes) used to be the large Neyther Field, one of three medieval glebe fields of Churchill.' Today, about two-thirds of this has become Churchill and Blakedown Golf Course. The early Club House was a corrugated iron hut, and the grass was kept short by grazing sheep! Now, much enlarged, and with Viscount Cobham as President and 380 members, the golf club has a splendid club house.

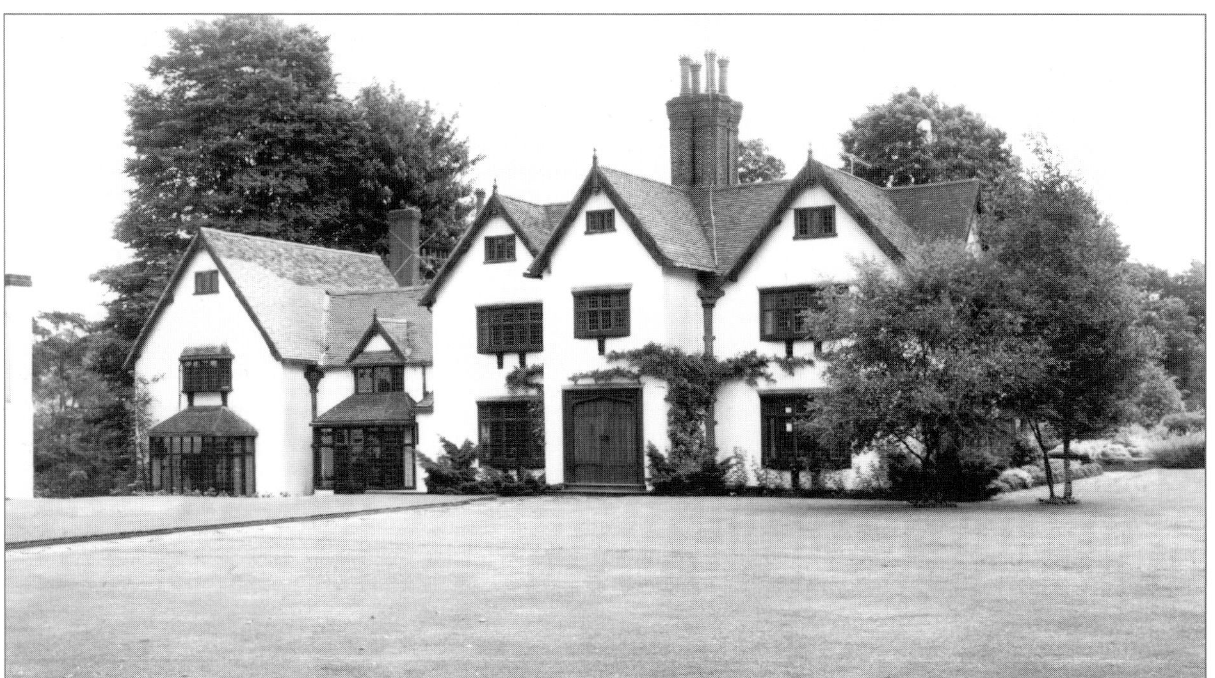

**BLAKEDOWN,** *Harborough Hall c1960* B419004

The gabled front was once half-timbered, but because the timber is no longer exposed it looks quite different today. Over the doorway was the date 1635 and the initials W A P, standing for William and Anne Penn. There was a hiding place in the garret, and later in the 19th century a second priest hole was found. One daughter married the minor poet William Shenstone. By the 1950s, when Harborough Hall was bought by Birmingham corporation, radical repair work was necessary to the timber, wattle and daub.

# INDEX

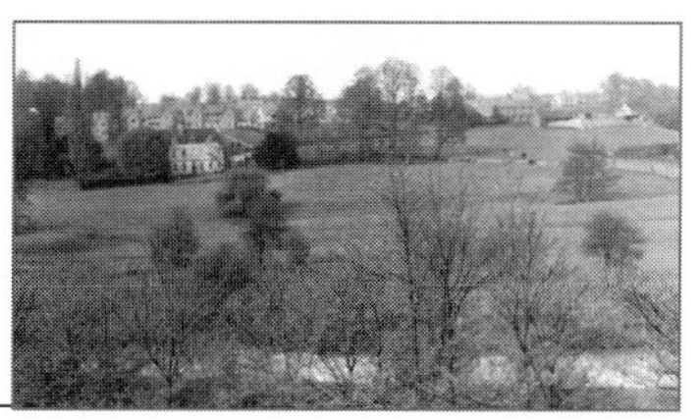

# Frith Book Co Titles

## www.francisfrith.co.uk

The Frith Book Company publishes over 100 new titles each year. A selection of those currently available is listed below. For latest catalogue please contact Frith Book Co.
***Town Books*** 96 pages, approximately 100 photos. ***County and Themed Books*** 128 pages, approximately 150 photos (unless specified). All titles hardback with laminated case and jacket, except those indicated pb (paperback)

| Title | ISBN | Price |
|---|---|---|
| Amersham, Chesham & Rickmansworth (pb) | 1-85937-340-2 | £9.99 |
| Andover (pb) | 1-85937-292-9 | £9.99 |
| Aylesbury (pb) | 1-85937-227-9 | £9.99 |
| Barnstaple (pb) | 1-85937-300-3 | £9.99 |
| Basildon Living Memories (pb) | 1-85937-515-4 | £9.99 |
| Bath (pb) | 1-85937-419-0 | £9.99 |
| Bedford (pb) | 1-85937-205-8 | £9.99 |
| Bedfordshire Living Memories | 1-85937-513-8 | £14.99 |
| Belfast (pb) | 1-85937-303-8 | £9.99 |
| Berkshire (pb) | 1-85937-191-4 | £9.99 |
| Berkshire Churches | 1-85937-170-1 | £17.99 |
| Berkshire Living Memories | 1-85937-332-1 | £14.99 |
| Black Country | 1-85937-497-2 | £12.99 |
| Blackpool (pb) | 1-85937-393-3 | £9.99 |
| Bognor Regis (pb) | 1-85937-431-x | £9.99 |
| Bournemouth (pb) | 1-85937-545-6 | £9.99 |
| Bradford (pb) | 1-85937-204-x | £9.99 |
| Bridgend (pb) | 1-85937-386-0 | £7.99 |
| Bridgwater (pb) | 1-85937-305-4 | £9.99 |
| Bridport (pb) | 1-85937-327-5 | £9.99 |
| Brighton (pb) | 1-85937-192-2 | £8.99 |
| Bristol (pb) | 1-85937-264-3 | £9.99 |
| British Life A Century Ago (pb) | 1-85937-213-9 | £9.99 |
| Buckinghamshire (pb) | 1-85937-200-7 | £9.99 |
| Camberley (pb) | 1-85937-222-8 | £9.99 |
| Cambridge (pb) | 1-85937-422-0 | £9.99 |
| Cambridgeshire (pb) | 1-85937-420-4 | £9.99 |
| Cambridgeshire Villages | 1-85937-523-5 | £14.99 |
| Canals And Waterways (pb) | 1-85937-291-0 | £9.99 |
| Canterbury Cathedral (pb) | 1-85937-179-5 | £9.99 |
| Cardiff (pb) | 1-85937-093-4 | £9.99 |
| Carmarthenshire (pb) | 1-85937-604-5 | £9.99 |
| Chelmsford (pb) | 1-85937-310-0 | £9.99 |
| Cheltenham (pb) | 1-85937-095-0 | £9.99 |
| Cheshire (pb) | 1-85937-271-6 | £9.99 |
| Chester (pb) | 1-85937-382 8 | £9.99 |
| Chesterfield (pb) | 1-85937-378-x | £9.99 |
| Chichester (pb) | 1-85937-228-7 | £9.99 |
| Churches of East Cornwall (pb) | 1-85937-249-x | £9.99 |
| Churches of Hampshire (pb) | 1-85937-207-4 | £9.99 |
| Cinque Ports & Two Ancient Towns | 1-85937-492-1 | £14.99 |
| Colchester (pb) | 1-85937-188-4 | £8.99 |
| Cornwall (pb) | 1-85937-229-5 | £9.99 |
| Cornwall Living Memories | 1-85937-248-1 | £14.99 |
| Cotswolds (pb) | 1-85937-230-9 | £9.99 |
| Cotswolds Living Memories | 1-85937-255-4 | £14.99 |
| County Durham (pb) | 1-85937-398-4 | £9.99 |
| Croydon Living Memories (pb) | 1-85937-162-0 | £9.99 |
| Cumbria (pb) | 1-85937-621-5 | £9.99 |
| Derby (pb) | 1-85937-367-4 | £9.99 |
| Derbyshire (pb) | 1-85937-196-5 | £9.99 |
| Derbyshire Living Memories | 1-85937-330-5 | £14.99 |
| Devon (pb) | 1-85937-297-x | £9.99 |
| Devon Churches (pb) | 1-85937-250-3 | £9.99 |
| Dorchester (pb) | 1-85937-307-0 | £9.99 |
| Dorset (pb) | 1-85937-269-4 | £9.99 |
| Dorset Coast (pb) | 1-85937-299-6 | £9.99 |
| Dorset Living Memories (pb) | 1-85937-584-7 | £9.99 |
| Down the Severn (pb) | 1-85937-560-x | £9.99 |
| Down The Thames (pb) | 1-85937-278-3 | £9.99 |
| Down the Trent | 1-85937-311-9 | £14.99 |
| East Anglia (pb) | 1-85937-265-1 | £9.99 |
| East Grinstead (pb) | 1-85937-138-8 | £9.99 |
| East London | 1-85937-080-2 | £14.99 |
| East Sussex (pb) | 1-85937-606-1 | £9.99 |
| Eastbourne (pb) | 1-85937-399-2 | £9.99 |
| Edinburgh (pb) | 1-85937-193-0 | £8.99 |
| England In The 1880s | 1-85937-331-3 | £17.99 |
| Essex - Second Selection | 1-85937-456-5 | £14.99 |
| Essex (pb) | 1-85937-270-8 | £9.99 |
| Essex Coast | 1-85937-342-9 | £14.99 |
| Essex Living Memories | 1-85937-490-5 | £14.99 |
| Exeter | 1-85937-539-1 | £9.99 |
| Exmoor (pb) | 1-85937-608-8 | £9.99 |
| Falmouth (pb) | 1-85937-594-4 | £9.99 |
| Folkestone (pb) | 1-85937-124-8 | £9.99 |
| Frome (pb) | 1-85937-317-8 | £9.99 |
| Glamorgan | 1-85937-488-3 | £14.99 |
| Glasgow (pb) | 1-85937-190-6 | £9.99 |
| Glastonbury (pb) | 1-85937-338-0 | £7.99 |
| Gloucester (pb) | 1-85937-232-5 | £9.99 |
| Gloucestershire (pb) | 1-85937-561-8 | £9.99 |
| Great Yarmouth (pb) | 1-85937-426-3 | £9.99 |
| Greater Manchester (pb) | 1-85937-266-x | £9.99 |
| Guildford (pb) | 1-85937-410-7 | £9.99 |
| Hampshire (pb) | 1-85937-279-1 | £9.99 |
| Harrogate (pb) | 1-85937-423-9 | £9.99 |
| Hastings and Bexhill (pb) | 1-85937-131-0 | £9.99 |
| Heart of Lancashire (pb) | 1-85937-197-3 | £9.99 |
| Helston (pb) | 1-85937-214-7 | £9.99 |
| Hereford (pb) | 1-85937-175-2 | £9.99 |
| Herefordshire (pb) | 1-85937-567-7 | £9.99 |
| Herefordshire Living Memories | 1-85937-514-6 | £14.99 |
| Hertfordshire (pb) | 1-85937-247-3 | £9.99 |
| Horsham (pb) | 1-85937-432-8 | £9.99 |
| Humberside (pb) | 1-85937-605-3 | £9.99 |
| Hythe, Romney Marsh, Ashford (pb) | 1-85937-256-2 | £9.99 |
| Ipswich (pb) | 1-85937-424-7 | £9.99 |
| Isle of Man (pb) | 1-85937-268-6 | £9.99 |
| Isle of Wight (pb) | 1-85937-429-8 | £9.99 |
| Isle of Wight Living Memories | 1-85937-304-6 | £14.99 |
| Kent (pb) | 1-85937-189-2 | £9.99 |
| Kent Living Memories(pb) | 1-85937-401-8 | £9.99 |
| Kings Lynn (pb) | 1-85937-334-8 | £9.99 |

**Available from your local bookshop or from the publisher**

# Frith Book Co Titles (continued)

| Title | ISBN | Price |
|---|---|---|
| Lake District (pb) | 1-85937-275-9 | £9.99 |
| Lancashire Living Memories | 1-85937-335-6 | £14.99 |
| Lancaster, Morecambe, Heysham (pb) | 1-85937-233-3 | £9.99 |
| Leeds (pb) | 1-85937-202-3 | £9.99 |
| Leicester (pb) | 1-85937-381-x | £9.99 |
| Leicestershire & Rutland Living Memories | 1-85937-500-6 | £12.99 |
| Leicestershire (pb) | 1-85937-185-x | £9.99 |
| Lighthouses | 1-85937-257-0 | £9.99 |
| Lincoln (pb) | 1-85937-380-1 | £9.99 |
| Lincolnshire (pb) | 1-85937-433-6 | £9.99 |
| Liverpool and Merseyside (pb) | 1-85937-234-1 | £9.99 |
| London (pb) | 1-85937-183-3 | £9.99 |
| London Living Memories | 1-85937-454-9 | £14.99 |
| Ludlow (pb) | 1-85937-176-0 | £9.99 |
| Luton (pb) | 1-85937-235-x | £9.99 |
| Maidenhead (pb) | 1-85937-339-9 | £9.99 |
| Maidstone (pb) | 1-85937-391-7 | £9.99 |
| Manchester (pb) | 1-85937-198-1 | £9.99 |
| Marlborough (pb) | 1-85937-336-4 | £9.99 |
| Middlesex | 1-85937-158-2 | £14.99 |
| Monmouthshire | 1-85937-532-4 | £14.99 |
| New Forest (pb) | 1-85937-390-9 | £9.99 |
| Newark (pb) | 1-85937-366-6 | £9.99 |
| Newport, Wales (pb) | 1-85937-258-9 | £9.99 |
| Newquay (pb) | 1-85937-421-2 | £9.99 |
| Norfolk (pb) | 1-85937-195-7 | £9.99 |
| Norfolk Broads | 1-85937-486-7 | £14.99 |
| Norfolk Living Memories (pb) | 1-85937-402-6 | £9.99 |
| North Buckinghamshire | 1-85937-626-6 | £14.99 |
| North Devon Living Memories | 1-85937-261-9 | £14.99 |
| North Hertfordshire | 1-85937-547-2 | £14.99 |
| North London (pb) | 1-85937-403-4 | £9.99 |
| North Somerset | 1-85937-302-x | £14.99 |
| North Wales (pb) | 1-85937-298-8 | £9.99 |
| North Yorkshire (pb) | 1-85937-236-8 | £9.99 |
| Northamptonshire Living Memories | 1-85937-529-4 | £14.99 |
| Northamptonshire | 1-85937-150-7 | £14.99 |
| Northumberland Tyne & Wear (pb) | 1-85937-281-3 | £9.99 |
| Northumberland | 1-85937-522-7 | £14.99 |
| Norwich (pb) | 1-85937-194-9 | £8.99 |
| Nottingham (pb) | 1-85937-324-0 | £9.99 |
| Nottinghamshire (pb) | 1-85937-187-6 | £9.99 |
| Oxford (pb) | 1-85937-411-5 | £9.99 |
| Oxfordshire (pb) | 1-85937-430-1 | £9.99 |
| Oxfordshire Living Memories | 1-85937-525-1 | £14.99 |
| Paignton (pb) | 1-85937-374-7 | £7.99 |
| Peak District (pb) | 1-85937-280-5 | £9.99 |
| Pembrokeshire | 1-85937-262-7 | £14.99 |
| Penzance (pb) | 1-85937-595-2 | £9.99 |
| Peterborough (pb) | 1-85937-219-8 | £9.99 |
| Picturesque Harbours | 1-85937-208-2 | £14.99 |
| Piers | 1-85937-237-6 | £17.99 |
| Plymouth (pb) | 1-85937-389-5 | £9.99 |
| Poole & Sandbanks (pb) | 1-85937-251-1 | £9.99 |
| Preston (pb) | 1-85937-212-0 | £9.99 |
| Reading (pb) | 1-85937-238-4 | £9.99 |
| Redhill to Reigate (pb) | 1-85937-596-0 | £9.99 |
| Ringwood (pb) | 1-85937-384-4 | £7.99 |
| Romford (pb) | 1-85937-319-4 | £9.99 |
| Royal Tunbridge Wells (pb) | 1-85937-504-9 | £9.99 |
| Salisbury (pb) | 1-85937-239-2 | £9.99 |
| Scarborough (pb) | 1-85937-379-8 | £9.99 |
| Sevenoaks and Tonbridge (pb) | 1-85937-392-5 | £9.99 |
| Sheffield & South Yorks (pb) | 1-85937-267-8 | £9.99 |
| Sherborne (pb) | 1-85937-301-1 | £9.99 |
| Shrewsbury (pb) | 1-85937-325-9 | £9.99 |
| Shropshire (pb) | 1-85937-326-7 | £9.99 |
| Shropshire Living Memories | 1-85937-643-6 | £14.99 |
| Somerset | 1-85937-153-1 | £14.99 |
| South Devon Coast | 1-85937-107-8 | £14.99 |
| South Devon Living Memories (pb) | 1-85937-609-6 | £9.99 |
| South East London (pb) | 1-85937-263-5 | £9.99 |
| South Somerset | 1-85937-318-6 | £14.99 |
| South Wales | 1-85937-519-7 | £14.99 |
| Southampton (pb) | 1-85937-427-1 | £9.99 |
| Southend (pb) | 1-85937-313-5 | £9.99 |
| Southport (pb) | 1-85937-425-5 | £9.99 |
| St Albans (pb) | 1-85937-341-0 | £9.99 |
| St Ives (pb) | 1-85937-415-8 | £9.99 |
| Stafford Living Memories (pb) | 1-85937-503-0 | £9.99 |
| Staffordshire (pb) | 1-85937-308-9 | £9.99 |
| Stourbridge (pb) | 1-85937-530-8 | £9.99 |
| Stratford upon Avon (pb) | 1-85937-388-7 | £9.99 |
| Suffolk (pb) | 1-85937-221-x | £9.99 |
| Suffolk Coast (pb) | 1-85937-610-x | £9.99 |
| Surrey (pb) | 1-85937-240-6 | £9.99 |
| Surrey Living Memories | 1-85937-328-3 | £14.99 |
| Sussex (pb) | 1-85937-184-1 | £9.99 |
| Sutton (pb) | 1-85937-337-2 | £9.99 |
| Swansea (pb) | 1-85937-167-1 | £9.99 |
| Taunton (pb) | 1-85937-314-3 | £9.99 |
| Tees Valley & Cleveland (pb) | 1-85937-623-1 | £9.99 |
| Teignmouth (pb) | 1-85937-370-4 | £7.99 |
| Thanet (pb) | 1-85937-116-7 | £9.99 |
| Tiverton (pb) | 1-85937-178-7 | £9.99 |
| Torbay (pb) | 1-85937-597-9 | £9.99 |
| Truro (pb) | 1-85937-598-7 | £9.99 |
| Victorian & Edwardian Dorset | 1-85937-254-6 | £14.99 |
| Victorian & Edwardian Kent (pb) | 1-85937-624-X | £9.99 |
| Victorian & Edwardian Maritime Album (pb) | 1-85937-622-3 | £9.99 |
| Victorian and Edwardian Sussex (pb) | 1-85937-625-8 | £9.99 |
| Villages of Devon (pb) | 1-85937-293-7 | £9.99 |
| Villages of Kent (pb) | 1-85937-294-5 | £9.99 |
| Villages of Sussex (pb) | 1-85937-295-3 | £9.99 |
| Warrington (pb) | 1-85937-507-3 | £9.99 |
| Warwick (pb) | 1-85937-518-9 | £9.99 |
| Warwickshire (pb) | 1-85937-203-1 | £9.99 |
| Welsh Castles (pb) | 1-85937-322-4 | £9.99 |
| West Midlands (pb) | 1-85937-289-9 | £9.99 |
| West Sussex (pb) | 1-85937-607-x | £9.99 |
| West Yorkshire (pb) | 1-85937-201-5 | £9.99 |
| Weston Super Mare (pb) | 1-85937-306-2 | £9.99 |
| Weymouth (pb) | 1-85937-209-0 | £9.99 |
| Wiltshire (pb) | 1-85937-277-5 | £9.99 |
| Wiltshire Churches (pb) | 1-85937-171-x | £9.99 |
| Wiltshire Living Memories (pb) | 1-85937-396-8 | £9.99 |
| Winchester (pb) | 1-85937-428-x | £9.99 |
| Windsor (pb) | 1-85937-333-x | £9.99 |
| Wokingham & Bracknell (pb) | 1-85937-329-1 | £9.99 |
| Woodbridge (pb) | 1-85937-498-0 | £9.99 |
| Worcester (pb) | 1-85937-165-5 | £9.99 |
| Worcestershire Living Memories | 1-85937-489-1 | £14.99 |
| Worcestershire | 1-85937-152-3 | £14.99 |
| York (pb) | 1-85937-199-x | £9.99 |
| Yorkshire (pb) | 1-85937-186-8 | £9.99 |
| Yorkshire Coastal Memories | 1-85937-506-5 | £14.99 |
| Yorkshire Dales | 1-85937-502-2 | £14.99 |
| Yorkshire Living Memories (pb) | 1-85937-397-6 | £9.99 |

**See Frith books on the internet at www.francisfrith.co.uk**

# Frith Products & Services

Francis Frith would doubtless be pleased to know that the pioneering publishing venture he started in 1860 still continues today. Over a hundred and forty years later, The Francis Frith Collection continues in the same innovative tradition and is now one of the foremost publishers of vintage photographs in the world. Some of the current activities include:

### *Interior Decoration*

Today Frith's photographs can be seen framed and as giant wall murals in thousands of pubs, restaurants, hotels, banks, retail stores and other public buildings throughout the country. In every case they enhance the unique local atmosphere of the places they depict and provide reminders of gentler days in an increasingly busy and frenetic world.

### *Product Promotions*

Frith products are used by many major companies to promote the sales of their own products or to reinforce their own history and heritage. Frith promotions have been used by Hovis bread, Courage beers, Scots Porage Oats, Colman's mustard, Cadbury's foods, Mellow Birds coffee, Dunhill pipe tobacco, Guinness, and Bulmer's Cider.

### *Genealogy and Family History*

As the interest in family history and roots grows world-wide, more and more people are turning to Frith's photographs of Great Britain for images of the towns, villages and streets where their ancestors lived; and, of course, photographs of the churches and chapels where their ancestors were christened, married and buried are an essential part of every genealogy tree and family album.

### *Frith Products*

All Frith photographs are available Framed or just as Mounted Prints and Posters (size 23 x 16 inches). These may be ordered from the address below. From time to time other products - Address Books, Calendars, Table Mats, etc - are available.

### *The Internet*

Already fifty thousand Frith photographs can be viewed and purchased on the internet through the Frith websites and a myriad of partner sites.

For more detailed information on Frith companies and products, look at these sites:

www.francisfrith.co.uk
www.francisfrith.com
*(for North American visitors)*

See the complete list of Frith Books at:

***www.francisfrith.co.uk***

This web site is regularly updated with the latest list of publications from the Frith Book Company. If you wish to buy books relating to another part of the country that your local bookshop does not stock, you may purchase on-line.

***For further information, trade, or author enquiries please contact us at the address below:***

**The Francis Frith Collection, Frith's Barn, Teffont, Salisbury, Wiltshire, England SP3 5QP.**
Tel: +44 (0)1722 716 376 Fax: +44 (0)1722 716 881 Email: sales@francisfrith.co.uk

**See Frith books on the internet at www.francisfrith.co.uk**